CW01305868

THE EXCISE CRISIS

THE EXCISE CRISIS

*Society and Politics
in the Age of Walpole*

PAUL LANGFORD

CLARENDON PRESS · OXFORD

This book has been printed digitally and produced in a standard specification
in order to ensure its continuing availability

OXFORD
UNIVERSITY PRESS

Great Clarendon Street, Oxford OX2 6DP
Oxford University Press is a department of the University of Oxford.
It furthers the University's objective of excellence in research, scholarship,
and education by publishing worldwide in

Oxford New York

Auckland Bangkok Buenos Aires Cape Town Chennai
Dar es Salaam Delhi Hong Kong Istanbul Karachi Kolkata
Kuala Lumpur Madrid Melbourne Mexico City Mumbai Nairobi
São Paulo Shanghai Singapore Taipei Tokyo Toronto

with an associated company in Berlin

Oxford is a registered trade mark of Oxford University Press
in the UK and in certain other countries

Published in the United States
by Oxford University Press Inc., New York

© Oxford University Press 1975

The moral rights of the author have been asserted
Database right Oxford University Press (maker)

Reprinted 2002

All rights reserved. No part of this publication may be reproduced,
stored in a retrieval system, or transmitted, in any form or by any means,
without the prior permission in writing of Oxford University Press,
or as expressly permitted by law, or under terms agreed with the appropriate
reprographics rights organization. Enquiries concerning reproduction
outside the scope of the above should be sent to the Rights Department,
Oxford University Press, at the address above

You must not circulate this book in any other binding or cover
and you must impose this same condition on any acquirer

ISBN 0-19-822437-0

Preface

IN carrying out this study I have incurred many debts of gratitude. I should like to express my appreciation of the assistance rendered by the staff of the following institutions: the British Museum; the Public Record Office; the Bodleian Library, Oxford; Cambridge University Library; the Archives du Ministère des Affaires Étrangères, Paris; Gloucestershire, Norfolk and Norwich, and Northamptonshire Record Offices; Gloucester, Norwich and Newcastle upon Tyne City Libraries; Bury St. Edmunds, Derby and Northampton Public Libraries. I also acknowledge the gracious permission of Her Majesty The Queen to print extracts from the Stuart Papers at Windsor Castle. Similarly I wish to record the kindness of the Duke of Devonshire, the Marquess of Cholmondeley and Lord Walpole in granting me access to their collections and permission to publish quotations.

To many colleagues and friends I have particular obligations. Mr. Michael Mahony gave me a reference, and Mr. Ian Doolittle assisted me in a statistical analysis of pollbooks. Many others, too numerous to acknowledge by name, have discussed aspects of the excise crisis with me. However, my greatest obligation is to Dame Lucy Sutherland, Dr. Aubrey Newman and Mr. John Walsh, who read the typescript of this book and were kind enough to offer their comments. I am also grateful to Dr. Newman for permission to quote from his unpublished thesis. In addition I cannot let this opportunity pass of recording my debt to Dr. John Owen and Mr. John Brooke. To their guidance and knowledge of eighteenth-century politics I owe a very great deal. Finally I wish to thank the Rector and Fellows of Lincoln College, who made me a research grant which greatly facilitated the more technical side of my research for this book.

PAUL LANGFORD

Lincoln College,
Oxford

Contents

	ABBREVIATIONS	viii
	NOTE ON DATES	viii
I.	Introduction	1
II.	The Background to the Excise Crisis	4
III.	Walpole and the Excise	26
IV.	The Public and the Excise	44
V.	Parliament and the Excise: I	62
VI.	Parliament and the Excise: II	77
VII.	The Court and the Excise	87
VIII.	The Electorate and the Excise	101
IX.	The Impact of the Excise	124
X.	Public Opinion and the Excise Crisis	151
	APPENDIX A: LIST OF INSTRUCTIONS AGAINST THE EXCISE	172
	APPENDIX B: DIVISION LISTS ON THE EXCISE	173
	APPENDIX C: COURT ABSTENTIONS IN THE DIVISION OF 10 APRIL 1733	175
	INDEX	181

Abbreviations
(*For Principal Sources used*)

Add. MSS.	British Museum, Additional Manuscripts.
C(H) MSS.	University of Cambridge Library, Cholmondeley (Houghton) Manuscripts.
Corr. Pol. Angl.	Archives du Ministère des Affaires Étrangères, (Quai d'Orsay), Correspondance Politique d'Angleterre.
Coxe	W. Coxe, *Memoirs of the Life and Administration of Sir Robert Walpole, Earl of Orford* (London, 1798, 3 vols.).
Hervey Memoirs	R. Sedgwick, ed., *Some Materials towards Memoirs of the Reign of King George II By John, Lord Hervey* (London, 1931, 3 vols.).
Parl. Hist.	*Cobbett's Parliamentary History of England*, vols. viii, ix (London, 1811).
P.R.O.	Public Record Office.
RA Stuart	Royal Archives (Windsor Castle), Stuart Papers.

Note on Dates

ALL dates in this book are Old Style; however, 1 January, not 25 March, is treated as the beginning of the new year.

I

Introduction

IT is one of the more surprising features of eighteenth-century history that the excise crisis of 1733 should have received relatively little detailed investigation.[1] Comparable episodes in the politics of the period—the Jew Bill affair, the Wilkesite agitations of the 1760s, the Association movements of the 1770s and 1780s—have been minutely studied.[2] Yet the excise crisis looms at least as large as any of these. It was, for example, one of the most shattering defeats ever suffered by a minister of the crown at the bar of public opinion. Sir Robert Walpole's hack journalist, William Arnall, described it to his master as 'one of those very few measures wherein your Success hath not been equal to your Good Intentions'.[3] Others were less restrained. James Ralph considered that 'Never, in the Memory of Man, was the Nation so alarm'd at the Design of a Minister, as in the Case of the projected *Excise* on Wine and Tobacco in 1733'.[4] Even before the defeat of the excise bill contemporaries recognized the importance of the crisis blowing up. The *Historical Register* called it 'the most material publick Event that has happen'd in our own Country ... in many Years last past'.[5] 'You never saw', wrote one observer, 'a greater ferment in this nation than there is at present on account of the project for a new excise on Wine and Tobacco'.[6]

By its influence on later events, too, the excise crisis signalized its

[1] The only monograph, which is concerned largely with the polemical literature of the excise crisis, is E. R. Turner, 'The Excise Scheme of 1733', *Eng. Hist. Rev.* xlii (1927), 34–55. The best accounts are to be found in P. Vaucher, *La Crise du Ministère Walpole en 1733–1734* (Paris, 1924) and J. H. Plumb, *Sir Robert Walpole: The King's Minister* (London, 1960).

[2] See, for example, T. W. Perry, *Public Opinion, Propaganda and Politics in Eighteenth Century England* (London, 1962) which is actually a study of the Jew Bill affair; G. Rudé, *Wilkes and Liberty* (Oxford, 1962); E. C. Black, *The Association* (Cambridge, Mass., 1963); I. R. Christie, *Wilkes, Wyvill and Reform* (London, 1962), and H. Butterfield, *George III, Lord North and the People, 1779–80* (London, 1949).

[3] C(H) MSS. Corr. 1965: 12 Apr. 1733.

[4] J. Ralph, *A Critical History of the Administration of Sir Robert Walpole, Now Earl of Orford* (London, 1743), p. 256.

[5] xviii. 130.

[6] Add. MS. 21500 (Carte Papers), f. 94: Rev. T. Carte to C. Kynaston, 12 Mar. 1733.

outstanding importance. For one thing its defeat effectively made impossible further extensions of the excise law. When Lord Bute introduced a cider excise in 1763 the result was a storm of protest which ended in its repeal three years later; the arguments employed were almost identical to those used in 1733, and the constant inspiration of the West Country in its opposition to the cider tax was 'the glorious victory of 1733 over the most *hellish* design that was ever projected'.[7] Even in America the excise became legendary. A political crisis over taxation in Massachusetts Bay in 1754 was 'decisively conditioned by a similar upheaval which had occurred in Great Britain two decades earlier'.[8] As late as 1790, after Pitt the Younger had finally broken the embargo on a tobacco excise, and so provoked a flood of references to 1733, an election candidate at Hull assured the voters that 'had he been in Parliament at the time when the Tobacco Bill passed, he never would have consented to that article being excised'.[9] Not until well over half a century after the event were the prejudices established or at least reinforced by the excise crisis eradicated.

And yet there are questions about the excise crisis which have scarcely been adequately answered. It is intriguing, for example, that although the immediately succeeding generations agreed on the long-term effects of the crisis they were nonetheless mystified by it. In retrospect it became difficult to see quite why Walpole's scheme had been so contentious a measure. The Elder Pitt declared later in Parliament that 'the more I reflect on my conduct, the more I blame myself for opposing the excise bill—let those who are ashamed to confess their errors laugh out'.[10] Adam Smith's frequently quoted approbation of the excise was in fact the conventional wisdom of the late eighteenth century.[11] Yet this raises problems. If the excise scheme was so unexceptionable, why was it defeated? Was it the force of public opinion or was it, as many thought, a tribute to the malignancy of Walpole's enemies among the opposition and the merchants—'Faction, combined with the interest of smuggling

[7] *Gloucester Journal*, 28 Mar. 1763.

[8] P. S. Boyer, 'Borrowed Rhetoric: The Massachusetts Excise Controversy of 1754', *William and Mary Quarterly*, 3rd Ser., xxi (1964), 328–9.

[9] G. Hadley, *A New and Complete History of the Town and County of the Town of Kingston-upon-Hull* (Hull, 1788), p. 487. For Pitt's measure, which was passed in 1789, see S. Dowell, *A History of Taxation and Taxes in England* (London, 1884), ii. 192.

[10] Coxe, i. 748.

[11] See, for example, J. Tucker, *Four Tracts, together with Two Sermons, on Political and Commercial Subjects* (Gloucester, 1774), pp. 71–2.

INTRODUCTION

merchants', as Smith called it?[12] More particularly, did Walpole really need to climb down? 'Why he finally yielded', remarked the second Earl of Hardwicke, no mean historian and political observer, 'I have never clearly understood.'[13] Even a hardened Tory like Dr. King was surprised by Walpole's surrender. 'He seemed to have great resolution; and yet he was once so much intimidated by the clamours of the people without doors, that he thought it expedient to give up one of his most favourite schemes'.[14] Again, if the excise was so unpopular and so unsuccessful, why did Walpole adopt it at all, and how does his miscalculation affect one's assessment of his political character? In the following pages some attempt is made to answer these questions. Yet they are not all. At base the interest of the excise crisis as an episode in eighteenth-century history is that it presents an ideal opportunity to examine Georgian politics in a wide social dimension. It has become something of a truism that the key to eighteenth-century politics is to be sought in the restricted world of Whitehall and Westminster, in the gilded corridors of St. James's and the smoke-laden chamber of St. Stephen's. No doubt this is imposed by the character of the times. The politics of oligarchy are scarcely to be studied in the market-place, and it is understandable that the activities of the eighteenth-century historian should be concentrated in the areas where the important decisions were made. Yet there was another politics, a politics which contemporaries referred to generally by the term 'out of doors', which rarely played a vital part in day-to-day decision-making but which nonetheless existed and at times turned out to be crucial. The excise crisis represented one of these rare moments. The events of 1733-4 did not merely signify great happenings in the corridors of power, though they did that too; they also revealed a ferment in society at large. In that crisis there was room for many more besides the politicians; every county, every borough, every parish was in some sense involved. The word excise united, briefly but significantly, the entire nation from the peasant to the peer. If any generalizations are possible about the nature of politics in English society at this time, they are those which can be elicited from the excise crisis.

---

[12] *An Inquiry into the Nature and Causes of the Wealth of Nations*, by A. Smith, ed. E. Cannan (London, 1950, 6th edn.), ii. 370.
[13] P. Yorke, 2nd Earl of Hardwicke, *Walpoliana* (London, 1781), p. 12.
[14] W. King, *Political and Literary Anecdotes of his Own Times* (London, 1819, 2nd edn.), p. 40.

II
The Background to the Excise Crisis

IN some ways the most essential exercise in understanding the excise crisis is to clarify its place in relation to the pattern of politics at the time. Normally that pattern is seen in terms of the growing stability which was after all England's principal constitutional achievement in the eighteenth century and which so clearly marks the period off from the preceding one. Unfortunately this stability is sometimes misinterpreted as tranquillity, though the two are not necessarily synonymous. According to one of the most respected accounts of the period, the reigns of George I and George II formed 'an oasis of tranquillity between two agitated epochs'.[1] On this reading and against this background the excise crisis appears as a curious, indeed inexplicable aberration on the part of Englishmen, a strange atavistic throwback to the ferments of an earlier age. Yet this is an interpretation which stretches credulity. Although contemporaries were struck by the intensity of the excise crisis, the phenomenon itself did not surprise them. They were not amazed that Walpole's ministry could be shaken in this way, nor that politics out of doors could leap into such prominence. It is at least worth asking therefore whether the excise crisis was quite as unpredictable as the usual diagnosis might suggest.

There can be no question of course that it was this period which saw the most significant phase in the growth of political stability in England.[2] It is possible to view this process at two quite different levels. At one level the achievement of the age was one of pure political mechanics, in which the outlines are familiar. The problem of the seventeenth century had been a basic failure of the executive to find a *modus vivendi* with the legislature. What happened in the early eighteenth century was that the former, which had been taught a hard lesson in 1642 and 1688, discovered that management could do what less subtle methods could not. The combination of

[1] B. Williams, *The Whig Supremacy, 1714-60* (Oxford, 1962, 2nd edn.), p. 1.
[2] See J. H. Plumb, *The Growth of Political Stability in England, 1675-1725* (London, 1967), to which the following account is much indebted.

expert management and judicious use of patronage created a powerful Court and Treasury party which was generally able to control the House of Commons, especially since the monarchy was no longer foolish enough to provoke the extreme anger of the propertied classes by exploiting its prerogative. The result was the creation of something like a modern system of government buttressed by a majority in Parliament, a developing Cabinet system, and an emerging Prime Minister, with something like the modern stability in the working of politics. At another level this pattern was merely part of a broader development, the growth of oligarchy. Economically as well as politically the early eighteenth century was a period of prosperity for the great landowners, the great merchants, and the great financiers, a period in which the rich became richer and more powerful.[3] This was reflected locally in the growing control of the smaller constituencies by the wealthy, with a gradual but corresponding reduction of electoral independence and volatility; at the centre it was associated with the creation of a gigantic spoils system for aristocratic politicians and their clients. There were of course other long-term factors—the establishment of a stable financial system, the growth of government bureaucracy and patronage, the Union with Scotland, and so on. As Professor Plumb has shown, though the early years of the eighteenth century were exceptionally violent in terms of political conflict, the underlying trends were all towards the stability of Pelhamite England.

Whatever means is used to identify the foundations of the political stability which characterized the years after the accession of George I, it is impossible to ignore the decisive role of Sir Robert Walpole. Walpole dominated the politics of the twenties and thirties in a way which is given to few politicians in any age, and only the Elder Pitt, of other eighteenth-century statesmen, achieved comparable pre-eminence. It is interesting, for example, that these were the only two politicians of the period who were regularly referred to, half in sarcasm half in seriousness, as 'the Great Man'. They were the giants of the eighteenth century. Of the two, Walpole's was the greater political accomplishment; certainly his hold on the power

[3] See especially H. J. Habakkuk, 'English Landownership, 1680–1740', *Econ. Hist. Rev.*, x (1939–40), 2–17; G. E. Mingay, *English Landed Society in the Eighteenth Century* (London, 1963); P. G. M. Dickson, *The Financial Revolution in England: a Study in the Development of Public Credit, 1688–1756* (London, 1967), and W. E. Minchinton, ed., *The Growth of English Overseas Trade in the Seventeenth and Eighteenth Centuries* (London, 1969).

politics of his day was astonishing. No other Prime Minister has ever had such a long tenure of office, and Walpole himself had reason to boast to one of his bitterest opponents, Samuel Sandys, 'that perhaps they might get the better of him, but he was sure no other minister would ever be able to stand so long as he had done'.[4]

However, this achievement did not earn him the unstinted admiration of contemporaries. Walpole, almost more than any other eighteenth-century politician, unless it be his protégés, Henry Fox and George Bubb Dodington, was a byword for corruption. The Tory view, as summarized by Thomas Hearne, was clear; 'a wicked man, and imployed to do all the dirty tricks that can be thought of to inrich miserably covetous Princes, and to drain the Subject'.[5] Dr. King went still further; 'It is certain, that all our national misfortunes since the accession of the House of Hanover must be chiefly ascribed to Walpole's administration. He unhinged all the principles and morals of our people, and changed the government into a system of corruption'.[6] Walpole had grown up in the bitterness and violence of post-Revolution politics. He was not squeamish, nor, to put it no more strongly, was he high-minded. On the other hand, he claimed that he had personally taken no more by way of reward for his services than was reasonable,[7] and his friends felt that he was much maligned in this respect. According to Lord Hardwicke 'he often contrived to pass for a much more profligate man than he really was'.[8] If this is so he had only himself to blame. Walpole's notorious conviction that 'Every man has his price', may be partly explained away,[9] but it is not untypical of the man.

What can be said of him is that his well-known brashness and unscrupulousness were set off by widespread recognition of his abilities. Lord Chesterfield, one of his enemies, nonetheless recorded a glowing tribute to his capacity as a parliamentarian. 'He was the best parliament-man, and the ablest manager of parliament, that I believe ever lived. An artful rather than eloquent speaker, he saw as by intuition, the disposition of the house, and pressed or receded

---

[4] W. King, ed., *Memoirs of Sarah, Duchess of Marlborough* (London, 1930), p. 326.
[5] *Remarks and Collections of Thomas Hearne*, ed. H. E. Salter (Oxf. Hist. Soc. lxxii), xi. 175.
[6] King, *Anecdotes*, p. 39.
[7] RA Stuart, Unbound MSS, 1/125: debate of 16 Mar. 1733.
[8] Hardwicke, *Walpoliana*, p. 16.
[9] There are various accounts of the origin of this phrase; see, for example, King, *Anecdotes*, p. 44.

accordingly'.[10] George II from a different viewpoint made a similar assessment: 'Sir Robert Walpole was, by so great a superiority, the most able man in the kingdom, that he understood the revenue, and knew how to manage that formidable and refractory body, the House of Commons, so much better than any other man, that it was impossible for the business of the Crown to be well done without him'.[11] In this respect Walpole outdid almost all eighteenth-century ministers, and set a pattern which all the more successful ones were to follow. Much of the importance of his position was the result of his electing to stay in the House of Commons to lead the government there. This decision, so simple on the face of things, was epoch-making. Previous managers had moved on to the Lords to signalize their elevation in the royal councils. Walpole, though generally expected in 1721 to follow suit by taking the title of Earl of Walsingham,[12] decided to remain a member of the lower house and so set a precedent which was to be unbroken for the rest of the century, except by the disastrous decision of Pitt the Elder in 1766.[13]

It is understandable that Walpole's skill as a parliamentarian should be stressed. But equally significant was his prowess as a courtier. No minister could be appointed or remain in office without the support of the monarch, and Walpole was adept at the art of obtaining and retaining such support. In 1721–2 he had won the favour of George I after a bitter spell in opposition, partly it must be admitted by good fortune, the death of his rivals Stanhope and Sunderland, but partly by the dazzling way in which he nursed the government and the dynasty through the South Sea crisis.[14] In 1727, when George I died, he again demonstrated his ability. The new king's own favourite, Spencer Compton, was comprehensively outmanoeuvred by Walpole, who obtained a massively increased civil list for the Crown, exploited his old association with the Princess (now Queen) Caroline, and pushed Compton into the background. In part the fault was that of Compton, who gave Walpole a crucial chance to seize the initiative. 'Affairs, abroad', according to

[10] M. Maty, ed., *Miscellaneous Works of Chesterfield* (London, 2nd edn., 1779), App., 36.
[11] *Hervey Memoirs*, pp. 177–8.
[12] *HMC Portland*, vii. 306.
[13] R. Sedgwick, 'Sir Robert Walpole', *Times Lit. Supp.*, 24 Mar. 1945. Walpole also set a precedent by taking the Garter, despite the fact that he was a commoner; since a peerage was out of the question, other marks of honour had to be found.
[14] See J. H. Plumb, *Sir Robert Walpole: The Making of a Statesman* (London, 1956), chaps. vii–x.

Walpole's brother, 'were in so bad situation that Lord Wilmington (Compton) would not venture to be premier Minister, and Sir Robert then offered to act in conjunction with him, to help on the common good'.[15]

Even so Walpole's speed of action in this crisis was impressive. Before it he had expected no favour in the new reign; after it he worked himself rapidly into an impregnable position in the royal closet. This was not easy. George II was by no means the most manageable of monarchs. He was intelligent, but testy and prone to jealousy of those who sought to wield the power which he in theory possessed and which his continental brethren certainly exercised. For Walpole, constant attendance on the royal family, with the exception of his brief visits to Houghton, was essential, and he was continually threatened by the tempests, the plotting, the factiousness of the court. As he told Lord Hervey, 'he never could turn his back for three days',[16] and even in the closet itself extreme delicacy was required. 'You, my Lord, are enough acquainted with this Court to know that nothing can be done in it but by degrees; should I tell either the King or the Queen what I propose to bring them to six months hence, I could never succeed. Step by step I can carry them perhaps the road I wish; but if I ever show them at a distance to what end that road leads, they stop short, and all my designs are always defeated.'[17] The king especially was awkward. 'You are always teasing me to do things that are disagreeable to me, and for people I dislike',[18] he told Walpole on one occasion. The Queen was more dependable but also had to be managed with care. Fortunately long before the reign of George II, when Walpole had been in opposition with the future king and his wife as Prince and Princess of Wales, he had learned to handle them. As early as 1720 Lady Cowper had analysed the relationship which was later to underpin the stability of the Walpole administration between 1727 and 1737: '*Walpole* has engrossed and monopolised the *Princess* to a Degree of making her deaf to Everything that did not come from him', and 'The *Prince* . . . is guided by the *Princess* as she is by *Walpole*'.[19] This area of Walpole's primacy was every bit as important as his

[15] *HMC Egmont Diary*, i. 375.
[16] *Hervey Memoirs*, p. 295.
[17] Ibid., p. 361.
[18] Ibid., p. 407.
[19] *Diary of Mary, Countess Cowper, Lady of the Bedchamber to the Princess of Wales, 1714–20* (London, 1865, 2nd edn.), pp. 134, 164.

THE BACKGROUND TO THE EXCISE CRISIS

mastery of the Commons. No eighteenth-century minister could endure without combining the control of the royal prerogative with that of parliament.

It is not denying either the strength or importance of the Walpole establishment to point to some of the factors which detracted from them. Not everyone in George II's England was altogether enamoured of Walpole and his work. There was, for example, the parliamentary opposition. In the mid-1720s this had threatened to disappear altogether, and certainly after Walpole's successful takeover from Spencer Compton in 1727 it had shown few signs of revival. After the General Election of that year the government could boast an immense majority of more than 270 in the Commons, and its opponents rarely managed to win even 100 votes there.[20] The later 1720s represented the height of Walpole's power and were appropriately crowned by his ditching of Lord Townshend, long his political ally and by now his only real rival in the ministry. This moment, in 1730, which signalized Walpole's arrival at the very pinnacle of his fame, was also the moment at which the opposition began to revive. The gravity of the changed situation in the Commons became clear in the session of 1730 when Walpole's foreign policy was challenged on a sensitive issue—the alleged refusal of the French to destroy the harbour of Dunkirk in accordance with treaty obligations. Eventually the ministry won by a substantial majority of 270 to 149, but only after Walpole had taken drastic measures with the French court. In the same session a division on British employment of German troops earned the opposition a vote of 169 against the ministry's 248. This was still a secure majority for the government, but the contrast with earlier sessions was obvious. As Hervey remarked, at this time 'the whole House was in a flame, and the ministry stronger pushed than they had ever been on any occasion before'.[21] It is possible to explain this growth of opposition between 1727 and 1730 in several ways. In part it was simply the result of growing hostility among those elements at court which for some time had been considering the possibility of rebellion. The ostensible reason was Walpole's pacific foreign policy which, with the associated displacement of Lord Townshend, split the Whigs as surely as Walpole and Townshend's own revolt in 1717 had done at that time.

---

[20] R. Sedgwick, ed., *The History of Parliament: The House of Commons, 1715-1754* (London, 1970), i. 37.
[21] *Hervey Memoirs*, p. 116.

Pulteney, who found himself leading the dissident Whigs, put his finger on this as the crucial factor. 'The quarrel between Lord Townshend and Sir Robert Walpole has so shattered their strength at home by the subdivision of the before divided Whig party that their mutual endeavours to ruin each other must end in the ruin of both'.[22] In fact Walpole weathered this storm, but the rift opened or rather widened in the parliamentary Whig party in 1730 was not to be even partially healed until his fall in 1742; throughout the 1730s he was faced with an opposition in which Whigs were almost as numerous as Tories.

It would be tempting to suggest that the growth of opposition in the late 1720s and early 1730s was merely a parliamentary phenomenon. In reality it was representative of a general trend which was as marked without doors as within. Essentially this was the product of the gradual dissolution of those restraints which had in preceding years prevented an outbreak of political violence comparable to that of Queen Anne's reign. In the first place it was becoming difficult by 1730 to claim that Jacobitism was sufficient of a threat alone to justify Walpole's system of government. Ever since the Revolution the lure of Jacobitism had been a millstone around the necks of those who opposed the Whig establishment. Since this included much of the Tory party in particular and a substantial section of English public opinion in general, its significance is clear enough. Certainly since 1714 it had done much to divide and paralyse the Tories, and had given a perfect handle to government to discredit those Whigs who were foolish enough to venture into opposition. This is not to imply that Walpole's incessant harping on the Jacobite danger was necessarily either dishonest or unjustified. 'In fact', as Lord Hardwicke commented, 'his fears of Invasions and of Jacobitism were real; though his enemies affected to say they were state artifices'.[23] Moreover Walpole's well-known prediction that 'if there was a war, the King's crown would be fought for on this land',[24] was amply fulfilled in 1745. That alone would justify his policy of peace and alliance with France, if not his political exploitation of the dynastic issue.

However, it is important to distinguish between the immediate threat of Jacobitism at home and that abroad. Actual support for the

[22] Ibid., p. 105.
[23] Hardwicke, *Walpoliana*, p. 9.
[24] Ibid., p. 7.

Pretender in England was extremely limited in the sense of real conspiracy. A successful invasion would no doubt have produced a dramatic change in the general climate, but for the moment active supporters were few and less resolute friends deterred by the risks involved. Moreover, in this area there was a distinct lessening of tension during the 1720s. While the '15' was on, at the time of the Swedish plot of 1718, during the South Sea crisis of 1720, following the Atterbury plot of 1722, the Jacobite danger was obviously real and acted as a powerful argument for supporting the establishment. But the danger decreased in following years. It is evident that by 1730 much of the vigour was draining from the Jacobite camp. For one thing the conspirators were hopelessly divided. 'It is not to be described', Lord Cornbury wrote to James III, 'what animosities there are amongst the king's friends in England'.[25] The minds of the leaders 'ran much upon Projects'[26] which lacked organization and any prospect of success. In any event it was generally clear that the dangers posed by the Pretender were scarcely of a particularly immediate kind, and as this awareness grew, the constraints on opposition to George II's court on the one hand and alliance with the Tories on the other loosened. By the time of the excise crisis many Whigs were merely irritated by the stress which Walpole placed on the Jacobite threat. Lord Haddington complained bitterly of the way in which 'if a man cannot think the same way with two or three men in power he shall be looked as much down on as if he had been not only a Jacobite but a rebell'.[27] Another Whig, Lord Bristol, took a similar view: 'God forbid that every man, who woud but cannot approve of what are calld his M——y's or M——r's measures, shoud, as hath been injustly done, be markd for and numberd among the Jacobites'.[28]

Closely connected with the diminishing importance of the succession as an issue was another and most important development, the decline of traditional party antipathies. In an age in which parties were not related to mass politics in the modern way, nor organized on the central and national basis of the monolithic parties, they were of course at most temporary and fluid forms of political organization.

---

[25] RA Stuart, 154/104: 29 June 1732.
[26] Ibid., 164/226: Mist to O'Brien, 30 Oct. 1733.
[27] *HMC Polworth*, v. 81: Haddington to Marchmont, 5 Feb. 1734.
[28] *Letter-Books of John Hervey, First Earl of Bristol* (Wells, 1894), iii. 100: Bristol to Hervey, 18 Aug. 1733.

It is true that the reign of Queen Anne in particular had been dominated by the rivalry of Whig and Tory. Yet in many ways this had been a most misleading and artificial situation, brought about by the exceptional economic tensions and political issues of the day. Moreover, it began to disintegrate quite rapidly after the death of Anne in 1714. The accession of George I had a far more fundamental effect on the party situation than that of most monarchs in the modern period, simply because the new king opted so unreservedly for the Whig party. In retrospect this seems natural enough, yet at the time it was remarkable. After all, William III, who had been expected to act very much in favour of the Whigs, had in practice preferred to keep his options open, while Queen Anne too, despite her Tory prejudices, favoured a balanced or mixed government. George I was less equivocal, and the result was a gigantic victory for the Whigs. Bolingbroke called 1714 'the *Millenary year* of *Whigisme*, because it is manifest that the Whigs intended to make it such'.[29]

In the following decade Toryism was divided and discredited by the problem of the succession and the Whig monopoly at court was amply reinforced. However, as the years passed it became apparent that what was initially a victory for one party was truly a blow for the party system in general. In the 1720s and 1730s it grew increasingly clear that the new 'Whig' system was closed not so much to those who had been Tories as to those who persisted in describing themselves as Tories. Moreover, Walpole's own principles turned out to have a peculiarly Tory air, once he was in power. His policy of peace and alliance with France, his stress on financial retrenchment and reduction of the land tax, his refusal to disturb the establishment in church as well as state, all these contrasted violently with traditional Whig policy in the age of the Junto, and indeed with the conduct of Stanhope and Sunderland before 1720. Walpole's only clear 'Whig' principle was unwavering attachment to the new dynasty, and this imposed no great ideological strain on the many Tories who had always preferred the prospect of a Protestant Succession to the risks of a Stuart Restoration. It was not surprising therefore that the Tories gradually returned to the fleshpots of power. Throughout the 1720s a steady stream of Tories quietly came into government, just as many Whigs were going into opposition. 'I can't help thinking', wrote one of the Tory Finches, 'since this country must be governed why one had not better govern than be governed', a sensible argu-

[29] Add. MS. 4948A (Bolingbroke's Works), f. 423.

ment which appealed very strongly to many aristocratic Tory families.[30]

One of the most obvious results of this change in the party situation was simply enormous confusion. The *Craftsman*, for example, remarked on the strange reversal of roles by which Whiggism had become the defender of monarchy and Toryism its enemy. 'I think nothing more demonstrable than that the *Court-Whigs* of this Age are exactly the same kind of Creatures with the *Court Tories* before the *Revolution*; that, *vice versa*, the *Body* of the *present Tories* have adopted the Spirit of the *old Whigs*, etc.'.[31] The press conducted bitter debates as to who had the better right to be considered a true Whig, William Pulteney who was in opposition with the Tories, or Walpole who was in office.[32] Lord Bristol, an old Whig if ever there was one, had nothing but detestation for the regime which ruled the Whig promised land under Walpole. He saw himself as 'one of those few old and steady Whiggs . . . opposing his even worse than Tory schemes of standing armies, revenues, Parliaments etc., whilst he and his have quite deserted those noble English principles they once professed'.[33] The final word may come from Bristol's son, Lord Hervey, another Whig but one who as a close friend of Walpole and the court, found himself in the opposite camp to that of his father:

WHIG and TORY had been the denominations by which men opposite in their political views had distinguished themselves for many years and through many reigns. Those who were called Whigs had been in power from the first accession of the Hanover family to the Crown; but the original principles on which both these parties were said to act altered so insensibly in the persons who bore the names, by the long prosperity of the one, and the adversity of the other, that those who called themselves Whigs arbitrarily gave the title of Tory to every one who opposed the measures of the administrations or whom they had a mind to make disagreeable at Court; whilst the Tories (with more justice) reproached the Whigs with acting on those very principles and pushing those very points which, to ingratiate themselves with the people and to assume a popular character, they had at first set themselves up to explode and oppose.[34]

---

[30] Quoted in A. N. Newman, 'Elections in Kent and its Parliamentary Representation, 1715–1754' (Oxford Univ. unpub. D. Phil. thesis, 1957), p. 180.
[31] 6 Oct. 1733.
[32] *Hyp-Doctor*, 7 Mar. 1732.
[33] *Letter-Books of Bristol*, iii. 105: Bristol to Lady Bristol, 29 Oct. 1733.
[34] *Hervey Memoirs*, p. 3.

In themselves these weakening elements in the traditional party structure might have strengthened rather than weakened Walpole's regime. If the Tories could be demoralized and destroyed, or at any rate reduced to an impotent rump of country gentlemen, so much the better from his point of view. The difficulty was that, though the Tory party gradually lost its strength, by the late 1720s there were so many Whigs who no longer felt any fundamental objections either to opposing Walpole or consorting with the Tories that a new danger began to emerge. This was the threat of a novel alignment based not on the traditional enmities, but on one still older, that of court and country. If the meaning of Tory and Whig were debased, if the old parties had lost their real identity, this was a rivalry which could well fill the party vacuum. As early as 1721, the celebrated radical tracts, *Cato's Letters*, had urged

'Forget . . . the foolish and knavish Distinction of *High Church and Low Church*, *Whig and Tory*, Sounds which continue in your Mouths when the Memory of them is gone, and are now only used to set you together by the Ears, that Rogues may pick your Pockets. I own myself to be one of those, whom one Side in Respect, and the other in Contumely, call Whig; and yet I never discoursed with a candid and sensible Tory, who did not concur with me in Opinion, when we explained our Intentions'.[35]

This was a theme which Bolingbroke and his colleagues took up with vigour in the late 1720s when opposition began to grow.[36] It was also one which was most alarming to the government. A really strong country opposition could make considerable difficulties for the court, as the exclusion crisis of 1679-81 and the last years of William III's reign had demonstrated. Understandably, the government press did its best to encourage an alternative rivalry between Whig and Tory, one which since 1714 had invariably favoured the ministerialists.

We have been charg'd [declared the *London Journal*] with conjuring up the Spirit of *Whiggism, and Toryism*; *Distinctions* which all good Men wish'd were buried in Oblivion. To this we answer; That the *Distinctions* ought to be kept up as long as *the Difference* remains; . . . While there are Papists, Jacobites, and Tories in the Kingdom, they ought to be

[35] J. Trenchard and T. Gordon, *Cato's Letters* (London, 1733, 3rd edn.), iii. 9.
[36] See H. T. Dickinson, *Bolingbroke* (London, 1970), chaps. 11, 12, and I. Kramnick, *Bolingbroke and his Circle* (London, 1968).

THE BACKGROUND TO THE EXCISE CRISIS 15

call'd *Papists, Jacobites, and Tories*; and while *Whig and Tory* last, they ought to be called *Whig and Tory*.[37]

To some extent, of course, circumstances still favoured such appeals to the old antipathies. In many places party labels were still the stuff of politics. In a city like Norwich, every local election, whether of common councillors, of sheriffs, of mayor, or of M.P.s, was the signal for the traditional type of conflict. In Oxford too the venom which Whig and Tory dons injected into their customary bickering showed no signs of lessening. More than politics was affected. Sir George Savile, for example, had severe doubts as to the wisdom of prosecuting the divorce of his wife for adultery with the young M.P. William Levinz, because 'Mr. Levinz was a Tory, and the Lawyers of the Spiritual Court were all such, and he had experience how far Party governed their judgments. To sue there for a divorce might be attended with ill success'.[38] However, all these symptoms of apparently bitter party strife were in reality little more than the last vestiges of ancient feuds, which at least at national level were slowly but steadily receding before the advance of a conflict at once older and newer, that of court and country.

Even so this conflict could only become a real threat to Walpole and his regime if it were fed with the issues needed to create sustained discontent. Fortunately for Walpole's opponents the conditions in the early 1730s were not unpropitious. Despite the immense strength and apparent security of the Walpolian system, it had many features which were likely to alarm its potential enemies and provoke considerable debate. In the first place it must be stressed that the dynasty, which Walpole supported by his efforts and consolidated by his policies, was far from being the object of popular affection. In large measure the king himself was responsible for the odium which he incurred. It was doubtless inevitable that George I, a foreign prince who could speak English only badly, who made plain his dislike of Tories, who had none of the charisma which tempered the unpopularity of the Stuarts, should be badly received, but George II had far less excuse. In 1727 indeed he missed a great chance to ingratiate himself with the uncommitted. As Prince of Wales he had dabbled in opposition politics and given great cause for expectations of change. At the death of George I many expected that the new

[37] 4 Mar. 1732.
[38] *HMC Egmont Diary*, ii. 224–5.

king would discourage divisions and bestow his favours on both parties in the manner of William III. 'Joy', one commentator reported, 'is the universal fashion, without any mixture of concern; all parties seem pleased and full of hopes. The malcontent clergy who were so in the late reign (I know not why) now preach obedience, loyalty and unity'.[39] Yet George II disappointed all. Not only did he continue his father's minister, but his prejudies were also similar. His predilection for Hanover, his appallingly bad manners, his lack of interest in most things English, all made him hated in a short time. His personal unpopularity with those outside the charmed circle of the court was remarkable. 'The king's not speaking to the country gentry when they come to Court', it was commented, 'tries them, and makes them declare they have no business to come there, since they are not regarded, and so they betake themselves to the discontented party'.[40] Just how great an opportunity George II missed in such matters is clearly demonstrated by the reign of his successor. George III was eventually to become immensely popular with almost all classes because his natural amiability and his strong sense of duty made him indefatigable in his social obligations. Had George II possessed half his grandson's conscientiousness and half his ability to conciliate those who were little acquainted with courts, he would have been a better-loved king.

The loathing quite unnecessarily accumulated by George II was reinforced by that which Walpole earned. Some of this merely stemmed from dislike of Walpole's character. But it also sprang logically from Walpole's position and policies. In retrospect it can be seen, for example, that Walpole's pioneering work as Prime Minister was to establish an important and useful institution. But at the time few were prepared to admire it. The length of Walpole's tenure, of which he was so proud, was distinctly alarming to others, and in this respect again the episode of 1727 worsened matters. The *Craftsman* in 1734 argued that Walpole's entry into his fourteenth year of power since taking office on 1 April 1721 ('of all Days in the Year') was in itself intolerable.[41] Moreover, the concept of a 'sole' or 'prime' minister had long been odious, smacking, as it supposedly did, of 'foreign' slavery. It was still the common belief at this time that the constitution required a king who was his own prime minister advised

---

[39] *HMC Savile*, p. 125: Gertrude Savile to Sir G. Savile, 20 June 1727.
[40] *HMC Egmont Diary*, i. 41.
[41] 11 May 1734.

by privy councillors answerable to Parliament. Such was the doctrine for which Clarendon had held out,[42] and such was the 'correct' prevailing view. 'It would be best', Sarah Churchill argued, 'for a King, as well as the nation and everybody that has any property or love to their posterity, to have all things done in council without a Premier Minister, which I have often heard is the law. In that case many great officers would be answerable for what they did'.[43] This was already an obsolete view of the constitution, but it was still commonplace, and Walpole as well as others knew how unpopular prime ministers and cabinets were in theory, however essential in practice. In this as in much else he paid the penalty of the pioneer. Where he led others followed, and what seemed unnatural in his position was later to be accepted as the normal practice under Pelham, North and the Younger Pitt.

By his policies, too, Walpole incurred censure. From the point of view of traditional 'country' attitudes there was much to complain of. It is easy in retrospect to forget how the preoccupations of the seventeenth century lingered on in the early eighteenth century. In many ways the crucial dividing line lay in the 1740s and 1750s, when many of the aspects of Georgian politics established under Walpole came to be fully accepted. But until that happened there was a tremendous potential opposition to much of the Hanoverian system. Political memories were long—the Rump, Commonwealthmen, Presbyterians, Papists, Roundheads, not to say more recent figures like William III, Queen Anne, Sacheverell and Ormonde, figured prominently in the slogans of Walpole's age. Political violence did not seem as dead at the time as it has since. Quite apart from the Jacobite danger, some contemporaries still feared that political conflicts could turn into 'a rebellion or civil war'; the newspapers were not above speculating about the possibility of assassinations, and even in Parliament there were apt to be 'great heats'.[44] Nor were the issues particularly novel or trivial. There was for example a perfectly genuine fear of standing armies, which makes little sense with hindsight but meant much at the time; as Lord Hervey pointed out, 'there was certainly nothing so odious to men of all ranks and

[42] W. C. Costin and J. S. Watson, eds., *The Law and Working of the Constitution: Documents 1660–1914* (London, 1961, 2nd edn.), i. 317–22.
[43] *Memoirs of Sarah, Duchess of Marlborough*, p. 310.
[44] *HMC Egmont Diary*, iii. 235; *Remarks on Fog's Journal of February 10, 1733. Exciting the People to an Assassination* (London, 1733); E. Calamy, *An Historical Account of my own Life, with some Reflections on the Times I have lived in* (London, 1829), ii. 511.

classes in this country as troops'.[45] Sensible country gentlemen could not be reassured on this point. 'We are and are like to be', wrote George Clarke, by no means the most extreme of Tory gentry, 'under a military government, for there does not seem to be any more prospect of disbanding troops than lessening the Public Debt'.[46] Debates on the standing army in Parliament are indeed an 'open sesame' to the assumptions of the time about the dangers to the constitution. 'I believe', it was declared in one such debate in 1734, 'it will be granted, that the prerogative, even within these last 30 or 40 years, has grown pretty considerably. I believe every gentleman will admit, the power of the crown is now infinitely greater than it was for some years after the revolution'.[47] On the other side a member 'had never heard of any motion made in parliament, which tended so directly towards establishing a commonwealth, as the present does, except some of those famous motions which were made in the years forty and forty-one'.[48] Even Walpole, when it suited his convenience as it did in this particular debate, warned: 'we should be in continual danger of falling entirely under the government of our army'.[49] Such arguments, however absurd in retrospect, struck a potent chord at the time, and while the realists voted annually for the standing army, not all of the public could be expected to be very realistic.

There were of course other issues which struck very similar chords. The national debt with its allegedly colossal subsidy for the commercial and financial interests, septennial parliaments, introduced only in 1716 and arguably the cause of immense corruption, alliance with the national enemy, France, all these were the subject of incessant debate in an age which loathed change of any kind. But the conflict which both dwarfed and absorbed these matters, and which inspired so much of the political violence of the day, involved a more general problem, in a word that of corruption. Today it is customary to qualify the significance of the crown's influence as a sinister force at work in the constitution. It may be pointed out, for example, that no minister lived by bribery alone, that the House of Commons was rarely the docile servant of the court, and that the actual amount of influence at the crown's disposal was in practice

---

[45] *Hervey Memoirs*, p. 525.
[46] *HMC Leybourne-Popham*, p. 289.
[47] *Parl. Hist.*, ix. 291: Samuel Sandys, 13 Feb. 1734.
[48] Ibid., 294: Martin Bladen.
[49] Ibid., 322.

relatively small.[50] At the same time it can be argued that patronage in any case played a vital role in constitutional development, making possible precisely that harmony between executive and legislature which had been lacking in the seventeenth century and was to prepare the way for the emergence of parliamentary democracy in the nineteenth.

Neither of these arguments could be expected to appeal to contemporaries, however. If it is clear to us now that under Walpole the Court and Treasury party was as strong in terms of places and pensions as it was ever to be, we can scarcely expect contemporaries to be equally sure that it would stop growing at the pace of preceding years. 'If some stop be not put to it,' declared Perceval, 'in a few Parliaments more [than] two-thirds of the lower House may consist of absolute dependents on the Court'.[51] Since the power of patronage in Parliament had grown so much in the years of the early eighteenth century, why should it not grow still further in the middle and late eighteenth century? Admittedly such growth could be defended. Even at the time the possible political value of the system of spoils could be seen. They 'tell us', remarked the *Craftsman*, 'that the *Influence* They plead for is necessary to strengthen the Hands of Those, who govern; that *Corruption* serves to oil the Wheels of Government, and to render the Administration more smooth and easy'.[52] This argument was indeed familiar to many. William Stukely, the celebrated antiquarian and a Whig, urged a clerical correspondent to beware of opposing government. 'This is the zeal of a high churchman, which runs through your whole letter. PENSIONS and PLACES, writ in capitals to render it more formidable, shows what political papers you read. . . . My friend, what are pensions and places, but wages? Doe you serve your livings the worse because you receive the tythes and offerings?'[53] Even so such arguments were not unanswerable. For one thing contemporaries did not all accept the premise that ministerial stability was worth having for the surrender of traditional liberties. For another it was generally felt, and increasingly so in the years before the excise crisis, that corruption was getting altogether out of hand. In the

[50] See, for example, J. B. Owen, *The Rise of the Pelhams* (London, 1957), pp. 56-7.

[51] *HMC Egmont Diary*, ii. 37. John, Viscount Perceval (1683-1748) is better known as Earl of Egmont, a title which he received 6 Nov. 1773. However, to avoid confusion, he is throughout this book described as Perceval.

[52] 26 Jan. 1734.

[53] *The Family Memoirs of the Rev. William Stukely, M.D.* (Pubs. Surtees Soc., lxxiii (1880)), 274: Stukeley to Rev. A. Pimlow, 9 Mar. 1734.

conventional nightmare of the period the perpetuation of the existing system, as one opposition M.P. put it,

> would indeed make the Election of a House of Commons a Very Easy Task for any first Minister here after: He might sitt at home in his great Chair, and order such and such Persons to be elected, as he shoud think most proper. He did not doubt but that in a little time he would see all the little inferior Clerks of the treasury and other offices coming to that house in the morning to Vote taxes upon the People, and in the afternoon attending at Dinner behind the Chair of the Chancellor of Exchequer nay he did not know, but the Oldest of them might live to see some Vain, overgrown first Minister of State driving along the Streets with Six Members of Parliament behind his Coach.[54]

It must be admitted that this growing sentiment of alarm and disgust at the apparent degradation of political life was partly the fault of Walpole. Almost everything he did reinforced the popular belief that the politics of courts were disgusting to a degree. It happened, for example, that the early 1730s witnessed a whole series of major scandals which worried even Walpole's friends and supporters. Four major public trusts, the South Sea Company, the York Building Company, the Charitable Corporation and the Derwentwater Trust, found themselves in difficulties which involved considerable sums of public and government money on the one hand, and M.P.s who were supporters of the ministry on the other. The result was a political sensation in which a good deal of the mud stuck to Walpole. In the case of the Charitable Corporation, for example, where the guilty party was Robert Sutton, a supporter of Walpole's, who was eventually expelled from the House of Commons for his misdemeanours, Walpole went out of his way to defend Sutton and alienated many of his most loyal friends in doing so. The Derwentwater case was equally alarming. There two of the M.P.s involved, Denis Bond and John Birch, were in so deep that nothing could save them; but Sir John Eyles, a prominent figure in the city and a great friend of Walpole's, was saved by his efforts. Such conduct was most damaging to Walpole. Even if he had no real interest involved, even if, as he claimed, the government bore none of the responsibility for such scandals, his defence of the culprits could only make the general opinion of him and his system worse. Opponents could hardly be expected to interpret Walpole's activities charitably. Hence allega-

---

[54] RA Stuart, Unbound MSS 1/125: Pulteney in Commons' debate of 16 Mar. 1733.

tions like 'dissipating and grossly embezzling the publick money, by vile stockjobbing, protecting openly every rapacious villain, and all the gross horrid frauds in the trading companies'.[55] Even Lord Hervey, Walpole's close friend, had to admit that his propensity for opposing any kind of enquiry into abuse was 'the weakest part of his character and policy'.[56] This was reinforced in other ways. Walpole's ruthless exploitation of political advantage against all considerations of justice came out particularly in election disputes. Perceval thus described one episode in 1730 when Walpole sought to seat his friend Brereton, unsuccessful candidate for Liverpool.

Sir Robert Walpole stayed till the division was over, in order to influence the House for Brereton, but he found there are certain occasions where he cannot carry points; it is this meanness of his (the prostitution of the character of a first Minister in assisting and strenuously supporting the defence of dunghill worms, let their cause be ever so unjust, against men of honour, birth, and fortune, and that in person too), that gains him so much ill-will; formerly, when the first Minister appeared in any matter, he did it with gravity, and the honour and service of the Crown appeared to be concerned, but Sir Robert, like the altars of refuge in old times, is the asylum of little unworthy wretches who, submitting to dirty work, endear themselves to him, and get his protection first, and then his favour, which as he is first Minister, is sure to draw after it the countenance of the Court; in the meantime, the world, who know the insignificancy, to say no worse, of these sort of tools, are in indignation to see them preferred and cherished beyond men of character and fortune, and set off in a better light to the King, and this with men of small experience, which are the bulk of a nation, occasions hard thoughts of the Crown itself.[57]

Hervey and Perceval were both basically friends of Walpole. What then was the verdict of 'the bulk of the nation' who had no particular reason to love him?

If there was much in Walpole's regime to arouse considerable resentment, there was also at hand a powerful weapon with which to inflame and concentrate it. Few developments in early eighteenth-century England were more striking or more important than the growth of the press. Ever since the formal machinery of state censorship set up by the Licensing Act had been allowed to lapse in 1695

[55] 'Letters of Lord Grange', *Miscellany of Spalding Club*, iii (Aberdeen, 1846), 46: Grange to Erskine, 5 and 6 Aug. 1732.
[56] *Hervey Memoirs*, p. 186.
[57] *HMC Egmont Diary*, i. 85–6.

(as much by accident as design), the world of pamphlets and newspapers had flourished. The first decade of the century undoubtedly stands out in the history of Grub Street if only by virtue of the galaxy of talents which presided over it. Yet in some ways more significant was the period of consolidation which succeeded it. Some contemporaries expected that the stamp tax of 1712 and the end of the War of Spanish Succession, which was generally supposed to have sustained popular interest in the newspapers, would effectively smash the press.[58] In fact after an initial setback the newspapers prospered during the reigns of George I and George II as it quickly became clear that they had a growing as well as an enduring audience. However, what is surprising in retrospect is not the growth of the press but its relative independence of government. In theory almost all the advantages in this area belonged to the court. Though formal censorship was at an end, the law still acted as a powerful and partisan restraint on the freedom of the press. Walpole's administration was indefatigable in detecting and prosecuting anything that smacked of libel or sedition. However, it was not invariably successful. Juries could still be found to defy the crown,[59] and the opposition newspapers became adept at evading prosecution. 'As for the *Craftsman*', one Attorney-General complained, 'tho' it is a very impudent Paper, I think it is so guarded, That an Information cannot be brought on any part of it'.[60]

Even so the law was not the only threat to the opposition press. The government propaganda machine was no less forbidding. Walpole was ever a great believer in the power of the printed word. In the 1730s he spent on average well over £5,000 per annum (mostly from the king's secret service fund) on pamphlets and newspapers. Journals like the *Free Briton*, the *London Journal* and the *Corn-Cutter's Journal* were little more than propaganda sheets, and even 'newspapers' proper like the *Daily Courant* and *Daily Journal* were heavily subsidized. In addition the Post Office was shamelessly employed to distribute and advertise officially approved publications.[61] The opposition press was also subsidized by leading opponents of Walpole, but they could hardly compete with the resources of the ministry. Yet the fact was that the opposition press flourished.

---

[58] L. Hanson, *Government and the Press, 1695–1763* (London, 1936), pp. 11–12.
[59] Ibid., p. 19.
[60] P.R.O., S.P. 36/30, f. 345: Willes to Newcastle, 15 Dec. 1733.
[61] K. Ellis, *The Post Office in the Eighteenth Century* (London, 1958), chap. 5.

Even in the technical problem of distribution it proved capable of beating the court at its own game. Thus at the height of the excise crisis one government supporter in Sussex complained bitterly of the opposition's superiority in this respect. 'I wish we had some proper news Papers etc: to disperse here . . . We have no news Papers here except the London Journal on our side tho' the Craftsman is very industriously sent down to the Tory Coffeehouse every weeke.'[62] Particularly striking in this context was the emergence of a provincial press. At the beginning of the century there were no regular newspapers outside London. By 1733 there were nearly thirty representing practically all the major towns.[63] This crucial extension of the media from the metropolis to the provinces was most important, especially in relation to opposition. The great mass of the public at large was generally little inclined to favour the court in the age of Walpole, as even the ministerialists admitted.[64] Most of the local newspapers were either hostile to the government or quickly became so,[65] and took pains to see that the arguments set forth in the more violent London papers, particularly the *Craftsman* and *Fog's Weekly Journal*, were relayed up and down the country. Simultaneously reflecting and fanning popular opposition, they did not a little to prepare the public for a ferment such as the excise crisis was to unleash.

A factor which might be thought wanting in the background to the excise crisis was the economic one. Though the ancient grievance of the country gentleman—that his land was taxed to feed the avarice of the merchant and the corruption of the court—was much voiced in this period, it scarcely had the force of earlier days when almost continuous war had severely burdened the country's financial system. Yet even in the 1730s there was something of a strain, though without the backdrop of war. It was, after all, precisely at this time that there began that boom on the land which paradoxically depressed the landowner's fortunes. The extraordinary series of good harvests in the 1730s and 1740s, which did so much to raise the labourer's standard of living on the one hand and give a crucial impetus to population growth on the other, hit many farmers very hard. In these years the price of grain, the ultimate index of the farmer's profits,

[62] Add. MS. 32689 (Newcastle Papers), f. 9: T. Ball to Newcastle, 4 Nov. 1733.
[63] G. A. Cranfield, *The Development of the Provincial Newspaper, 1700–1760* (Oxford, 1962), pp. 19–21.
[64] See below, p. 131.
[65] Cranfield, op. cit., chap. vi.

dropped catastrophically. In 1728 wheat stood at 6s. 8d. a quarter; thereafter it fell progressively until it reached 4s. in 1730, 3s. 3d. in 1732 and 3s. 6d. in 1733, the period of the excise agitation.[66] The figure for 1732 was indeed the lowest of the entire century with the exception of 1706 and 1744. Under this pressure rents fell severely as landlords were forced to reduce the burden on their tenants.[67] There is ample evidence of distress. In 1733 in Lancashire, for example, the Quaker William Stout noted appallingly low prices for wheat, meat and fruit. 'This went hard with poor farmers, and broke many, and lessned the rent of lands'.[68] The following year it was reported in Kent that 'Barley sells almost for nothing'.[69] This was the economic background to the general election which followed the excise crisis, an election in which, as will be seen, the county electorates, dominated by small farmers and landowners, swung dramatically against government. The correlation involved is scarcely incontestable, but it does suggest that Walpole was unfortunate in launching a major measure of taxation at a time when the rural landowner, a critically important figure in extra-parliamentary politics, was suddenly and seriously distressed.

A final pointer to the discontent which was mounting is to be found in another significant sector, the city of London. At least since 1715 London, though politically divided, had been tolerably loyal to government. Walpole's alliance with the financiers, his appeal to the merchants, and his stress on the dangers of Jacobitism had had their effect. In 1727, for example, the general election had produced two opposition M.P.s and two ministerialists, and Tories rejoiced even at their partial triumph. 'The carrying of two in the City', it was commented, 'under the present circumstances, is a great victory'.[70] Yet soon after this there were seen the beginnings of a movement away from government. Rumours abounded of discontent among the great mercantile interests which had so far supported Walpole, and

[66] T. S. Ashton, *Economic Fluctuations in England, 1700-1800* (Oxford, 1959), p. 181; the view that there was a striking contrast between food prices before and after 1750 is challenged in D. E. C. Eversley, 'The Home Market and Economic Growth in England, 1750-1780' in E. L. Jones and G. E. Mingay, eds., *Land, Labour and Population in the Industrial Revolution* (London, 1967), pp. 240-6.

[67] G. E. Mingay, 'The Agriculteral Depression, 1730-1750', *Econ. Hist. Rev.*, 2nd Ser., viii (1955-56), 323-38.

[68] J. D. Marshall, ed., *The Autobiography of William Stout, of Lancaster, 1665-1752* (Manchester, 1967), p. 213.

[69] *London Evening Post*, 9-11 Apr. 1734.

[70] *HMC Portland*, vii. 453: Dr. W. Stratford to Oxford, 28 Nov. 1727.

significantly Micajah Perry, one of the government M.P.s, defected in the course of this Parliament. In other areas, elections of Lord Mayor, sheriffs, and other officers, there was a marked swing away from the court.[71] Even in the Court of Aldermen, the preserve of the Whigs, government support declined sufficiently to endanger its majority. According to some contemporaries this trend took place in other cities as well, and certainly some were aware which way the wind was blowing. One moderate Tory observed,

There is one thing too at home that may deserve some reflections . . . the strange spirit that continues in the city of London. We find too it is a contagious spirit, and has infected the city greatest in extent and trade next to London, that of Norwich. I cannot imagine any reason for the uneasiness of such bodies, but some decay which they feel in their trade. That is the only article that uses to affect them. But it is plain here are great uneasiness ready to be increased and to break out, upon any juncture proper to inflame and favour them. And should not things abroad go to our wishes, I will not answer that there may not be a ferment run again through the nation, somewhat like that which was in Sacheverell's case.[72]

This most perceptive comment, written several years before the excise crisis, was mistaken only in the issue it predicted. Had the Dunkirk affair of 1730 blown up, the prophecy might well have been fulfilled in its entirety. Instead it was smothered in good time by Walpole, and the forces which were building for an explosion in these years had to await the advent of a major domestic issue.

[71] A. J. Henderson, *London and the National Government, 1721–1742* (Durham, N.C., 1945), p. 132.
[72] *HMC Portland*, vii. 465: Stratford to Oxford, 6 July 1728.

III
Walpole and the Excise

THOUGH it is possible in retrospect to analyse the accumulation of factors in the early years of George II's reign which made the excise scheme so dangerous, it does not necessarily follow that Walpole's timing of his project cannot be defended. His opponents were naturally quick to condemn his folly once the extent of the storm which he had raised became apparent. Arbuthnot, for example, recalled the Sacheverell affair of 1709-10, when the young Walpole and his fellow Whigs had 'putt all to the test by an experiment of a silly project of the tryal of a poor parson. the same Game, in my mind, is playing again from a wantonness of power'.[1] Ever since, Walpole's decision has been seen as a gigantic miscalculation, one of the most extraordinary instances in British political history of a complete failure of judgment by a leading statesman. Nonetheless, an examination of Walpole's position in the early 1730s, and particularly of the considerations which led him to propose new duties, suggests that this verdict is not without its dangers.

Walpole's own account of the reasons which led him to attempt an extension of the excise was simple and straightforward. When he outlined his proposals for an excise on imported wine and tobacco in the Commons he insisted that the pressures for the change had come from outside the government. 'It was the frequent advices I had of the shameful frauds committed in these two branches, and the complaints of the merchants themselves, that induced me to turn my attention to discover a remedy for this growing evil'.[2] This claim was not totally implausible. The battle between the smuggler and the government in the eighteenth century was of course a ceaseless one. However, while any attempt to quantify the volume of smuggled goods is difficult, there are indications that the early 1730s were a particularly prosperous period for customs evasion.[3] Especially on

[1] H. Williams, ed., *Correspondence of Jonathan Swift* (Oxford, 1963-65), iv. 102: Arbuthnot to Swift, 13 Jan. 1733.
[2] *Parl. Hist.*, viii. 1270: 14 Mar. 1733.
[3] W. A. Cole, 'Trends in Eighteenth Century Smuggling', in W. E. Minchinton, ed., *Growth of English Overseas Trade*, and T. C. Barker, 'Smuggling in the Eighteenth

the south-east coast, smuggling was reaching new heights of intensity. The newspapers reported pitched battles between the coast-guards and gangs thirty or forty strong, while in Kent it was even alleged that smuggling provided such an attractive career to the labouring classes that farmers found it impossible to hire casual help at harvest time.[4] In a number of cases troops had to be deployed to deal with smugglers who, as the *London Magazine* observed, 'are arriv'd to such an intolerable Pitch of Insolence, as to bid Defiance to the civil Magistrates'.[5] Not until the 1770s was this problem to be so grave again as it was under Walpole. A prolonged period of peace and prosperity, high duties on luxury articles, and low standards of public morality and service in the customs administration combined to produce particularly favourable conditions for fraud on a large scale. It was argued by many that the only satisfactory answer to this situation was the gradual extinction of customs duties in favour of excises. There were in fact a great variety of frauds quite apart from straightforward smuggling. In the case of tobacco, for example, these covered false declarations of weights and measures in order to minimize import duties and maximize export rebates, clandestine unloading from ships waiting to dock, bogus re-exports achieved either by the substitution of worthless stems for tobacco leaves, or by immediate re-landing from nearby smuggling havens like the Channel Islands and Flanders, in both cases with the object of illegally obtaining drawbacks, and extremely complex accounting 'fiddles'. However, what all these practices had in common was the system which they preyed on. As Walpole told the Commons, 'Frauds become practicable by having but one check at importation, and one at exportation'.[6] The fatal failing of the customs system was that it operated only at the point of entry. Once past a lax and overstretched coastguard system, the smuggler was safe. Excise duties by contrast were levied basically on internal consumption; they could be applied and checked at a number of stages between landing and retail sale. In practice, it is true, even the excise could be evaded

---

Century: The Evidence of the Scottish Tobacco Trade', *Virginia Mag.*, lxii (1954) 387-99.

[4] *Fog's Weekly Journal*, 15 Sept. 1733.

[5] 1732, p. 37: see also C(H) MSS. 41/20: Customs memorial on use of dragoons in Suffolk.

[6] *Parl. Hist.*, vii. 1275: 14 Mar. 1733; for Walpole's papers relating to frauds, see C(H) MSS. 41.

with more ease than governments ever admitted, but it was undeniable that it presented the dishonest trader with more difficulties than did the customs.

Though Walpole could legitimately claim that his measure would at least assist the revenue departments to deal with the problem of fraud, his additional statement that it had been suggested by those who suffered through such frauds is more contentious. He appears to have had friends among the traders in the commodities affected by his scheme, who plied him with information about the frauds in their trade.[7] But these merchants scarcely represented more than a tiny minority; most of them were doubtless small dealers with an interest in conciliating the administration. In fact only one very important interested party in either the tobacco or wine industry gave strong support to Walpole's project of an excise. The Virginia Council and House of Burgesses, on behalf of the planters of that province, actually petitioned King and Parliament in the summer of 1732 in favour of an excise on their product.[8] John Randolph was commissioned to carry the petition to London, and it was indeed his arrival in October which formed the first clear indication to the public that a major change in the taxation laws was contemplated. Randolph was knighted by the King when presenting the petition at court on 3 November, and thereafter the supporters of the government made a great deal of this apparently unanimous approval of the excise by the tobacco-growers. Walpole himself actually planned to have Randolph interrogated by the Commons to make the most of his evidence,[9] and he and his colleagues on the government benches laid great stress on the need to satisfy the demands of the Virginia and Maryland planters.

Even so this development provoked considerable controversy. According to the opposition the Virginia petition was an elaborate fraud. Micajah Perry, the doyen of London tobacco merchants and one of the M.P.s for the city, claimed in the Commons that 'the representation from Virginia was formed and cooked up here; not only the President (of the Virginia Council), Mr. Carter, now dead, repented the signing it, as he wrote me himself, but most of the planters have repented it too'.[10] The *Craftsman* also alleged that the

[7] See, for example, C(H) MSS. 41/46, 50.
[8] For the Virginian representation, see C. Headlam and A. P. Newton, eds., *Calendar of State Papers Colonial Series; America and West Indies, 1732* (London, 1939), pp. 178–80.
[9] C(H) MSS. 90/20: notes.   [10] *HMC Egmont Diary*, i. 352–3: 4 Apr. 1733.

Virginians had been deceived into drawing up their protest. 'We have received Accounts from *Virginia* that when they were made acquainted with the Consequences of an EXCISE, They were as much alarmed at it as the People in *England*.'[11] On the other side of the argument it was pointed out that the grievances of the Virginians were so obvious that such allegations were absurd. 'Can anyone be so weak, as to imagine the *Planters* requir'd *ministerial* Spurs, and Artifices, to excite them to what must so manifestly tend to their general Interest.'[12] Nonetheless, this connection between taxation reform in England and economic recovery in Virginia is not quite so clear as this implied. The basic cause of the slump which affected the Virginia and Maryland tobacco industry so severely in the 1720s and 1730s, and which so reduced the value of tobacco that the planters were allegedly 'hardly able to provide cloaths for the slaves that make it',[13] was chronic overproduction which flooded the European market with inferior produce and kept prices excessively low. According to Randolph fraud contributed in two principal ways to this problem.[14] Firstly, the customs system, with its involved bureaucratic methods associated with the re-export procedures, gave the dishonest tobacco merchants and factors in England an opportunity to lay unnecessary charges to the planters' accounts; secondly, dishonest merchants reduced the cost of their imported merchandize without passing on the benefit of their frauds to either the planters or consumers. The strict relevance of these points is not altogether obvious, and while the introduction of an excise might have dealt with them at least to some extent, it is difficult to see how it would have affected the underlying position. If there was any practicable solution to the problem of low prices and overproduction it lay in America rather than in England.

The suspicion that colonial interests were less involved in the question of the excise scheme than Walpole and his supporters claimed is reinforced by an examination of the process which led to the Virginian action. On the face of it the Virginian House of Burgesses' petition was a spontaneous demonstration in favour of

[11] 28 July 1733.
[12] *Englishmen's Eyes open'd; or, All made to See, who are not resolv'd to be Blind: Being the Excise Controversy Set in a new Light* (London, 1734, 2nd edn.), p. 68.
[13] *CSP Col. America and West Indies, 1732*, p. 179: Gooch to Newcastle, 20 July 1732.
[14] *The Case of the Planters of Tobacco in Virginia, As represented by Themselves*, signed by the President of the Council, and Speaker of the House of Burgesses (London, 1733).

Walpole's excise. In reality it was a carefully engineered piece of ministerial propaganda. The truth of a rumour picked up by the French ambassador, to the effect that the Governor of Virginia had received direct instructions from London, is amply confirmed by an entry in the Journals of the Virginia Council dated 15 December 1731:

The Gov[ernor] Communicated to the Council a Scheme projected in Great Britain for putting the Tob[acc]o under an Excise instead of the present method of paying the Duties thereof and desir'd their Opinion therein. Whereupon the Board are of Opinion that the Scheme propos'd would be greatly for the Interest of his Majesty in securing his Customs prevent the running of Tob[acc]o prove very beneficial to the Inhabitants of this Country.[15]

The Governor's informant was not named, though it is a reasonable supposition that it was Walpole's brother Horace Walpole. In his capacity as Auditor-General of the Plantations, Horace corresponded regularly with the colonial governors and, as Walpole's younger brother and general factotum, he was used to carrying out political commissions. Moreover, Horace made a particular point of stressing the Virginian interest in the excise to those in England who needed convincing as to its merits.[16] In addition, his correspondent in Virginia had particular reason to fall in with instructions from London. The acting governor of Virginia, Lieutenant-Governor Gooch, had his own solution to the problem of the tobacco depression. Essentially it consisted of a system of quality control calculated to improve the standard of tobacco exports, and so raise the price of tobacco in Britain. Unfortunately for Gooch, the project was not without its opponents. In Virginia many planters, especially the poorer ones, saw it as a direct assault on the smaller tobacco-grower.[17] In London the customs commissioners regarded any scheme intended to improve the quality of imports at the expense of quantity as a threat to revenue yields.[18] Consequently Gooch was

[15] H. R. McIlwaine, ed., *Executive Journals of the Council of Colonial Virginia* (Richmond, 1930), iv. 258; Corr. Pol. Angl., 380, f. 311.
[16] *HMC Egmont Diary*, i. 311.
[17] J. C. Rainbolt, '"The Case of the Poor Planters in Virginia" against the Law for Inspecting and Burning Tobacco', *Virginia Mag.*, lxxix (1971), 314–21.
[18] *Journal of the Commissioners for Trade and Plantations from January 1728–9 to December 1734, preserved in the Public Record Office* (London, 1928), pp. 164, 168, 175, 176, 179–80, 181.

compelled to tread carefully. Even after steering his scheme through the Virginian legislature he had needed the co-operation of the administration in England to ensure that it was endorsed by the Privy Council, and he would need it again for a renewal. Virginian approval for the excise scheme, especially if it could be argued that the excise was genuinely in the planters' interest, was a very small price to pay for such co-operation. That this was the origin of the excise petitions from Virginia can hardly be doubted. Ironically, Gooch himself was also responsible at least in part for the very conception of a tobacco excise. When he had requested the government's support for his Tobacco Inspection Act in 1730 he had stressed that one of its effects would be the reduction of fraud, which preyed severely on the inferior tobacco previously entered from Virginia. 'My Design is to prevent the Running of Tobacco in Great Britain, which if we can Compass, His Majesty's Customs will be very considerably augmented'.[19] At the time this had doubtless been intended as an argument to secure British support for his own scheme. But it may also have drawn the attention of Horace and Sir Robert Walpole to the political value of the Virginia planter's distress in the context of their plans for new excises.[20] In any event it is obvious that the Walpole Administration could not fairly claim to have been drawn into its excise proposals by the Americans. Whatever the Virginians thought of the excise scheme, and there is no particular reason why they should have opposed it, they had not spontaneously requested its enactment.

In fact the excise scheme is better seen as a logical part of Walpole's financial policy than as a sudden response to the needs of the fair trader and distressed planter. Basically it reflected two of the fundamental themes of Walpole's policy—the growing emphasis on efficient taxation of internal consumption in the form of inland duties, and the diminishing importance of direct taxes on propertied income. Both these processes had much to commend them. Ever since its introduction in 1643 the excise or inland duty had been one of the mainstays of government finance. Unlike the land tax, it was a tax on the community at large, affecting a wide variety of articles of consumption, unlike the customs, it was comparatively effective

[19] P.R.O., C.O. 5/1322, f.147: Gooch to Board of Trade, 9 Apr. 1730.
[20] See D. A. Williams, 'Anglo-Virginian Politics, 1690–1735', in A. G. Olson and R. M. Brown, eds., *Anglo-American Political Relations, 1675–1773* (New Brunswick, 1970).

against fraud and cost relatively little to enforce. By the Hanoverian period it was, despite recurrent bouts of unpopularity, an established and indeed essential item in the nation's budget. Under Walpole it also acquired a connection with commercial reform. Most of the inland duties had been traditionally levied on basic home-produced foodstuffs, notably alcoholic beverages. In short they were employed not as an alternative to customs duties, which applied only to imported goods, but as an addition to them. However, Walpole had demonstrated that they were also viable simply as a substitute for customs duties. His celebrated 'bonded warehouses' provided both a more liberal commercial policy and a more effective revenue machine by clearly distinguishing between goods intended for internal consumption and those destined for re-export. Those released on the home market could be taxed by the excise department, while those sent out of the country could be despatched with the minimum of bureaucracy. Thus duty-free storage in the bonded warehouses replaced a cumbersome and clogging system of bonds and drawbacks inherent in the old customs system. In 1723 Walpole had applied this so-called excise (though in purpose and function it differed radically from the traditional seventeenth-century excises) to tea, chocolate and coffee. The benefit conferred on the revenue was apparent in the initial stages of this experiment, less so later on.[21] Even so the administration clearly had strong grounds for its belief that an extension of the excise would be at least as useful in terms of revenue as the customs, and a clear gain to the empire's trading system. Walpole indeed always insisted that one of the great advantages of his proposed scheme was a major liberalization of trade as well as a great advantage to the Treasury. Bonded warehouses would attract ever-increasing amounts of commodities for re-export. Not only would the strain on other forms of taxation be eased, but London would quickly become a 'free port, and by consequence, the market of the world'.[22]

Even more important to Walpole himself was the precise branch of revenue which would be eased by a new excise. No part of Walpole's policy is more celebrated than his persistent stealing of Tory

[21] The statistics were capable of various interpretations. The eight years following the introduction of the excise on tea and coffee (the only significant items affected by the measure of 1723) produced over £1 million more than the preceding eight years' receipts from customs. On the other hand the three years 1729-32 showed a steady decline in revenue. See C(H) MSS. 27/2 for the detailed accounts.

[22] Coxe, i. 399: Walpole's speech on 14 Mar. 1733.

clothes on the issue of the land tax. It was always his aim to keep direct taxation to a minimum, and so draw the venom from the most contentious and dangerous problem of early eighteenth-century politics. In Anne's reign nothing had contributed more to the rage of the country gentry and thus to political instability than the growth of the land tax. In 1722 Walpole had managed to reduce it to 2s. in the £, half the wartime rate, and although the emergencies of the mid 1720s pushed it back briefly to 4s., by 1730 he had again reduced it by half. In that year he had also been permitted an additional luxury, a reduction in indirect taxation. The consequent abolition of the salt duty has been seen as a clearing of the decks for the excise scheme,[23] though it was scarcely this. Walpole himself had wanted the abolition of the candle tax; it was the House of Commons, which was apt to be particularly self-willed in matters of taxation, which chose to repeal the salt duty.[24] But 1730 was a turning-point. In that year Walpole's honeymoon period as George II's minister came to an end. Townshend and Carteret left the administration, the government's political base perceptibly narrowed, and in the House of Commons the rebel Whig opposition came into growing prominence. There were also financial problems. An increasingly tense diplomatic climate in Europe, which was to culminate in the War of Polish Succession, prevented significant reductions of British arms expenditure even given the ministry's determination to avoid involvement in continental warfare. But without such a reduction or comparable economies elsewhere there was little hope of further diminishing direct taxation. As a result Walpole was driven to unsatisfactory expedients in the last years of the 1727 Parliament. In 1732, in order to achieve his ambition of further reducing the land tax to 1s. in the £, he was compelled to resort to the reintroduction of the salt tax abolished in 1730.

Extraordinary reasons have been suggested for this move; it has been claimed, for example, that Walpole was moved to recreate the salt duty solely by compassion for the plight of those tax officials who

[23] N. A. Brisco, *The Economic Policy of Robert Walpole* (New York, 1907), p. 100.
[24] *HMC Egmont Diary*, i. 60, 63. It must be stressed that this tax reduction was not a piece of gratuitous ministerial generosity on Walpole's part. The reduction was a result of the statutory requirement to keep the Sinking Fund annual contributions to £1 million. By 1730 they had reached £1,130,000, and it became necessary to diminish their product accordingly. Walpole favoured the abolition of the candle duties because they yielded precisely £130,000, but the Commons preferred to repeal the salt tax, which was especially unpopular. See E. Hughes, *Studies in Administration and Finance, 1558–1825* (Manchester, 1934), p. 292.

had been unemployed since the disbandment of the salt department.[25] In fact there is no need to look further than the obvious. Walpole simply needed to find £500,000 of revenue to replace the loss of 1s. in the £ land tax. The salt duty revival was also a vital part of his excise plans. Though it was managed not by the Excise Commissioners but by a separate revenue department, it was of course an inland duty, and provided an opportunity to test possible reactions to further extensions of the excise. Moreover, Walpole did not conceal that he had every intention of devising further expedients. In the salt tax debates he and his brother, while denying that they had further specific proposals in mind, both applauded the principle of excise extension, and insisted that the policy of land tax reduction was to continue. As Perceval recorded in his diary, Walpole 'said he would not propose it if he did not intend that this ease in the land tax should continue'.[26] Unfortunately this was easier said than done. The salt duty was only a partial answer. As planned in 1732 it would yield £500,000 only over a period of three years; in short, to reduce the land tax by 1s. for just one year, the produce of the salt duty had to be mortgaged for three. In the event even this turned out to be wildly optimistic, as it quickly became clear that the yield of the salt duty would fall short by about £100,000.[27] Though the duty was renewed in 1734 and thereafter for the rest of the century, it was clearly inadequate to the limited task Walpole had initially set it, and to anything more ambitious correspondingly more so. As a result Walpole was again driven to a desperate measure even to maintain the land tax reduction essayed in 1732. In 1733 the missing £500,000 was provided by the first of many such raids on the theoretically sacrosanct Sinking Fund.[28] In this year as in 1732, Walpole specifically told the Commons that rejection of his proposals would mean an increase in the land tax. In each case he got his way, and in each he registered his failure to find a permanent substitute for 1s. of the land tax, let alone—the apparent summit of his ambitions—the entire 2s.

It is against this background that the origins of the excise must be

[25] Ibid., pp. 294 et seq.
[26] *HMC Egmont Diary*, i. 220.
[27] C(H) MSS. 30/5: salt duty accounts.
[28] It is sometimes stated that the raid on the Sinking Fund was itself necessitated by Walpole's miscalculation in regard to the salt tax. In fact the revived salt duty had never been intended to yield £500,000 in *one* year, and certainly played no part in the budgetary decisions of 1733.

seen. It was a logical extension of the system which Walpole had already employed and found useful, and above all it provided the one apparent means of escape from the financial dilemma in which Walpole found himself. Walpole was always cautious not to commit himself on the score of the exact results of a new excise. He was never precise as to whether he planned to maintain the reduction of the land tax to 1s. for example, or whether he wished to go further and abolish it altogether.[29] Nonetheless, his message was clear. Again and again in the excise debates of 1733 he stressed the impact which this new initiative would make on the land tax. There were naturally many other arguments in favour of the excise; all of them he mentioned and all of them he doubtless believed in, but at base his scheme was designed to bring to life the dream of country gentlemen throughout the period—the destruction of the land tax. Lord Hervey's description of Walpole's great excise project simply as 'a project of Sir Robert Walpole's to ease the land-tax of one shilling in the pound' has much to commend it.[30]

The fact that the excise scheme of 1733 was a logical part of Walpole's financial policy does not of course fully explain its introduction, nor does it satisfactorily answer those who criticized Walpole for his foolhardiness. The main charge against Walpole then as now concerned not the intrinsic merits or defects of the excise extension but rather the political inexpediency of its timing. It has become commonplace to regard it as a colossal blunder and one which reflects Walpole's uncertain grasp of matters involving public opinion. The view that 'for once Sir Robert had allowed his desire for financial efficiency to get the better of his political judgment' is perhaps the usual one.[31] What seemed particularly inopportune was Walpole's decision to introduce his project less than two years before a dissolution of Parliament, at a time when the political atmosphere both in and out of Parliament was bound to be extremely sensitive,

---

[29] The probable yield of the excise scheme was a matter of surprising confusion. Walpole himself mentioned a figure of £300,000 (*HMC Egmont Diary*, i. 353) which, as the *Craftsman* pointed out (17 Feb. 1733), was insufficient to replace 1s. of the land tax even for one year. Some government supporters expected a revenue of up to £600,000 (Add. MS. 27732 [Essex Papers], f. 137: Delafaye to Essex, 15 Mar. 1733), though this was probably unrealistic. Presumably Walpole's main concern was to avoid repeating his error in the revival of the salt duties, by declining to anticipate the exact yield of the new excises. As a result any effect which his scheme might be expected to have on the land tax would be delayed for at least a year until the actual figures were available.
[30] *Hervey Memoirs*, p. 132.
[31] D. Marshall, *Eighteenth Century England* (London, 1962), p. 150.

and when a public outcry could have serious consequences for M.P.s. As one pamphleteer pointed out, Walpole apparently 'did not sufficiently consider what Influence an *approaching Election* might naturally have on the Fate of *such a Project*'.[32] And what makes this blunder even more surprising is the degree of deliberation and calculation which Walpole put into it. The excise scheme was not after all a piece of ill-considered policy. Walpole was not the man to risk unnecessary and superfluous reforms, not, as Lord Hervey remarked, 'one of those projecting systematical geniuses who are always thinking in theory, and are above common practice'.[33] The excise went through a long period of gestation before emerging in public. Walpole himself had probably been seriously considering new inland duties for a long time. Certainly the letter which Gooch received in Virginia in December 1731 shows that by the summer of that year the administration had resolved on a tobacco excise, while the cautious statements which Walpole and his brother made about a general excise in the debates on the salt tax in 1732 represented careful preliminary testing of the public temperature. Characteristically Walpole himself gave the whole scheme immensely careful consideration, to which the notes left among his manuscripts bear ample testimony.[34] When he unveiled his scheme in the Commons in March 1733 his speech was generally acknowledged to be a masterly performance, a brilliant exposition in detail of the state of the country's finances. Only months and indeed years of thought and planning with the assistance of the Secretary to the Treasury, John Scrope, and the other revenue officials, made possible Walpole's excise project.

If the excise scheme had been long in preparation its timing was no less deliberate. It is unthinkable that Walpole, one of the most politically minded of eighteenth-century statesmen, can have failed to take into account the importance of the proximity of a general election at the time he was introducing his excise scheme. Indeed he made regular use of the election argument in a different context. In 1732, for example, it was employed in a clash with the Presbyterians, Congregationalists and Baptists, in their attempts to secure the repeal of the Test and Corporation Acts. As Walpole himself told the Bishop of Salisbury,

[32] *A Review of the Excise Scheme; ... with Some Proper Hints to the Electors of Great Britain* (London, 1733), p. 33. The author may have been William Pulteney.
[33] *Hervey Memoirs*, p. 19.   [34] C(H) MSS. 43.

in this country, which was in reality a popular government that only bore the name of monarchy, and especially in this age where clamour and faction were so prevalent over reason and justice, he said a minister sometimes must swim with the tide against his inclination, and that the current was too strong at present against this proposal of the Dissenters for any judicious minister to think of stemming it. He further added, that if he were wholly unconcerned as a minister, and only considered this thing as a friend to the Dissenters, he should certainly rather advise them to try it at the beginning of a new Parliament than at the end of an old one, as people would be less afraid of the ferment in the country seven years before elections were again to come on, than one.[35]

The man who said this was scarcely likely to ignore the electoral consequences of a major reform like the wine and tobacco excise barely a year before a general election.

The fact that the excise scheme was meticulously planned and timed and that Walpole himself was particularly conscious of the importance of the coming dissolution only aggravates the underlying problem. Why did Walpole so wilfully court disaster? Why at a moment of especial political sensitivity did he essay a major programme of financial reform? For whatever else it was, the excise scheme was that. Later on, when he had been proved so disastrously wrong, his friends in the press insisted that the excise was a mere administrative triviality, the conversion of a few customs duties into a more convenient bureaucratic form. But before this Walpole clearly planned the excise as a great reform. Through all his speeches on the excise, and indeed in the build-up of the salt tax debates, he stressed the importance and novelty of his project. In these circumstances it is simply not possible to plead a straightforward oversight on his behalf. The only plausible answer is that Walpole regarded his project not as a liability but as a positive vote-catching measure, that he deliberately launched it in time to catch the electoral tide, and that he regarded it as a master-stroke of political strategy. In retrospect no doubt this seems a curiously aberrant piece of judgement on his part. At the time it must have borne a quite different appearance.

For this there were good reasons. It has become customary to regard the excise as an inherently unpopular measure, predestined to arouse public fury in whatever form it was extended. But this is

[35] *Hervey Memoirs*, pp. 128-9.

something of an injustice to the excise as well as to Walpole's judgement. The excise had been badly received when introduced 'after the manner of the Low Countryes for the maintenance of the Warre', in 1643.[36] But after 1660 it had become a normal part of the state's financial machinery. No taxes are ever popular, and the inland duty, which bore heavily on popular consumption, was less likely than any to be so. But it would be a great mistake to imagine that the uproar which greeted the appearance of Walpole's excise scheme in 1733 could have been readily predicted beforehand. As Hervey pointed out, excises had not in recent times been particularly controversial except among the financial pundits. 'There never was the least clamour raised in the country, or any opposition to them in Parliament, on any other foot than a dispute whether they would answer the charge of collection by their produce.'[37] This was perhaps an exaggeration, but not grotesquely so. After all Walpole himself had launched a major reform in this area with his excise on tea, chocolate and coffee in 1723. That reform had produced no public outcry and barely a whimper even from the dealers in those commodities. Still more recently the re-establishment of the salt duty in 1732 had been a significant pointer to the probable public reaction to further excises. True, it was the revival of an old duty, not the introduction of a new one. On the other hand the duty on salt affected a staple consumer article more genuinely relevant to the pockets of the country at large than the new excises on tobacco and wine, and these in any case could be represented as basically a recasting of existing duties.

In short there was every reason to assume that the reaction to the salt duty would be a fair test of the likely reception to the new excises. As such it was most reassuring. The government faced some stiff divisions in the House of Commons, though no stiffer than it had become accustomed to face on issues of major importance, especially in relation to taxation. The opposition ranted to little apparent effect about the danger of new excises leading to a general excise on all commodities, and there was a relatively minor pamphlet war about the significance of the trend towards excises. As a result Walpole could reasonably feel that the excise scheme would obtain popular

[36] Add. MS. 31116 (Whitacre Diary), f. 38: Pym in Commons' debate of 28 Mar. 1643.
[37] *Hervey Memoirs*, p. 147; for the arguments involved in seventeenth-century discussions of the excise, see E. R. Turner, 'Early Opinion about English Excise', *Am. Hist. Rev.*, xxi (1915–16), 314–18.

support. In so far as he entertained doubts, they concerned not the essential features of the excise but what must appear in retrospect a relatively unimportant consideration. The wine and tobacco customs contributed substantially to the King's civil list, ever the object of suspicion and hostility on the part of the public and Parliament. An increase in the efficiency and yield of these duties would, it might be argued, inflate the value of the civil list and so make the King increasingly independent of parliamentary control. When he spoke to the question of excise extensions in 1732 Walpole clearly regarded 'the great clamours that have been raised upon that head' as the only serious objection.[38] In consequence he carefully kept up his sleeve a special measure to ensure that the increase in yield anticipated from the introduction of wine and tobacco excises would go entirely to the Treasury. As it turned out this was the least of his worries, but his advance provision for it demonstrates strikingly how little he had forecast the extent and nature of opposition to the excises, and yet how carefully he had reconnoitred the ground.

If Walpole had little reason to anticipate the unpopularity of the excise, he had excellent grounds for predicting the popularity of its basic purpose, the reduction and, if possible, abolition of the land tax. Walpole, who as a young man had seen the party warfare of Queen Anne's reign and the conflict and emotion aroused by heavy land taxes, had a strongly rooted conviction that the abolition of the land tax was the surest road to ministerial popularity. The distress of the landed gentry and the extreme urgency of their relief, traditionally a Tory preoccupation, was a theme which he never tired of hammering home not merely in the Commons, but even in the closet. Thus he informed the King that the land tax

> was the most unequal tax, and the most generally complained of, of any tax now subsisting; and as this measure would make every landowner and country gentleman a zealous friend to his Government, so it would be the glory of his reign, and one not to be paralleled by any reign since the Revolution, that he had reduced the land-tax to one shilling in the pound, which was not only lower than ever it had been since it was first laid, but lower than the most sanguine landowner in the kingdom ever hoped to see it.[39]

The electoral significance of Walpole's strategy as embodied in the salt duty of 1732 and the excise scheme of 1733 is sufficiently obvious

[38] *Parl. Hist.*, viii. 961: 9 Feb. 1732; see also Corr. Pol. Angl., 379, f. 320.
[39] *Hervey Memoirs*, p. 149.

against this background. However, the comments of Charles Delafaye, the ministry's loyal servant and aide, drive the point home. In March 1732, after the revival of the salt duty, he pointed out to Lord Waldegrave, the ambassador in Paris, 'Half the land tax taken off, and no more remaining than 1*s.* in the pound, which was never known before since the revolution, must be popular in the country, let the Pulteneyans say what they will against it in the house, and must be of service against the next election; for no doubt it will be known who voted pro and con'.[40] This firm conviction that the public out of doors would actually prove more enthusiastic than Parliament in their support for the excise is a remarkable comment on Walpole's activities at this time. It is reinforced by a similar remark of Delafaye's just a year later, when the new tobacco and wine excise was being considered by the Commons. 'The taking off this Tax', Delafaye then told the Earl of Essex, the British envoy in Turin, 'ought surely to reconcile all those who are eased by this means, to the present Administration, and will incline them to wish for such another *parliament* when a new one shall be chosen, and to contribute their Interest towards it.'[41] Such comments convey an intriguing picture of Walpole's project. For Walpole and his friends, whose concern with public opinion is apt to receive little recognition, the excise scheme was a stroke of genius, the culmination of Walpole's attempts to cut the ground from beneath his opponents' feet and make the Whig Hanoverian establishment a popular as well as parliamentary success.

This hypothesis is reinforced by an examination of Walpole's own position in relation to the general election of 1734, the second since the accession of George II. In it he would have to deal with the rebellious Whig groups which had sprung up in opposition in the course of the 1727 Parliament. This was by no means impossible, but it required address. Certainly nothing would more facilitate success than a popular reforming measure such as Walpole believed the excise to be. Moreover, the preparations for this election forcibly suggest the drift of Walpole's calculations. In the first place there is a strong possibility that Walpole originally planned to maximize the propaganda value of his project and surprise the opposition by calling an early election, one year before the expected termination of the Parliament. Rumours of such a coup were flying about in July 1732 and

[40] Coxe, iii. 125: 3 Mar. 1732.
[41] Add. MS. 27732, ff. 139–40: 15 Mar. 1733.

seemed to receive considerable support from the extraordinary excitement in many constituencies fully two years before the expected elections.[42] In Hampshire, for example, there were complaints of 'the early and unusual Application for Knights of the Shire, so long before the natural Determination of this present Parliament', while in London it was reported in November 1732 that 'People begin already to talk of Candidates to represent this City in Parliament, as if a new one would be chosen after next Session'.[43] In Gloucestershire too it was noted that 'Here is as great a stir about elections as if there was to be a new parliament presently'.[44] Still more suggestive was the extraordinary electoral activity of the Walpole family in its own county of Norfolk. Walpole himself sat for King's Lynn, his brother Horace for Great Yarmouth. But in the summer of 1732 there were manoeuvres which indicated that they had an extension of their political influence in view. Both Yarmouth and King's Lynn were practically close boroughs, neither particularly prestigious. But the county town was in a different category. Traditionally containing a strong Tory element, Norwich had been steadily won over to the Whigs, and by 1732 the Walpole brothers evidently felt that the process had been carried far enough to justify them in committing their own prestige to a contest there. Thus on 25 August it was publicly announced that one of the city's Whig M.P.s, Robert Britiffe, a prominent lawyer and a particular associate of the Walpoles, was to retire at the ensuing election to permit Horace Walpole to stand in his place. The announcement was accompanied by great junketing and the presentation of the freedom of the city to Horace.[45] The resulting vacancy for Yarmouth was to be filled by yet another Walpole, Sir Robert's son, Edward. In gratitude for this 'Extraordinary favour' on Walpole's part that corporation presented Edward with its freedom in a silver box as a 'Testimony of our Esteem for Sir Robert and his Family'.[46]

Still more intriguing was the possibility of taking the county seats, the most prized possession of all. Like many other counties, Norfolk had a mixed tradition in which Whiggism had more recently played a growing part. The sitting members were Sir Edmund Bacon,

[42] Corr. Pol. Angl., 378, f. 6.
[43] *Northampton Mercury*, 8 Jan. 1733, 20 Nov. 1732.
[44] Add. MS. 31142 (Strafford Papers), f. 45: Berkeley to Strafford, 16 Oct. 1732.
[45] *Norwich Mercury*, 26 Aug. 1732.
[46] Norfolk and Norwich Record Office, Yarmouth Corporation MSS, Assembly Book 1724–32: 10 Oct. 1732.

a rank Tory, and Harbord Harbord, a friend and supporter of the Walpole family. And yet in the autumn of 1732 it began to be put about that a new and more distinguished candidate was to appear. In December 1732 the ministerial newspapers declared that the Prime Minister himself would stand for the county at the next election.[47] How seriously this should be taken is difficult to estimate. Though the report went uncontradicted, Walpole himself had previously been chary of standing for his home county. In 1710 he had burnt his fingers by standing rashly and losing heavily. Thereafter he wisely took the view that a borough seat, for which re-election on acceptance of office was easy, was a wiser haven for a minister.[48] But he may have felt in 1732 that the time had come to change his tactics. His election as knight of the shire for Norfolk would represent a huge triumph and, with Horace Walpole's in Norwich, would raise the fame and power of the Walpole family to new heights. Moreover, if Walpole's great stratagem, the excise, was to pay anywhere it would be in the counties. In these circumstances it would not be surprising if Walpole indeed widened his options in this direction. He committed himself to nothing of course. If all went well in the 1733 session he could have dissolved early, taken advantage of the careful preparations made in advance by government candidates, and exploited his achievement to the maximum both on a national scale and in Norfolk.

As it happened these plans went awry. The excise project turned out disastrously and there could be no question either of an early general election or a Walpole candidate for Norfolk.[49] In these circumstances Walpole's intentions must remain matter for conjecture. The one thing that is reasonably certain is that he saw his excise scheme not as a trivial piece of administrative tinkering nor as a mere fiscal expedient. Walpole was nothing if not the politician's politician, and his excise scheme was fully intended to be a political triumph. The fact that he was mistaken in his assessment does not make him a hopelessly inadequate judge of public opinion; few foresaw the

---

[47] *St. James's Evening Post*, 19–21 Dec. 1732. The opposition responded with the announcement in the *London Evening Post* for 30 Dec. 1732 that the sitting Tory M.P. for the county, Sir Edmund Bacon, would stand again.

[48] *HMC Onslow*, p. 518.

[49] The Whig cause in Norfolk was eventually represented by William Morden and Robert Coke, who were defeated by the Tories. Coke's comments on the election of 1734 (C(H) MSS. Corr. 2127, 2220) confirm the impression that he was unexpectedly called upon by Walpole to stand in for the Prime Minister.

débâcle which the excise precipitated. As Lord Hervey remarked, 'Those, . . . who accuse Sir Robert Walpole of want of penetration in not foreseeing the difficulties into which this scheme would lead him, are of that class (and a numerous one it is) who imagine that every event is so little casual, that whatever is, could not have been otherwise; and of course, with equal folly, impute all success to prudence, and all disappointments to indiscretion'.[50]

[50] *Hervey Memoirs*, p. 147.

IV

The Public and the Excise

NOT the least of the factors which wrecked Walpole's calculations and destroyed his excise scheme was the ample advance notice of his intentions which was given to his opponents. The *Craftsman* is usually credited with opening and developing the campaign against him. It did so with a series of articles which began on 28 October 1732 and continued for eight weeks. This was not, however, the first warning to the public that a new excise was contemplated. As early as 1731 the *Craftsman* itself had claimed to have got wind of a similar project,[1] and since the revival of the salt tax in January 1732 inland duties had been the subject of more than passing public discussion. The foundation for this debate was laid by the Walpole brothers in the Commons on 9 February 1732. In reply to the opposition's claim that the salt duty was the thin end of an excise wedge, Horace Walpole made no bones about lauding such a possibility. 'I must say, that I think many of our customs are heavy upon trade, and very troublesome to our merchants: and therefore, if some of the most grievous of them were turned into an excise, it would be of great advantage to the nation, and might, I believe, be easily done.'[2] It is possible that this was simply a gaffe. But even Sir Robert, while insisting that 'There are at present no thoughts of converting any duty into an excise', declared his approval in similar terms of 'changing the method of raising the taxes we now pay, and choosing that method which is most convenient for the trading part of the nation'.[3] The probability is that the Walpoles were cautiously testing the possible reaction to their projected scheme. In the following months they were certainly given the opportunity to complete the process. In a pamphlet war, which started with the subject of the revived salt duties but was extended to the wider problem of new excises, most of the arguments which were to preoccupy the public in 1733 were rehearsed a full year earlier.[4] In fact throughout the summer of 1732 there was much talk of the excises; it was the

[1] 28 Oct. 1732.   [2] *Parl. Hist.*, viii. 951.   [3] Ibid., 961.
[4] The principal pamphlets were, on the opposition side, *The Case of the Revival of the*

rumour that the administration definitely intended to initiate a new project that launched this discussion to a new level. Before October all was speculation, and not even the rabid opposition press actually committed itself to the assertion that Walpole would bring in a new excise at once. What changed the situation was the arrival of John Randolph with the Virginian petition, which was reported by the press in the middle of October, though curiously the first accounts alleged that wine, not tobacco, was to carry the new duty.[5] Yet a great deal of caution and uncertainty remained. The *Craftsman* itself hedged its bets by attacking the standing army as well as the excise, and by remarking that it could not be certain that an excise would ensue at once, but 'it may be too late to oppose it *without Doors*, when it is brought into the *House*'.[6] Only after the Virginian emissary had been knighted, a sure sign that his mission had Walpole's backing, was the situation made clearer. Even then it was far from certain what commodities would actually be excised apart from tobacco. As late as 2 January 1733, only a few days before the opening of the parliamentary session, the *London Evening Post* was confidently asserting that sugar as well as tobacco and wine would carry the new duties.

If the excise scheme emerged in the public consciousness as anything but a bolt from the blue, it is also remarkable how late general interest was really fired by it. Even after the *Craftsman*'s articles in October and November there was little or no indication of the storm in the offing. In fact it broke quite suddenly at the end of the year. At one moment the main issue in the newspapers and coffee-houses was the agitation among the more extreme sections of the nonconformist community for a new initiative in favour of Church reform. 'The most common Topick of Discourse in all Companies', it was reported just before Christmas, 'is the Attempt of the Dissenters to get the *Corporation* and *Test Acts* repealed'.[7] Three or four weeks later the excise had dramatically moved to the centre of the stage. 'The business of religion and the Test Act is quite dropped amongst us', one clerical observer noted, 'and the Excise is now the private

---

Salt Duty fully stated and, on the government side, *The Reduction of the Land Tax*. Both were plundered for extracts and arguments by the newspapers.

[5] *Gloucester Journal*, 24 Oct. 1732; *Northampton Mercury*, 23 Oct. 1732.
[6] 28 Oct. 1732.
[7] *The Miscellany*, 23 Dec. 1732.

and public care'.[8] The resulting furore is one that is not easily captured in retrospect. All that is clear is that contemporaries were unanimous as to its intensity, which they could compare only with that of the Sacheverell affair, nearly a quarter of a century before. Among the newspapers scarcely an edition failed to comment on the excise in the winter of 1732-3, while the ballad-writers and cartoonists were untiring in their exploitation of the subject. Again, according to the *Northampton Mercury* 'more Pamphlets continue to be published against as well as for it, than have been seen perhaps on any Occasion'.[9] Nor was the press the only barometer of the public reaction to the excise. The *Craftsman* published a far from romanticized account of a tour of the city of London, passing through Lincolns Inn Fields and observing the print shops' exclusive concentration on the excise project, buying tobacco from a shop in Holborn which dispensed its wares in paper bearing lampoons against the excise, past a vintner whose rebus caricatured the excise, through a quadrille party where the excise was the subject of an oath, and meeting dissenters who compared the Test Act to 'an Excise upon Conscience'.[10] Such a picture was only partially exaggerated. Up and down the country in the early part of 1733 there were mob demonstrations and meetings involving the ritual burning of government newspapers and, particularly after the news of the ministry's defeat, riotous celebrations centring on the parading and destruction of ministerial effigies. Even in the New Theatre in the Haymarket, 'one of the Comedians took the Liberty to throw out some Reflections upon the Prime Minister and the Excise, which were not design'd by the Author; Lord Walpole being in the House, went behind the Scenes, and demanded of the Prompter whether such Words were in the Play, and he answering they were not, his Lordship immediately corrected the Comedian with his own Hands very severely'.[11]

Yet manifestations such as these, however significant, were not of themselves sufficient to direct political events. What was needed to translate the general atmosphere into effective action was some more specific and compelling pressure from the propertied classes. Such pressure could take various forms. The most characteristic type of out-of-doors political activity in the eighteenth century was the

---

[8] Mrs. Thomson, ed., *Memoirs of Viscountess Sundon* (London, 2nd edn., 1848), ii, 97: Dr. A. Clarke to Mrs. Clayton, 21 Jan. 1733.
[9] 19 Mar. 1733.
[10] 10 Feb. 1733.
[11] *St. James's Evening Post*, 24-27 Mar. 1733.

petition, either to Parliament, where legislation was concerned, or to the Crown, where executive action was involved. However, in 1733 petitions were not at all to the point. No legislative measure concerning the excise had formally come before the consideration of Parliament, and to wait until it did was to give the initiative to government. Equally, addresses to the Crown would have been wide of the mark and indeed offensive. In these circumstances the obvious course was to draw up formal constituency instructions to M.P.s. Instructions had good precedents, having been used to great effect, for example, in the Exclusion crisis. Even so there were inevitably attempts by the government's supporters to cast aspersions on their validity. It was alleged that the instructions were '*introducing* a new Legislative Power', and there were learned sermons addressed to the electorate on the independence of M.P.s who 'when ye have chose them they are as absolute in their legislative Capacities, as yourselves were in your Election of them'.[12] On the other side the opposition took a rather dramatic view of their importance, picturing them as the practical example of the revolutionary but respectable authority bestowed on the people in Lockian political theory, 'a *supreme Power* of saving Themselves from the Attempts and Designs of any Body, even of their *Legislators*'.[13] But despite these disputes instructions had too good a pedigree and were plainly too important to be safely ignored even by the administration's friends. Indeed it is not too much to claim that the instructions of 1733 were among the most massive demonstrations of extra-parliamentary opinion in the entire century. In the early part of 1733 instructions came from some fifty-four constituencies,[14] an extraordinary mark of the popular concern. The instructions against the Jew Bill of 1753, the petitions and instructions following the loss of Minorca in 1756, even the petitions and addresses associated with the Wilkes and reform agitations of the sixties and seventies were scarcely on this scale.

The incidence of the instructions, not to say the more varied evidences of popular opposition to Walpole's excise scheme, made it impossible to claim on behalf of the government that the general reaction was anything but hostile. In the circumstances the only possible attitude was one of scepticism not about the extent of the

[12] *The Rise and Fall of the Late Projected Excise, Impartially Consider'd* (London, 1733), p. 28; *A Letter to the Freeholders, etc. of Great Britain, concerning Their Duty before and after the Election of their Representatives* (London, 1733), pp. 5–6.
[13] *A Review of the Excise Scheme*, p. 49.
[14] For a list of these see Appendix A.

campaign against the excise but rather about its authenticity. Throughout the excise crisis there was bitter controversy as to the precise significance of the instructions. Naturally the administration's opponents claimed that they were a clear reflection of the nation's views. When Walpole revealed his plans in the House of Commons, Sir William Wyndham insisted that 'the very proposing of such a scheme to the House of Commons, after so many remonstrances against it, I must think most audacious; it is in a manner flying in the face of the whole people of England; and since they have already declared against it, God forbid that we who are their representatives should declare for it'.[15] Walpole's reply on this occasion was an uncompromising rejection of the validity of the instructions as an expression of the general will.

As to those clamours which have been raised without doors, and which are now so much insisted on, it is very well known by whom and by what methods they were raised, and it is no difficult matter to guess with what views; but I am very far from taking them to be the sense of the nation, or believing that the sentiments of the generality of the people were thereby expressed. The most part of the people concerned in those clamours did not speak their own sentiments, they were played by others like so many puppets: it was not the puppets that spoke, it was those behind the curtain that played them, and made them speak whatever they had a mind.[16]

At the heart of such allegations was the charge that opposition propaganda had misled the people. According to the *London Journal*, 'had not some Gentlemen, *out of Power*, set up *Incendiary Journals* to *deceive* and *inflame*, not one Man in a thousand would have said a Word against the Administration'.[17] Inevitably the *Craftsman* was selected for particular attention. 'T'is remark'd', the *Northampton Mercury* noted, 'that hardly any Scheme ever met with a more general Aversion throughout the Nation than this for a new excise; which is look'd upon to be owing in some Measure to the *Craftsman*, and 'tis believed he will be called to account for his Misrepresentations'.[18]

It is true enough that the opposition's principal journal conducted a great campaign against the excise, and went out of its way to en-

---

[15] *Parl. Hist.*, viii, 1304: 14 Mar. 1733.
[16] Ibid., 1305–6.
[17] 10 Feb. 1733.
[18] *Northampton Mercury*, 15 Jan. 1733.

courage instructions. When the commercial community in London decided late in December to put pressure on the city's parliamentary representatives, the *Craftsman* approvingly remarked that 'This is a laudable Precedent for reviving the antient Practice of the People in giving their Representatives Instructions upon all great Occasions, and We hope will be followed by every County and Borough in England'.[19] On the other hand the opposition could legitimately claim that the government had laid its case before the people and lost it after fair and extensive debate, though it was admittedly argued by some of the friends of government that the administration had been unnecessarily handicapped in its propaganda effort. 'Some blame Sir Robert Walpole for omitting to have something printed to explain his Scheme', Charles Delafaye remarked.[20] It is true that Walpole did not commit himself to a clear statement of his project until he was ready to unfold it formally in the Commons Committee of Supply. This was partly tactics, in that he believed the opposition to be at a disadvantage while they were attacking what might turn out to be a chimera and in that it permitted him to withdraw if necessary with relatively little loss of face. It was also to some extent a matter of necessity; it would have been strange for the minister of the crown to outline in the press a scheme which was intended for Parliament's deliberation.

In any case it is doubtful whether the consequences were very disastrous, though some journalists found themselves in a dilemma as a result of their uncertainty as to Walpole's intentions. The *Daily Courant* as late as November 1732 was not sure whether to dismiss the opposition's alarms as superfluous or to defend the excise as a valuable measure.[21] But this was the exception. In general Walpole's friends in Grub Street argued strongly for the excise and made by no means a poor showing against the *Craftsman*. Moreover, in some respects the administration had distinct advantages in the press war. It did not scruple, for example, to use the conventional machinery in favour of its own writers. The Post Office gave its customary assistance to the ministry and equally customary obstruction to the opposition. Indeed some of the constituencies which instructed their members against the excise specifically referred to the propaganda which the administration had dispensed through the Post Office.

[19] 30 Dec. 1732.
[20] Add. MS. 27732, f. 94: Delafaye to Essex, 18 Jan. 1733.
[21] 14 Nov. 1732.

Thus the Mayor, Aldermen and Burgesses of Wigan informed Peter Bold M.P. that 'The Proposal for increasing or extending the Laws of Excise, that has been of late much talk'd of, has been the Cause of some Dissatisfaction here; and the Pamphlet handed about amongst us in favour of it, has rather increas'd than diminish'd our Apprehensions, by giving us a nearer Prospect of the Danger that seems likely to attend the Execution of it'.[22] Similarly the Mayor, Jurats and Communalty of Rye referred to 'Books dispers'd from the publick Offices endeavouring to prepare our Minds quietly to suffer ourselves to be fetter'd', and the inhabitants of Daventry to 'Pamphlets given away and dispersed about'.[23] The *Craftsman* and its allies could not match the immense resources of the administration in this respect. Nor indeed could they conduct their own activities without interference. It was the prerogative of the Post Office clerks in London to despatch the tri-weekly evening papers, on which the provinces relied so heavily for their news, at reduced charge. But in the course of the excise crisis it was made clear that this privilege would be extended only to loyal supporters of the ministry. The *London Evening Post*, which had grown increasingly outspoken in its criticism both of the government and the excise scheme, found itself suddenly deprived of this right in October 1733 and was compelled to launch a campaign in favour of country orders for the paper.[24] Similarly the administration took particular care at this time to employ its legal advantages against its opponents. In January 1733, for example, three women were arrested in London for 'dispersing and crying about the Streets, a Seditious Libel, called *Britannia Excisa*'.[25] In the event the magistrate concerned, Sir Thomas Clarges, discharged the offenders,[26] but such experiences were not calculated to increase the ease with which Walpole's opponents in the press carried out their activities. All in all there is little reason to suppose that the opposition had any particular advantage in the realm of propaganda.

A more serious charge made by the court was that in various ways the campaign was not representative of the electorate at large. Where

---

[22] *London Evening Post*, 20–22 Feb. 1733.
[23] Ibid., 24–27 Feb. 1733; Northampton Record Office, Isham MSS., IL 1851A: 28 Mar. 1733.
[24] G. A. Cranfield, 'The "London Evening Post", 1727–1744: A Study in the Development of the Political Press', *Hist. Jnl.* vi (1963), 25.
[25] *Daily Post-Boy*, 12 Jan. 1733.
[26] *London Evening Post*, 11–13 Jan. 1733.

there were no actual instructions at all, for example, it was possible for the ministry to put on a brave front. Thus the House of Commons was treated to a difference of opinion as to the views of Devonians. Sir William Yonge, one of Walpole's most loyal supporters, claimed that Honiton, 'the Borough he represented, and which he and his family had represented for near 90 Years, had signified to him their approbation of the Scheme'. But the knight of the shire for Devon, Sir William Courtney, a strong Tory, contested this. 'He knew the borough the hon. Gent. stood for; He knew almost every man in it, he had but lately come from thence, and he knew that they were all against it. The whole People of that County were against and had joyned in their Sollicitations for him to come up of Purpose to Oppose it.'[27] In such a case it was at least possible for those well inclined towards the ministry to give it the benefit of the doubt. But where constituencies had actually despatched instructions to their M.P.s the administration's position was plainly more difficult, though it did its best even then. 'What Letters and Instructions to Represenatives', asked one pamphleteer, 'tho' most of them clandestinely, surreptitiously, or by more scandalous Methods, obtained and published, have the World been Witness to?'[28] Involved in such charges there were several elements. There was firstly the claim that some of the instructions were simply fabricated by the press and were not in fact drawn up by their alleged authors. There was secondly the allegation that many instructions had been obtained by political skulduggery, and failing these there was the argument that even bona fide instructions at best represented sectional interests.

None of these charges is easy to adjudicate on. Even the first one is by no means clear. Many of the instructions came from 'inhabitants' or 'traders' who kept no record of their transactions; in such cases the press report, however suspect, is the only possible evidence, apart from occasional comments by contemporaries. Even where the authors of instructions were members of corporate bodies, whether municipal, as in most cases, or merchantile, as in some, the absence of a formal record does not necessarily mean that the press report is unreliable. Corporate procedures were not sufficiently regular to ensure that the despatch of parliamentary instructions, a transaction which did not normally require the expenditure of corporation funds,

[27] RA Stuart, Unbound MSS. 1/125: debate of 16 Mar. 1733; this report is incorporated in a letter of Nathaniel Mist at Corr. Pol. Angl., 380, ff. 128–30.
[28] *The Occasional Writer, to the People; and for the People* (London, 1733), p. 26.

nor even necessarily the application of the corporation seal, was automatically recorded. In consequence some caution must be exercised in scepticism as to the reliability of the newspapers on this point. There was in fact only one clear case of falsification by the press. This concerned the somewhat impudent assertion by the London newspapers that King's Lynn, the constituency for which Walpole himself sat and practically a family borough, not only instructed its M.P.s against the excise but sent a deputation to town to reinforce its point.[29] This was so implausible that even the opposition newspapers admitted their error. No comparable cases of sheer invention were detected by the extremely vigilant government press,[30] and on the other side there were instances of instructions which were not actually reported in the press at all but which were amply attested to by other evidence.[31] In the circumstances it is reasonable to assume that the more than fifty parliamentary instructions reported in the press represented, if anything, an under-estimate.

More interesting was the claim that some of the instructions were politically inspired. This would be difficult to prove, though there are some suggestive indications. It must be more than coincidence, for example, that the only Welsh instructions came from Denbigh and Denbighshire, a county in the pocket of Watkin Williams Wynn, one of Walpole's most bitter and intemperate opponents.[32] The sceptic might note similar examples—the curious fact that two small Northamptonshire boroughs, Daventry and Towcester, neither with representatives in Parliament but both very much in the territory of the Tory M.P., Sir Justinian Isham, instructed their knights of the shire.[33] Again it is intriguing that the only English county as such to send instructions was Somerset, dominated by Sir William Wyndham and his friends, and long a centre of opposition to Hanoverian governments.[34] But these instances are by no means typical, and it is worth noting that many of the instructing corporations were represented in Parliament by government supporters. Boroughs like Coventry, Carlisle, Harwich, Bath, Wigan and York

[29] *B. Berington's Evening Post*, 16 Jan. 1733; *London Evening Post*, 13-16 Jan. 1733.
[30] This does not take into account the obviously spoof report in *B. Berington's Evening Post*, 18 Jan. 1733, that 'the several Ancient and Trading Boroughs' of Gatton, Hedon, and Old Sarum (three of the most rotten and insignificant corporations in the country) had instructed against the excise.
[31] For example, Carlisle and Harwich.
[32] *London Evening Post*, 24-27 Mar. 1733.
[33] Isham MSS., IL 1851, 1852.
[34] *London Evening Post*, 20-22 Mar. 1733.

were far from being nests of opposition; their instructions were anything but convenient for the recipients, torn between loyalty to a ministry from which in many cases they derived considerable benefits, and fear of their constituents' electoral power. Sir Roger Bradshaigh, M.P. for Wigan and a ministerialist, went out of his way to investigate the authenticity of the instructions he had received, and found no reason to question it, embarrassing though they were from his viewpoint. The Mayor of Wigan, it emerged, had raised the possibility of instructing and 'was so generally seconded that in all appearance it was become necessary'.[35]

Less easily dismissed are the cases of alleged skulduggery where the court's friends provided detailed evidence, as at Rochester and St. Albans. Rochester was a borough whose politics were traditionally governed by the proximity of the naval yards at Chatham and the consequent influence of the Admiralty. As a result its instructions against the excise were galling in the extreme to the administration. The essence of the government case was that the corporation had been assembled without proper notice and that the instructions then drawn up had not been approved by the mayor, himself apparently too ill to be present. Moreover, the city seal which formally authorized the instructions had been obtained from the mayor on the pretence that it was required for a property transaction. The result according to the *London Journal* was 'the Sense, or rather *Nonsense* and *Malice*, of eight or nine Persons, but not the Sense of the Inhabitants of the City'.[36] Comparisons between the corporation of an Admiralty borough and the general populace read oddly in a government newspaper, but in any case the allegations are somewhat unconvincing. In the *Craftsman*'s equally plausible version, the villain of the piece was the mayor himself, an agent of government who had sought to obstruct the wishes of what was after all a majority of the corporation.[37]

A similar case was that of St. Albans. There political excitement was particularly high at the time of the excise crisis as the result of a by-election in which the opposition, championed and financed by the Duchess of Marlborough, had triumphed. According to the government press the instructions were drawn up by the successful

---

[35] M. Cox, 'Sir Roger Bradshaigh, 3rd Bart., and the Electoral Management of Wigan, 1695–1747', *Bulletin of John Rylands Library*, xxxvii (1954–5), 140.
[36] 17 Mar. 1733.
[37] 31 Mar. 1733.

candidate, John Merrill, at a celebration party, sealed with the connivance of the mayor and distributed among a handful of aldermen for their signatures without a formal meeting.[38] Again, the *Craftsman* had some justification for pointing out that, whatever the technical deficiencies of this procedure, the fact was that the mayor and a great majority of aldermen signed the instructions.[39] If Rochester and St Albans were the best examples that the government's agents could unearth of political manipulation, there is little reason to accept their charges against the instructions in general. One of these charges, however, is of especial interest. This was the accusation, inevitable in the circumstances, that Jacobite activists were behind the whole affair. Walpole characteristically made much of this. 'Can gentlemen imagine', he asked the Commons in March 1734, 'that in the spirit raised in the nation but about a twelvemonth since, Jacobitism and disaffection to the present government had no share'.[40] Some even claimed to have definite proof. The *Daily Courant* declared that, in the riotous rejoicings and demonstrations which followed the abandonment of the excise in April 1733, Jacobite leaders had actually been identified.[41]

Where the truth lies is difficult to judge. Obviously Jacobites would not withhold support from such a promising movement as the anti-excise campaign. On the other hand the government's definition of what constituted a Jacobite was rather wide, and certainly opposition Whigs and Hanoverian Tories were as active in the agitation as Jacobites. Moreover, it is clear from the Pretender's papers that the activities of 'official' Jacobites in England were feeble in the extreme. The Prince was constantly assured from England that the excise crisis would lead to a 'General Insurrection' and that 'the people are so provoked that nothing is so much desyrd as a Restoration'.[42] Not surprisingly James himself grew enthusiastic at the opportunity apparently presented. 'It is impossible', he wrote to England, 'we can ever have a more favourable opportunity for an expedition'.[43] But French aid was not forthcoming in the tense international situation caused by the crisis over the Polish succession, and even in England there was little actually done by the Pretender's friends.

[38] *Hyp-Doctor*, 30 Jan. 1733; 6 Feb. 1733; *Daily Journal*, 6 Feb. 1733; *London Journal*, 10 Feb. 1733; 24 Feb. 1733.
[39] 17 Feb. 1733.   [40] *Parl. Hist.*, ix. 477: 13 Mar. 1734.   [41] 25 Apr. 1733.
[42] RA Stuart, 159/36: G. Robinson to James III, 2 Feb. 1733; 160/163: A. Cockburn to M. Russell, 19 Apr. 1733.
[43] Ibid., 161/32: James III to O'Brien, 28 Apr. 1733.

Individual Jacobites were of course prominent among those who stirred up the campaign of hate and hostility against the Walpole regime. Easily the most celebrated of these was John Barber, Lord Mayor of London. It was extraordinarily unfortunate for Walpole that such a bitter opponent happened to be in so influential a position in the year of the excise crisis. The Lord Mayoralty normally went by rotation among the aldermen, most of whom were staunch government Whigs. But in 1733 the succession fell to Barber and so did not a little to embarrass the administration. Barber had political and parliamentary ambitions and pushed the advantages of his office to the limit. While not actually responsible for initiating the city's vigorous attack on the excise, it was he who claimed the merit of aligning it officially behind the campaign launched by the merchants.[44] The instructions to the London M.P.s drawn up by the Common Council in January and later the even more important petition presented to the Commons in April owed much to Barber. Even so this was more in the nature of a political stratagem than a disaffected conspiracy. Despite his notorious record, which included a much-cited visit to the Pretender at Rome in 1722, Barber was too self-interested and too cautious to pursue a more thoroughgoing course in the interests of the Stuart family. He was astute enough to keep in touch with the Pretender's authorized agent, but on the one occasion when he sent an assurance to James that he would 'always promote his Interest in the City, and obey his Commands whilst he governs the City, and at all times as far as it is in his Power', it turned out that his real object was the Pretender's personal intercession with Lady Sandwich for her electoral interest at Huntingdon, where Barber had expectations as a candidate.[45] The general impression is irresistible that individual Jacobites did their best to inflame the situation, but that concerted conspiracy had no effective role to play in the excise crisis.

More plausible than the charge that the campaign against the excise was politically motivated is the allegation that sectional, and in particular commercial, interests were masquerading as public opinion. No one could deny the central role of mercantile bodies in the instructions against the excise. From Newcastle the Merchant

[44] For the charge that Barber unfairly took the credit from others in this respect, see *An Impartial History of the Life, Character, Amours, Travels, and Transactions of Mr. John Barber, City-Printer, Common-Councilman, Alderman, and Lord Mayor of London* (London, 1741), pp. 31–2.
[45] RA Stuart, 160/21: Ravell to Edgar, 13 Mar. 1733.

Adventurers Company instructed, and in Bristol instructions were transmitted separately by the city corporation and the local Merchant Venturers, both agreeing to share the expenses of campaigning against the excise and send deputations to London.[46] There was also a tendency for merchants to pass themselves off as representatives of the general feeling of their town, especially where they lacked the support of their municipal corporation. Thus when the *Gloucester Journal* first retailed the activities of the local instructors, it accurately reported that 'Several of the principal Traders of this City have wrote to our Representatives in Parliament desiring them to oppose any Attempt that shall be made to extend the Laws relating to the Excise'. But this was evidently not sufficiently emphatic for the local patriots, and a week later, when the letter of instruction was itself printed, it was accompanied by an assertion that the letter had been 'signed by a great Number of the principal Inhabitants of the City of Gloucester'.[47] No doubt there were other cases of a relatively small number of prominent businessmen who were anxious to see that their importance and representativeness was not under-estimated by the press. Even where it was the local corporation alone that instructed, the influence of the commercial interests was obvious. At Newbury, for example, the instructions, which came from the 'Mayor, Aldermen and Burgesses', were concerned almost exclusively with the particular effects which the excise would have on small businessmen. The anxiety expressed related not at all to the constitutional issue, nor even to the alleged damage which the excise would do to the national economic interest. Rather theirs was the authentic voice of the small retailer, concerned with such details as the problems of measuring and weighing groceries for the excise officers.[48] A similar note was sounded from Ripon, where the instructors claimed to be the 'People of Rippon' but ingenuously revealed themselves as the chief retailers there. Their complaint again concerned the petty inconveniences which the excise would inflict on inland trade and which, according to their own account, would 'reduce the Trade of this Town to the lowest Extremity'.[49]

[46] *Extracts from the Records of the Merchant Adventurers of Newcastle-upon-Tyne*' (Pubs. Surtees Soc., xciii (1894)), p. 256; *St. James's Evening Post*, 11-13 Jan. 1733; *London Evening Post*, 13-16 Jan. 1733.
[47] 13 Feb. 1733, 20 Feb. 1733; the second version was of course the one printed by the London newspapers: see *Craftsman*, 17 Feb. 1733.
[48] *St. James's Evening Post*, 25-27 Jan. 1733.
[49] Ibid., 3-6 Feb. 1733.

Such examples need not surprise. The small businessman was the central figure in most municipalities. Genuinely industrial towns like Leeds, Manchester and Birmingham rarely had the status of corporate boroughs, though the inhabitants of Birmingham, for example, instructed the Warwickshire M.P.s.[50] The characteristic borough represented in Parliament was either the great trading centre like Newcastle, or the small market town like Newbury, or a mixture of the two like Gloucester. In each case the result was similar; a town whose economic life was dominated by commerce and whose political life was conducted by businessmen. Its inhabitants tended to 'look upon Gentlemen out of trade [as] not proper persons to be in the Corporation'.[51] At Leicester the corporation was merely 'an organ through which the business community of the town expressed its views and policy'.[52] Among the twenty-four common councilmen in Southampton in the early eighteenth century, there were six merchants, two woollen drapers, two grocers, one goldsmith, one maltster, one pewterer, one shipwright, one baker and one apothecary, in short almost all involved in some description of trade.[53]

The significance of the attitudes of the trading boroughs is very much reinforced by the otherwise curious failure of the counties to join in the instructing campaign. In practically all the great petitioning movements of the eighteenth century the English counties were involved. And yet in the early part of 1733 only Somerset instructed its M.P.s against the excise, a single exception easily explained by the local influence of Sir William Wyndham. For this dearth of county instructions there were good reasons. In the first place the whole crisis blew up at a bad time for the county community. Its meetings normally took place in the summer at the annual assizes when the natural leaders of the countryside, the country gentlemen, were in residence. In the winter there were no very obvious opportunities to meet on political affairs, apart from the quarter sessions which were rarely well attended. Equally important was the fact that the excise agitation as it developed in the early stages was not strictly the affair of the counties. It was initially a matter for the merchant and manufacturer, not the farmer and freeholder. Only later in the crisis was the countryside to play its full part.

[50] *Northampton Mercury*, 5 Feb. 1733.
[51] 'Tiverton Letters and Papers', *Notes and Queries*, clxx (1936), 170.
[52] R. W. Greaves, *The Corporation of Leicester, 1689–1836* (Oxford, 1939), p. 77.
[53] A. T. Patterson, *A History of Southampton, 1700–1914* (Southampton, 1966), i. 13–14.

The heartfelt reaction of the provincial boroughs to the excise scheme was essential to the success of the agitation against it. But that reaction would not have been possible without skilled and vigorous leadership, such as came from the city of London, the home of the great plutocratic merchant houses as well as one of the strongest centres of opposition to government. It was Walpole's misfortune that his scheme affected not merely small businessmen up and down the country but also two of the biggest commercial interests in the capital, wine and tobacco. The starting-point was the decision of the vintners on 8 December 1732 to launch a full-scale campaign against the excise, financed by a 6*d*. per pipe levy on wines imported and directed by a Committee which included Aldermen Champion and Godschall, and two men who were to become important in city politics, Robert Willimot and William Chapman.[54] The tobacconists were also conferring at the same time, but more important was the great meeting at the Swan Tavern in Cornhill on 22 December. Though this meeting was attended by merchants, traders, and citizens generally, the lead came again from the great wine merchants.[55] The result was the establishment of a standing committee which was to meet regularly and perform a vital role in the subsequent agitation, especially in liaison with the city authorities. There followed further more specialized meetings, from that of the grocers on 3 January to that of the 'Hamburgh and Holland Merchants, and Linen-Drapers' on 11 January.[56] The grocers were particularly important. Both the wine and tobacco merchants had powerful connections up and down the country, and utilized them. But the grocers, through their association with the small businessmen, were especially useful. 'We will write', they resolved on 3 January, 'to our Chapmen and Friends in all the Cities and Boroughs to which we trade, that they will make it their earnest Request to their several Representatives, and other Friends and Neighbours who have a Seat in Parliament, that they will likewise oppose any new Excise, or any Extension of the Laws of Excise, under any Name or Title whatsoever'.[57]

If anything emerged in the early months of 1733 it was the astonishing unanimity of the business community both at metropolitan and provincial level. Beforehand, the government had

[54] *Weekly Register*, 23 Dec. 1732.
[55] *B. Berington's Evening Post*, 23 Dec. 1732.
[56] *London Evening Post*, 4–6 Jan. 1733; *B. Berington's Evening Post*, 11 Jan. 1733; *Weekly Register*, 13 Jan. 1733; *Whitehall Evening Post*, 11–13 Jan. 1733.
[57] *B. Berington's Evening Post*, 11 Jan. 1733.

flattered itself that the excise scheme would meet with approval from many sectors of the commercial world. Walpole distinguished between the 'sturdy beggars' who derived their profit from fraud, and the fair traders who would benefit by the scheme. The *Daily Courant*, one of the ministry's most reliable supporters in the press, had even committed itself in November 1732 to the statement that 'there would be few considerable Merchants or Dealers, that would think it for their Advantage to oppose it'.[58] This prediction was ludicrously mistaken. In the one instance where a government supporter was bold enough to test it he was proved disastrously wrong. John Neale, M.P. for Coventry and one of Walpole's loyal friends, openly declared in the Commons that his constituents' instructions were not representative, and that 'he had had a letter from his Borough approveing of the Scheme'.[59] The results of his action were dramatic. At Coventry, 'the whole City was almost in an Uproar upon it' and the authorities there were provoked into petititioning Parliament itself against the excise and compelling Neale's fellow M.P., Sir Adolphus Oughton, to make plain their true sentiments.[60]

For the unanimity of the business community on the score of the excise there were various reasons. At local level the small trader was naturally suspicious of a new tax which was bound to add to the bureaucracy involved in inland trade. Both wine and tobacco, though technically luxuries, were in practice almost staple commodities. Both were dispensed in one form or another in great quantities throughout the country—there can have been few small shopkeepers or dealers who did not deal in one of them to some extent.[61] Moreover, though London dominated the tobacco and wine trade, both were in the 1730s sufficiently dispersed to affect a very large number of outports and trading centres. In the case of the wine trade, for example, there were no less than fifty-two outports importing in 1731.[62] Nor were businessmen directly involved in the wine and tobacco trades the only ones involved. Both commodities were essential parts of intricate and important trading networks. In the Portugal trade, for example, wine and woollens were heavily interdependent. The huge textile exports to Portugal and Brazil were

[58] 9 Dec. 1732.
[59] RA Stuart, Unbound MSS. 1/125: Debate of 16 Mar. 1733.
[60] Ibid.; *Craftsman*, 24 Mar. 1733; *Weekly Register*, 7 Apr. 1733.
[61] See, for example, T. S. Willan, *An Eighteenth Century Shopkeeper, Abraham Dent of Kirkby Stephen* (Manchester, 1970).
[62] C(H) MSS. 28/13 (1): Wine import accounts 1710-31.

paid for by British wine purchases, and anything that affected the wine trade could reasonably be expected to affect English manufacturers.[63] It was not surprising then that the Leicester hosiers were among the first to make plain their hostility to the new excise.[64] All these fears were of course dependent on the assumption that the excise would have an adverse rather than a beneficial effect, but in an age when the businessman was normally ill disposed towards taxes and governments, this assumption was not easily shaken.

Walpole did not only under-estimate the genuine commercial opposition to his reform; he also badly miscalculated the importance of the metropolitan business interests. The great mystery which confronted his administration, and which also confronts the historian, lies in a comparison between the excise extension carried out in 1723 and that attempted in 1733. In 1723 the new excises had been superficially very similar to those proposed a decade later. Yet although the druggists had given some opposition to the excise on chocolate, coffee and tea, it had come to little. In part this was doubtless because in 1723 there had been no really well-organized and effective political opposition to Walpole, capable of using the opportunity presented. But it was also because the commercial interests affected in 1723 were in fact very different in character from those threatened in 1733. Neither coffee nor chocolate were articles of first-rate importance. Tea unquestionably was, but it was in one respect in an exceptional position. The merchandizing of tea was controlled by a great monopoly interest, the East India Company, which had little interest in fraud. Smuggling worked to the advantage of rival foreign tea and considerably embarrassed the trade of a company which in any case had to stay on good terms with government. In short, the most powerful interest in the tea trade was not in the least concerned to direct the activities of smaller and less well-organized dealers against an excise. In 1733 the situation was very different. The wine and tobacco excise was a direct challenge to two powerful commercial interests both of which had either direct or indirect financial interest in the existing system. It was common knowledge that large numbers of respectable merchants in both trades engaged very heavily in fraud, and, given the legal and moral laxity of attitudes towards tax evasion in the 1730s, it is very difficult indeed to believe that more than a handful of dealers in either commodity could claim to have

---

[63] H. E. S. Fisher, *The Portugal Trade* (London, 1971), chaps. 3, 5.
[64] R. W. Greaves, *The Corporation of Leicester*, pp. 71–2.

clean hands. Merchants like Micajah Perry were perpetually involved in brushes with the Treasury and its officials and had all too clear a motive for resisting the excise.[65] Such men had no interest whatever in co-operating with financial reforms. This perhaps was Walpole's greatest miscalculation in the excise crisis—his failure to perceive the importance of the wine and tobacco interests in a context of mounting political excitement. The great merchants of the city were the crucial link in the chain which connected the parliamentary opposition with provincial discontent.

It is understandable that Walpole and his supporters should have sought to explain their error by resorting to charges of chicanery. But when all is said and done there can be little question that the campaign against the excise which developed in the early part of 1733 was a bona fide expression of the general attitude both in the city and most provincial towns. It is difficult not to agree with Sir Thomas Saunderson, who thought 'the present discontents were too general to be the effect of contrivance', or Lord Tyrconnel, who considered that 'there must be something more in such an universal dissatisfaction than the bare artifice of interested men in London stirring them up'.[66] Perhaps the last word should be that of the opposition press who had some justification for ironically claiming that by the time all the allegedly dishonest, biased and ignorant opponents of the excise had been discounted there was precious little public opinion left.

To sum up the whole, there are no Persons who oppose an Excise, except Jacobites and Tories, and Whigs, and Dissenters, and Revolutioners, and Murmurers, and Grumblers, and *Portugal* and *Virginia* Merchants, and the Deluded and Disaffected, ... and the Rash and the Heady, and the Clamorous, and the Noisy (especially noisy Sheep) and Factious Writers, and those who write Letters to Members of Parliament, and Party Politicians, and Bugbears, and Scarecrows, and wooden Grenadiers, and Men of Sense, and Men of Honour, and the Fair Traders and Retailers, and the unfair Traders, and the Deceivers and Deceived, and the *Craftsman*, and *Fog*; who, if you take them altogether, will not amount to many more than 99 in 100.[67]

---

[65] It goes without saying that smuggled tobacco was sold at the same price as that imported legally; no benefit was passed on to the consumer. See T. C. Barker, 'Smuggling in the Eighteenth Century', p. 399.
[66] *HMC Egmont Diary*, i. 349, 348.
[67] *Fog's Weekly Journal*, 17 Feb. 1733.

V
Parliament and the Excise: I

WHATEVER the interest and importance of out-of-doors politics, the outcome would ultimately be decided in Parliament. The excise was the dominant issue of the parliamentary session of 1733, from the moment it began to the moment it ended. Both sides set the tone of the session when it opened on 16 January. The King's Speech stressed the need to 'avoid unreasonable heats and animosities'[1] and the opposition lost no time in preparing the ground for a full-scale assault on the excise. Sir John Barnard, the leading city M.P., and William Shippen, the notorious Jacobite, gave dark warnings of ministerial schemes to injure trade; Walpole obliquely accepted the challenge in this by replying that, while damage to commerce was by no means in his mind, improvements certainly were.[2] In the following weeks, while the political world outside Westminster grew increasingly agitated with the excise affair and Walpole held his fire, the opposition missed no chance of discussing the expected excise proposals, however slight the pretext. When the army estimates were debated on 2 February, for example, Shippen argued that the excise too must be discussed, since a standing army would 'make wicked ministers more audacious, than otherwise they would be, in projecting and propagating schemes, which may be inconsistent with the liberties, destructive to the trade, and burthensome on the people of this nation'.[3] By the end of the month the Paymaster-General, Henry Pelham, declared himself so irritated by the constant injection of the excise issue into less controversial debates, as to 'wish this scheme, be what it will, were laid before us; for till it is, I believe we shall every day be falling into some debate or other about it, without knowing anything of it'.[4] But the opposition's tactics were not designed solely to keep the issue of the excise firmly in the forefront of politics. On 8 March, for example, there was an unexpectedly

[1] *Parl. Hist.*, viii. 1168.
[2] Ibid., 1170–4.
[3] Ibid., 1186.
[4] Ibid., 1234: 27 Feb. 1733.

bitter wrangle over a subject which on the face of it was quite unconnected. The cause was a petition from the colony of Rhode Island against the sugar bill which was currently under consideration. The ministry attempted to reject the petition out of hand on the grounds that petitions against money bills could not be accepted by the Commons. There was a good deal in this argument, but the precedents left at least some room for dispute, and the opposition went to great lengths to get the petition received, not so much for the principle involved as for the fact that the excise scheme too would involve a money bill. Pulteney remarked in the course of the debate that 'he made no doubt but that Petitions would be sent up from all Parts of the Kingdom against that dangerous Scheme', and Perceval described the opposition's manoeuvre 'as a concerted thing, which if yielded to, would be confessing that the people have a right to petition against money Bills, and so the nation would be prepared to offer petitions against the intended excise of wine and tobacco'.[5] In fact the administration narrowly defeated Sir John Barnard's motion to accept the petition by 140 to 112 votes, and only then because the court got wind of the opposition's tactics just in time to whip in some government support on what would otherwise have been a very quiet day.

The the opposition was allowed to carry out this preliminary campaign against the excise was largely Walpole's fault. It was he who delayed introducing his project and in so doing gave his opponents their chance to prepare. Technically, as Walpole himself pointed out, the excise scheme did not need to be taken early in the session because it did not form part of the supply for the year 1733.[6] Not until the last week of February did he specifically mention his excise scheme, and only then to announce the establishment of a Committee on Frauds as a preliminary measure. A formal call of the House was twice delayed, and even when it took place on 7 March and Walpole opened his budget, he merely stated the bare bones of his plan, postponing the details for a further week. It is possible that he held back his announcement of the excise scheme because he was less than certain that he wished to go on with it, in the light of steadily mounting pressure out of doors. Certainly there were rumours that he intended to abandon his great reform prematurely,

[5] RA Stuart, 160/1: Ravell to Edgar, debate of 8 Mar. 1733; *HMC Egmont Diary*, i. 340.
[6] *Parl. Hist.*, viii. 1231–2: 27 Feb. 1733.

though it may be doubted whether such a change of plan was possible at this stage.[7] Unfortunately the attitude of Walpole and his colleagues is not easily determined in the absence of hard evidence. However, there was about the comments of the minister's friends a barely concealed concern at the turn events had taken, an anxiety to show them in their best light. Charles Delafaye remarked that Walpole's preliminary sketch of the excise in his budget speech of 7 March 'seemed to be received with much greater and more general approbation than could have been expected, after all the noise that has been made about it without Doors'.[8] Similarly, the best that Henry Pelham could find to say on 3 March was that 'my friend Sir Robert persists with that firmness, and that superiority of reason that truly belongs to him, that I think they are half beaten before they come to the battle'.[9] Such remarks savour rather of making the best of a bad job than of real confidence. More convincing perhaps is the testimony of Lord Hervey that Walpole adhered to his scheme only because he felt committed to it.[10] This was probably the case. After all, by this time nobody could imagine that Walpole had not been planning an excise extension of some kind. Apart from his remarks in the salt tax debates of 1732, apart from the affair of the Virginia petition and the arrival in England of John Randolph, Walpole had hinted sufficiently at his scheme in January and February 1733 for it to be impossible to claim that he had no reforms in mind. In these circumstances the issue was not whether Walpole could escape altogether from his dilemma, but whether he would suffer more by sticking to his plans or by backing down. Retreat might be more demoralizing and dangerous than pressing on. It was still doubtless possible to push the excise through by the superiority of the Court and Treasury party, and recover some popular credit before the last possible date for a general election in 1734. Walpole must have been aware throughout January and February that he had little option but to go on. His delays perhaps represented an attempt to let the storm blow itself out, before the launching of his by now rather fragile craft.

If this was Walpole's aim it was not achieved, though at least one government newspaper thought it detected a change in the climate

[7] *Gloucester Journal*, 20 Feb. 1733; *HMC Egmont Diary*, i. 329; *HMC Carlisle*, p. 102.
[8] Add. MS. 27732, f. 132: Delafaye to Essex, 8 Mar. 1733.
[9] Add. MS. 27733, f. 34: Pelham to Essex, 3 Mar. 1733.
[10] *Hervey Memoirs*, pp. 134–5.

in mid-February. 'This *popular Fury* begins to abate; the Passions, at least, of the better sort, begin to subside; and there seems to be a Disposition to hearken to the Voice of Reason, and receive Advice. . . . The *Scheme*, tho' *mysterious* at present, will shortly come into the House, where you will find it so *useful* to the Publick, and so *harmless*, with Regard to you, That, instead of *hating* the Ministry for their *Oppression*, you will *laugh* at yourselves for your *Credulity*.'[11] But this was whistling in the wind. So far as the public clamour was concerned there was little or no let-up during February. In any case, as so often in the eighteenth century, when matters were actively before Parliament the most important manifestations of out-of-doors pressure were bound to occur in London, and there in 1733 there was little hope of a relaxation of tension. The city authorities had already done their best to influence individual M.P.s against the excise; they now ensured that the House as a whole was well aware of opinion outside its walls. The political organization of the city was exploited to the full in this strategy. The Deputy and Common Councillors for Farringdon Ward Without even had printed for their constituents a circular which was sent out on 13 March. 'I have order'd our Beadle to summon those of our Ward to meet me this Night, to consider of making the best Appearance of eminent Citizens To-morrow in the Court of Request at *Westminster*.'[12] The results of such a carefully organized campaign were spectacular. On 14 March, the day set for the final unveiling of Walpole's project, Westminster was crowded with demonstrators. According to the *London Evening Post*, admittedly not the most impartial of sources, 'there was the greatest Appearance of eminent Merchants, and Traders of the Cities and Suburbs of London and Westminster, in the Court of Requests, and Parts adjacent to the House of Commons, the like not seen in the Memory of Man, in order to apply to their several Members to oppose the new intended Excise on Wines and Tobacco'.[13] Even one of Walpole's closest supporters, Colonel Howard, noted that 'The Court of Request, the Lobby, and the Stairs were filled with people from the City'.[14] Any hope entertained by the ministers that public excitement would be quelled by the time the excise scheme was actually before Parliament was effectively

[11] *London Journal*, 17 Feb. 1733.
[12] *London Evening Post*, 15–17 Mar. 1733.
[13] 13–15 Mar. 1733.
[14] *HMC Carlisle*, p. 104: Howard to Carlisle, 15 Mar. 1733.

crushed by this formidable demonstration of force on 14 March.

Interest within Parliament was as great as that without. Technically Walpole's proposals were to be put forward in a Committee of the Whole House in accordance with the conventions governing the introduction of financial legislation. The Committee naturally attracted a great audience. Perceval remarked that 'The House was crowded to an insupportable degree', and Charles Delafaye called it 'the fullest house that has been known this long time'.[15] In fact in the subsequent division 471 votes were cast, a spectacularly large total in an age when attendance in excess of 450 was exceptionally rare. The debate was also outstanding. Walpole opened in the morning with a lengthy oration lasting two hours, which 'was allowed to exceed any Speech he ever made'.[16] Though most of the arguments on the excise had been amply rehearsed in the press, Walpole's detailed exposition of the frauds which plagued the customs service in the tobacco and wine trades was relatively new and made considerable impact. It was fortunate for the opposition that their leading speaker in the ensuing debate was Micajah Perry, M.P. for the City and one of the wealthiest tobacco merchants in the country. Even so his reply to the mass of detail on frauds provided by Walpole was far from convincing.[17] The debate after Walpole's and Perry's speeches stretched out into the small hours. But though the interest of the debate was substantial that of the division which followed was still greater. The government secured a majority in favour of the tobacco excise resolutions (wine was to follow separately later) by 265 votes to 204. This was confirmed two days later on 16 March, when these resolutions were formally reported to the House to be accepted as the basis of a tobacco excise bill, by a majority of 249 to 189. Shortly afterwards the Commons retired for the Easter recess.

The main question which arises from the voting in March 1733[18] concerns the extent to which the campaign of instructions to M.P.s affected the outcome in the division lobbies. However, this is not easily answered. Many instructions were clearly inspired for propaganda reasons by M.P.s who were not likely to support the excise. The electors of Exeter cannot have been surprised that their two Tory M.P.s, John Belfield and Francis Drewe, hastened to obey

[15] *HMC Egmont Diary*, i. 343; Coxe, iii. 129: Delafaye to Waldegrave, 15 Mar. 1733.
[16] Add. MS. 27732, f. 137: Delafaye to Essex, 15 Mar. 1733. For Walpole's speech, see *Parl. Hist.*, viii. 1268-81.
[17] *Parl. Hist.*, viii. 1281-5.
[18] See Appendix B for the evidence as to voting in these divisions.

their instructions, nor can the readiness of Warwick's Tory M.P.s, William Bromley and Sir William Keyt, be attributed to their regard for their constituents' convictions. On the other hand it is undeniable that there were M.P.s who declined to be browbeaten by their constituents. Colonel Howard, for example, went to some lengths to explain his position to his electors at Carlisle, as he informed his father.

Yesterday they sent me instructions from Carlisle to oppose the Excising the Wine and Tobacco. I answered their Letter by this post, and told them, that as I was ignorant what the proposal would be, I believd they, at a greater distance, could not be much less so; that if the Scheme was right, to prevent frauds without detriment to the fair trader, or the liberty of the subject, their directions would prevent my giving my concurrence to it; if on the contrary, it was attended with any of these inconveniencies that alarmed them, of being prejudicial to trade and the liberty of the subject, it would have met with my negative, had I not received their instructions; so I desired to know, whether they expected me to oppose it, in what light soever it appeared to me.

In fact this moderate reply yielded a tolerant response from Carlisle. Twelve days later Howard was able to report to his father that 'the gentlemen at Carlisle, by answer to my letter, left me entirely at liberty to act for them as I thought right',[19] and in the subsequent divisions he did not hesitate to vote for the court. This is not the only example. Viscount Perceval, ever torn between fidelity to Walpole and independence, was concerned by the instructions which he received from Harwich, but nonetheless supported the excise scheme.[20] Sir Roger Bradshaigh, M.P. for Wigan and a government supporter, enquired as to the likely reaction of his constituents to disobedience, but remained loyal to the ministry.[21] In one or two cases, M.P.s positively made a point of flouting their instructions. Samuel Tufnell of Colchester conducted an acrimonious and very public quarrel with his corporation over the excise instructions, both sides publishing their correspondence in the newspapers, while John Neale of Coventry enraged his constituents by flatly declaring in the Commons that the instructions he had received were wholly unrepresentative of their true sentiments.[22] Unfortunately the most

[19] *HMC Carlisle*, pp. 102-4.
[20] *HMC Egmont Diary*, i. 311-12.
[21] M. Cox, 'Sir Roger Bradshaigh and the Electoral Management of Wigan', p. 140.
[22] *Whitehall Evening Post*, 6-8 Mar. 1733; *Craftsman*, 24 Mar. 1733.

impudent response of all was too good to be true. Anthony Henley of Southampton published a reply to the Mayor of that town which ran:

> Yours I received, and am very much surprized at your Insolence in troubling me about the Excise. You know what I know very well; that I bought you. I know what perhaps you think I don't know, that you are about selling yourselves to somebody else; and I know what perhaps you don't know; that I am buying another Borough—And now may the Curse of God light upon you all; and may your houses be as common to Excisemen, as your Wives and Daughters were to me, when I stood candidate for your Corporation.

In fact this turned out to be an elaborate joke. Henley was one of those who obeyed his instructions on 14 March.[23]

That the instructions had at best a limited impact by no means signifies that the campaign to pressurize M.P.s had no effect. On the contrary it is clear that in the excise divisions the government majority did suffer quite severely as the result, if not of instructions as such, at least of the general climate of opinion outside Westminster. The obvious reason for this was the fact that a general election lay at most eighteen months away. Electorates, then as now, had notoriously short memories; errors of conduct for which M.P.s might be forgiven six years before a general election were less likely to be forgotten only one year before. Right through the eighteenth century the last year or so of each Parliament was a peculiarly sensitive time for government. The Jew Bill affair of 1753, the anti-Spanish agitation of 1739–40, the petitioning movement of 1779, all owed much of their impact to this basic fact of political life. With the timing of his excise scheme Walpole had planned to turn this weakness into strength by producing a controversial but electorally attractive policy at the critical moment. But when this misfired, the natural corollary was an exceedingly dangerous electoral situation. Sir Richard Lane, a city merchant who sat for Worcester, warned Walpole that the tobacco excise 'will certainly disoblige—So that we shall loose our Elections—and may be attended with Ill consequences'.[24] Similarly, Perceval confided to Walpole's brother, Horace, his own anxieties on this score. 'I said the people were so

[23] *Weekly Register*, 31 Mar. 1733; see also *Swift Correspondence*, iv. 144.
[24] C(H) MSS. 29/29a.

possessed against [the excise] that it would unsaddle a great many of the Government's friends who should vote for it, and that already there were persons making interest against a new election on presumption that the electors would grow cool to their members that on this occasion should vote with the Court. That I did not know how safe my own election might be'.[25] Charles Delafaye, also, referred to the attempt to 'inflame the County Boroughs, and make them (tho' in several places it was done by Stratagem) write to their Representatives to oppose the Scheme; Which could not but influence several of the Members with an Eye to their future Resolutions'.[26]

These fears were reinforced by the by-elections which happened to fall in the early months of 1733. In Kent, for example, where the death of Sir Roger Meredith had necessitated a by-election for one of the county seats, it was confidently reported that 'both Whigs and Tories are determin'd not to elect any Person that shall Vote for an Excise, or Extension of Excise laws'.[27] The candidates were Sir Edward Dering, a staunch Tory, and Sir William D'Aeth, a Whig. The *London Evening Post* stated that 'as the former stands on the true Principles of Liberty, in Opposition to the Excise Scheme, it is thought he will carry it by a Considerable Majority', a prophecy which turned out to be accurate when he was returned without even a contest at the polls. Dering drove home the lesson of his victory by urging, in his maiden speech in the Commons, the obligation on M.P.s to obey their constituents' orders.[28] At Chester too there was a violent by-election contest between a ministerialist, Richard Manley, and a Tory, Sir Charles Bunbury, which was won by the latter. The opposition press, intent on alarming government M.P.s who sat for trading corporations, declared: 'it is computed, that if all those of that City, *who deal in Wine and Tobacco* had voted for Mr. Manley, he would have carried it by a considerable Majority'.[29] Nor was the lesson limited to the press. Sir Thomas Lyttelton, knight of the shire for Worcester, received a strong hint direct from Lord Coventry, one of the most influential figures in the county, that a vote for the excise would not be well received in the West Midlands.[30] Such pressures were not calculated to reassure the anxious administration

[25] *HMC Egmont Diary*, i. 312.
[26] Add. MS. 27732, f. 137: Delafaye to Essex, 15 Mar. 1733.
[27] *London Evening Post*, 22–24 Mar. 1733.
[28] 27–29 Mar. 1733; Corr. Pol. Angl., 380, f. 280.
[29] *Fog's Weekly Journal*, 31 Mar. 1733.
[30] M. Wyndham, *Chronicles of the Eighteenth Century* (London, 1924), i. 31–2.

supporter concerned about his prospects of re-election. Indeed, according to the French ambassador Walpole was visited by a deputation of such potential waverers, though he gave them short shrift, apparently informing them that 'Il ne pouvoit les regarder "tous que comme des canailles qu'il les avoit tous acheptes et qu'il les revendroit tous".'[31] Unsupported as this anecdote is by other evidence, it does not lack the authentic tone of Walpole's characteristic vulgar abusiveness.

This factor was bound to have some effect on voting. For M.P.s who normally supported administration but who sat for large and populous constituencies where commercial issues as well as constitutional points could tell against them, it was safer to vote against the excise, or at any rate abstain. Admittedly not all government deserters at this stage were in this category. Some of those who normally supported Walpole voted against the excise because their more immediate political bosses chose this moment to go into opposition. Walpole had a number of opponents at court who seized the chance of the excise crisis to declare their sentiments. Affected in this way were the three Dalrymples, Sir James, M.P. for Haddington Burghs and Auditor-General of the Scottish Exchequer, John, M.P. for Wigtown Burghs and a half-pay officer in the army, and William, M.P. for Wigtownshire and a former placeman. All three voted against the government on 14 March, not because they disliked the excise nor because they feared the electoral consequences of a vote for the court (on the contrary Scottish seats were more likely to be forfeited by disobliging the court than by offending the public), but because the head of their family, the celebrated Earl of Stair, instructed them to. A similar case was that of the three Stanhope brothers, respectively M.P.s for Derby, Nottingham and Buckinghamshire, whose politics were dictated by their elder brother the Earl of Chesterfield, or that of Lord Nassau Powlett, M.P. for Lymington and brother of the Duke of Bolton, himself a deserter at this moment. None of these M.P.s were really masters of their own political fate. However, more characteristic of the deserters on 14 March were the semi-independent supporters of government who sat for marginal or popular seats, and were naturally anxious about their electoral credit. Typical of these was the Eyles family, one of the wealthiest Whig houses in the city, with three representatives in Parliament. The head of the family, Sir John Eyles, was a prominent

[31] Corr. Pol. Angl., 379, f. 359.

alderman and a major figure in the affairs of the South Sea Company. He was also a reliable supporter of Walpole, as were his brother Joseph, a government contractor, and his cousin, Francis. But the excise crisis placed them in difficulties out of which there was only one possible route. Sir John sat for London and Joseph for Southwark, two of the most popular constituencies in the kingdom, and both had no hesitation in voting against Walpole for the first time on the excise issue. But their cousin sat for the family borough of Devizes where popular views could safely be ignored, a fact which enabled him to vote as usual with the administration. Equally significant was the case of Sir William Middleton, an independent friend of the ministry, who as knight of the shire for Northumberland was peculiarly vulnerable to popular opinion, as were John Hedworth, M.P. for County Durham, and Sir William Milner, M.P. for York. All three divided against the government on 14 March. Others simply abstained; Sir Adolphus Oughton, M.P. for Coventry but a man with expectations from government, did so, as did the M.P. for Harwich, Sir Philip Parker, who was conveniently ill at this time.[32] In short the divisions on the excise revealed many who, in Lord Hervey's words, 'without being enemies to Sir Robert Walpole, were against it from prudential views to their elections, and because they did not dare to be for it'.[33]

Despite these desertions the composition of the voting lists for 14 and 16 March gave the administration more cause for relief than for despondency. One most welcome feature was a marked tendency for some of the more hostile independents in the Commons to support Walpole on the excise issue. Typical was Sir William Lowther, M.P. for Pontefract, and by no means a slavish supporter of ministers. On 16 March Colonel Howard noted that 'Sir Will. Lowther spoke short, but close to the purpose, and had very loud heerum's from the Ministerial Bench. I really believe he and several more gentlemen that had no employments, and that I did expect to have seen of the Minority, voted entirely from the merit of the Question, as thinking it a right proposal.'[34] Similarly there was Perceval, who despite the pressure of his constituents was too impressed by Walpole's well-ordered arguments on 14 March to oppose the excise. 'The scheme of excising tobacco appeared when

[32] *HMC Egmont Diary*, i. 359.
[33] *Hervey Memoirs*, pp. 167–8.
[34] *HMC Carlisle*, p. 105: Howard to Carlisle, 20 Mar. 1733.

explained so very reasonable', he commented, 'that I wonder the majority was not greater'.[35] Most remarkable of all was the conduct of Sir Joseph Jekyll, Master of the Rolls and M.P. for Reigate. Jekyll had, as Speaker Onslow put it, 'much dislike to Sir Robert Walpole in many things and bore no great reverence to his character in general'.[36] In fact he generally voted against the government and was widely regarded as a prominent if somewhat quixotic opposition leader. His remarks on the excise on 14 March consequently created something of a sensation. 'Sir Joseph Jekyl', wrote Perceval, 'who is not used to vote with the Court, said he could not see one argument against it, and they who were against it had their own private advantage in their thoughts, not the good of the public'.[37] Jekyll's desertion was a great blow to the opposition and one which the government press exploited to the full.[38] Moreover, apart from Lowther, Perceval and Jekyll, there were other independents, who were converted by Walpole's speech on 14 March—Sir Roger Meredith, for example, whose death was shortly to produce the Kent by-election, John Ramsden, M.P. for Appleby, and John Yorke, M.P. for Richmond, all Whig independents.

These accessions to Walpole's strength were of the utmost significance, and not merely because they did something to offset the losses among those who looked to their electoral prospects. They suggested, for example, very forcibly that Walpole's original calculations about the electoral advantages of his project had been far from absurd. Though the business community had exerted every ounce of pressure it could command and though the opposition was determined to bring all its weight to bear, less-interested parties had too much to gain from a new excise to treat it lightly. A reduction in the land tax as a result of more effective and, in the minds of many, long overdue taxation of trade was by no means an unattractive proposition. The arguments of Walpole's opponents did not provide a very seductive alternative. It was one of the ironies brought about by Walpole's characteristic policy of adopting traditionally Tory policies that his opponents found themselves again and again in the early 1730s arguing in favour of heavier land taxes. While this line was swallowed by those totally committed to opposing the Walpole

[35] *HMC Egmont Diary*, i. 343.
[36] *HMC Onslow*, p. 470.
[37] *HMC Egmont Diary*, i. 343.
[38] See *A Political Conversation, which lately happened between A Couple of Staunch Patriots, and A Revolter to the Court Interest* (London, 1733).

regime regardless of measures, as the Tories were, it was not designed to appeal to those who were not particularly committed either way. Sir William Wyndham, the doyen of Tory country gentlemen, found one way out of the resulting dilemma; 'I know that since last session of parliament, it has been most industriously given about in the county, which I have the honour to represent, "O gentlemen! The knight of your shire was against easing you of one shilling in the pound land tax". . . . I shall always be against sacrificing the public happiness of the nation, or the security of our constitution, to any such mean and sordid views as that of a little present ease in the land tax'.[39] This was not an altogether barren line of argument, but it required a very clear demonstration that the public good and the security of the constitution were indeed at risk to convince the independents of its validity.

Yet such demonstration was scarcely forthcoming. Arguments about trade, for example, were not likely to make much impact among the independents. On the contrary, the tension between the landed and commercial interests, which was one of most marked features of post-Revolution politics, worked to the disadvantage of the opponents of excises. Wyndham bitterly described the excise scheme as 'an endeavour to set the landed interest in a manner at war with the trading interest of the nation', and government speakers certainly did their best to stoke the flames, with their assertions that 'the money arising by this tax [the land tax], is paid only by five out of six of those who possess the riches of this nation', and that the 'whole clamour . . . is in favour of the retailer or tradesman'.[40] Perhaps more likely to counterbalance the independent's understandable desire to reduce the land tax were the alleged constitutional dangers. The two outstanding arguments concerned juries and officials. In excise cases justice was summary and administered by the hated Excise Commissioners in London. This created a happy hunting-ground for those who sought to exploit the traditional pride in the Englishman's right to trial by his peers. Even so, the argument had limited appeal for country gentlemen who were themselves J.P.s and who were well aware that there were two sides to this question. Even the customs system involved some arbitrary procedures, and it was a notorious fact that, where juries were involved in smuggling cases, they were hopelessly reluctant to convict even in the face of the most

[39] *Parl. Hist.*, viii. 1211–12: 23 Feb. 1733.
[40] Ibid., viii. 1303, 1322, 1280.

flagrant guilt. The argument concerning officers was equally contentious. Nothing contributed more to the opposition's propaganda successes than the horrific tales associated with excise officers, either in their conduct towards the shopkeeper—an area in which no invasion of domestic privacy and no outrage against the dealer and his family was beyond credit—or in their role as electoral agents of government and purveyors of corruption. These fears were wildly exaggerated. The number of additional excise officers required to deal with the wine and tobacco excise would be at most 150. 'Is this nation to be enslaved by 150 little excisemen?' asked Philip Yorke, the Attorney-General.[41]

The electoral argument was particularly absurd. While Pulteney claimed that 'this scheme is absolutely inconsistent with a free election of members of parliament',[42] government supporters reasonably pointed out that excisemen were merely replacements for customs officers, themselves no less influential in elections. Moreover, customs officials were concentrated in the ports, where they could form an uncomfortably large proportion of the electorate. By contrast, excise officers would be scattered up and down the country and absorbed among the county and large borough electorates. On this calculation the gradual substitution of excise for customs officers would actually reduce the electoral influence of the administration. 'If all the *Officers* in a small *Borough* were disseminated, and thinly scatter'd over a large *County* in the Capacity of *Excise Officers*, their Interests would totally dwindle, and become very triffling and inconsiderable'.[43] Later on the government press had some justification for referring contemptuously to those 'who were against Inland Duties on Tobacco and Wine, because they thought Custom-house Officers would be less troublesome than Excise-Men'.[44] This is not to say that the arguments concerning liberty and the constitution were insincere on the part of the opposition. But they were not unanswerable, and independents like Sir Joseph Jekyll demonstrated on 14 March their belief that they had been grossly exaggerated by the press and the business world. If anything could vindicate Walpole's original conviction that the excise was fundamentally attractive to the genuinely uncommitted country gentlemen, it was the conduct

---

[41] Ibid., viii. 1289: 14 Mar. 1733.
[42] Ibid., viii. 1327: 16 Mar. 1733.
[43] *Applebee's Original Weekly Journal*, 18 Nov. 1732.
[44] *Flying Post*, 29 May 1733.

of those 'that voted for the Question, whose opinion carries them often with the Minority upon other occasions'.[45]

Quite apart from the relief provided by the unexpected support of some independently minded M.P.s, the administration had no need to feel particularly concerned when Parliament recessed for Easter. The majorities on the two crucial divisions of 14 and 16 March had been 61 and 60 respectively in a spectacularly crowded House. This was by no means a poor performance. Ever since the emergence of a strong combined Whig and Tory opposition three or four years before, the administration had had to face reduced majorities on the more important issues of the day. As recently as 1732 the small size of government majorities had been made plain in the voting on the salt tax. The crucial divisions then had registered majorities of 38 and 29. By comparison with these, two early majorities of 60 and 61 were bound to appear gratifyingly secure, especially in view of the clamour out of doors. 'I must own', Delafaye commented, 'the Majority was much greater than I expected', while Hervey had no hesitation in describing it simply as 'a great majority'.[46] The consequent relief and confidence of the ministers was strongly reflected in the despatches sent to ambassadors and envoys abroad. Even on 15 March Robinson, at the Vienna embassy, had been assured 'The House is now sitting upon the Report, and fighting the Battle over again, but there is no manner of Danger'.[47] Indeed the division of 16 March strongly suggested that the corner had been safely turned. On that day there were minor deviations from the pattern of voting in the first excise division two days previously. The opposition had succeeded in whipping in a number of backbenchers who had failed to put in an appearance originally and who could be relied upon to vote against the excise once they had been persuaded to attend—men like Sir George Beaumont, Tory M.P. for Leicester, Sir Charles and Edward Kemys, rabid Welsh Jacobites, and Edmund Pleydell, knight of the shire for Dorset. On the other hand the government too had made some gains. A few of its friends who had been constrained either to oppose or abstain on 14 March—such as Hedworth, Henley and Oughton—felt able to take out a modest reinsurance policy by returning to the ministerial fold in the less publicised division on the report. In so far as numbers fell they did so in equal

[45] *HMC Carlisle*, p. 105: Howard to Carlisle, 15 Mar. 1733.
[46] Add. MS. 27732, f. 137: Delafaye to Essex, 15 Mar. 1733.
[47] Add. MS. 23787, f. 303: Delafaye to Robinson, 15 Mar. 1733.

proportions on each side and indicated that interest in the issue was diminishing after the key debate in which Walpole had launched his project. Not surprisingly then, after the 16th the ministry looked forward to a safe, if no doubt contested, passage. The opposition would not give up the most important issue in years without a struggle, but after the divisions of March their chances of success were small. The backwoodsmen who had been lured to the Commons for the great debate would not turn out day after day in April to contest the excise bills stage by stage. 'So the main labour of that affair is over, though it must be carefully attended in all its steps through both houses, for the opponents will most probably dispute every inch of ground'.[48] The tobacco bill would turn out to be 'a nine Days' wonder' and the event would 'show, that neither the ministry nor the Parliam[en]t are to be deterred by the popular Clamour, from doing what is for the king's and the Country's Service'.[49]

[48] Coxe, iii. 131: Delafaye to Waldegrave, 19 Mar. 1733.
[49] Add. MS. 27732, f. 143: Delafaye to Essex, 22 Mar. 1733; f. 137: Delafaye to Essex, 15 Mar. 1733.

VI

Parliament and the Excise: II

UNFORTUNATELY for the ministry the Easter recess was not a success. Far from promoting a general relaxation of excitement out of doors, it gave the opposition the time it needed to reorganize its campaign, and particularly in London the popular furore showed no signs of diminishing. On 31 March, only a few days before the tobacco bill was due to come before the Commons, Colonel Howard noted, 'It's inconceivable the clamour and spirit of opposition there is in this part of the world to this Scheme; which hitherto I can see no reason for'.[1] The provinces too showed their continuing anxiety. By early April there were arriving in the capital deputations of business men from the major towns, a significant reinforcement of the earlier instructions; though the press exaggerated when it claimed that these came 'from most of the Cities and principal Corporations in England', the well-publicized presence in London of representatives from important trading towns like Bristol and Liverpool once again proved the concern with which the business community regarded the excise scheme.[2]

In this atmosphere there was little hope that the House of Commons would dispose of the remaining stages of the excise as quietly as had seemed likely at the beginning of the holiday. In fact for the administration the first two weeks of the resumed session were little short of a nightmare. Normally two successful divisions of the kind which had been registered in March would have ensured subsequent success. Instead, the story of the tobacco bill's progress through the Commons, beginning with its first reading on 4 April, was one of rapid deterioration for the court. The first division after the recess, on 4 April, produced a majority almost as large as those of March, 232 to 176. But both government and opposition votes were in fact down by about thirty, and when on the same day the opposition produced more supporters, the ministry was apparently not able to respond to this challenge. The result was two further divisions,

[1] *HMC Carlisle*, p. 105.
[2] *Fog's Weekly Journal*, 7 April 1733.

which the court won by reduced margins, 237 to 199 and 236 to 200. Whether at this stage the ministry could have found its missing thirty voters is doubtful, since it must be supposed that the government's managers worked as hard to pull in further votes as did the opposition. However, this must remain a matter for speculation. The next divisions, on 5 April, 128 to 112, 124 to 73, and 118 to 76, all in favour of the court, were meaningless. They were taken on opposition motions relating to procedure, and, as one ministerialist remarked, 'not many members were there, especially as no one expected that there would be anything of consequence to come on'.[3] Unfortunately there were no further divisions in the following days to test the situation, merely growing uneasiness that the government was losing control. The crisis finally burst, so far as Parliament was concerned, on 10 April. On that day the City of London presented a petition against the excise, a manoeuvre which represented a major advance on the previous tactics of instructions. The petition resembled the Rhode Island petition against the sugar bill presented a few weeks previously, in that it concerned a money bill, a subject on which the Commons generally refused to receive representations before enactment. As Lord Hervey remarked, 'this was the strongest point for the Court that had yet been debated in the whole progress of the Bill, as it was contrary to the rules and orders of the House to comply with petitions of this nature against taxes that are going to be laid'.[4] Yet the ministry's victory by a majority of 214 to 197 was pyrrhic, and on the following day Walpole informed the House that his project was to be postponed, and in effect dropped; the tobacco and wine excises were at an end. In fact he had taken the decision to drop the excise on 9 April, though without letting those beyond his own circle know it.[5] His announcement was delayed only until after 10 April because he regarded it as a matter of the first importance to resist and defeat the City's petition. Voluntarily to climb down on the excise was bad enough; to appear to do so because the City had officially thrown its weight into the struggle, would have been disastrous.

The fact that Walpole resolved to withdraw his excise scheme without actually waiting to be defeated before doing so raises certain problems. For example it enabled his loyal biographer, Archdeacon

---

[3] *HMC Carlisle*, p. 109: Sir T. Robinson to Carlisle, 14 April 1733.
[4] *Hervey Memoirs*, p. 160.
[5] *HMC Egmont Diary*, i. 359.

Coxe, to claim that he backed down, not under pressure from Parliament but in response to public opinion, though this is scarcely a plausible thesis.[6] Walpole himself was franker when he announced his decision to the Commons on 11 April. Though he admitted that 'it was not prudent to press a thing which the nation expressed so general a dislike to, however they were deceived', he also candidly stated that he had been compelled to change his mind by the collapse of his majority from 61 in March to 17 on 10 April.[7] Whether his judgement on this point was faulty is of course a matter for debate. Certainly some of his supporters had their doubts. Sir Thomas Robinson wondered whether it was 'an ill-judged retreat' and a hard-liner, Joseph Danvers, later asserted, 'I think the gentlemen concerned in the administration never did a thing so wrong, as the giving up that scheme'.[8] It also surprised many outside the Commons when the news filtered out 'that there was a Majority for the Bill in all the Questions that were put relating to it'.[9] Even so there was little doubt that Walpole was right in his conviction that his majority would vanish altogether unless he retreated. It was generally reckoned in the eighteenth century that when the opposition could turn in votes of about 200 the government was in serious trouble. On the excise issue the opposition had achieved this in March, and there was very good reason to believe that its total of 197 registered on 10 April would be pushed up substantially soon after. According to one ministerial supporter many fair-weather friends were preparing to defect on the 11th. 'Many of our deserters who had not voted at all the night before, and finding the affair droop (and the author thought by some in the same situation), that morn they came down with a resolution openly to join with the enemy'.[10] As early as 5 April Perceval noted that 'the minority gain ground so fast, that it is very doubtful whether this Bill will pass in any shape'.[11] Moreover, the bill had still to go through the Committee stage where it was traditionally far easier to harass the government. All in all it is difficult not to accept the elder Pitt's later assessment; 'Did not his

---

[6] Coxe, i. 403.
[7] *HMC Egmont Diary*, i. 360.
[8] *HMC Carlisle*, p. 111: Sir T. Robinson to Carlisle, 14 April 1733; *Parl. Hist.* ix. 262: 4 Feb. 1734.
[9] *Some Observations Upon a Paper, Intituled, The List. That is, Of Those who Voted for and against the EXCISE-BILL* (London, 1733), p. 5.
[10] *HMC Carlisle*, p. 110: Sir T. Robinson to Carlisle, 14 April 1733.
[11] *HMC Egmont Diary*, i. 354.

majority decrease upon every division? It was almost certain, that if he had pushed in any further, the majority would have turned against him'.[12] Walpole was not a coward, whatever else he was. It need not be imagined that there was any escape other than surrender in the second week of April.

The significance of this situation is only clear if the administration's apparent strength in the initial divisions on the excise is recalled. The excise scheme was actually defeated not by the swell of public opinion but by a dramatic change of fortunes for the government in the House of Commons. What had changed between 16 March, when the administration soundly defeated the opposition by a majority of 60, and 10 April, when the gap had been reduced to 17? This question is not easily answered. Though there is ample evidence of voting in the March divisions, no complete lists survive for 10 April. On the other hand there exists a list of government abstentions in the division of 10 April, which appears to have been the work of Walpole himself, and which when collated with the earlier and more detailed lists can yield a great deal of valuable information.[13] Together with the comments and observations of contemporaries, this list makes it possible to have a reasonably clear idea of the changes in the Parliamentary balance of power which brought Walpole nearer to defeat than at any time since the establishment of his regime.

One obvious possible explanation lies in a complete change of heart among some of those who had been content to cast their vote for the excise in March. It is true that there was a small number who actually changed sides, voting for the court on 14 March and against it in one or other of the subsequent divisions. But those involved were few and had plausible reasons for their conduct. George II characteristically resorted to mere abuse to account for their treachery, with epithets ranging from 'a whimsical fellow' to describe Sir William Lowther, through 'an Irish Blockhead' applied to Sir Thomas Prendergast, to simply 'a fool' for Lord James and 'half mad' for Lord Charles Cavendish.[14] Such terms were less than fair. The two Cavendishes, independent friends of the administration, had excellent reasons for changing their minds about the excise. Lord Charles sat for Westminster, a large and popular constituency,

[12] Quoted by E. R. Turner, 'The Excise Scheme of 1733', p. 45.
[13] See Appendix C.
[14] *Hervey Memoirs*, p. 162. On Lowther see Appendix C.

which had not attempted to influence him earlier, but which issued clear instructions against the excise after his vote on 14 March.[15] A similar factor may account for Lord James's attitude. At the time he sat for Derby, but the Cavendish family was currently planning a campaign to take one of the county seats for Derbyshire, in the next general election. It would have been madness on the part of the Cavendishes to continue to flout popular opinion in two large constituencies a matter of months before a general election. Of others who changed their vote, Sir Thomas Clarke, M.P. for the large and volatile constituency of Hertford, may also have had his electoral prospects in mind; Sir Thomas Prendergast, the new M.P. for Chichester, rebelled out of pique at failing to obtain a lucrative place in the ministry; while Lord Tyrconnel, Sir William Lowther and John Yorke were all thoroughgoing independents, whose minds were doubtless changed for them by the growing clamour. This handful of M.P.s who altered their sentiments completely in the course of a month were, however, relatively unimportant. The essential element in the destruction of the government's majority was large-scale abstention, rather than outright rebellion. If the figures of 14 March and 10 April are compared it is obvious that the opposition did not actually increase in strength but merely maintained its position, with 205 on the former occasion and 197 on the latter.[16] By contrast the administration's numbers fell from 264 to 214, despite Walpole's desperate efforts to whip in supporters for the rejection of the City's petition on 10 April. The court strained every nerve to get a respectable majority on this occasion. Sir Adolphus Oughton, a government supporter who sought to absent himself from the excise divisions in deference to the pressures of his Coventry constituents, bore testimony to Walpole's vigour on this occasion. 'On m'a mis le marché en mains, and if I do not vote for the wine bill at least . . . I must renounce all hopes and thoughts of any present or future recompense for all my life spent in the service, a hard lesson this'.[17] Yet despite all the weight which the court could bring to bear, as many as fifty

---

[15] *Craftsman*, 24 Mar. 1733.
[16] This is not to say that the opposition did not find any new votes between these two dates. On the contrary there appear from the division lists printed (see Appendix B) to have been a number of Tory country gentlemen who only presented themselves for the voting in April. However, these merely replaced others of their kind who had voted in March but were absent in April.
[17] Quoted in R. Sedgwick, ed., *History of Parliament: House of Commons 1715–1754*, ii. 316.

or sixty of those who had voted for the excise on 14 March declined to do so a month later.

A glance at the list of those whom Walpole noted as abstaining on 10 April is sufficient to show that the defections of that date were of a novel and, from his viewpoint, a sinister kind. In March the characteristic desertions had been of independent friends of government anxious to insure against disaster at the ensuing general election by voting on the popular side. No doubt what Perceval called 'the ill-will the members who vote for it will get in their countries' was a factor throughout the excise crisis, but in April there must have been an additional factor operating.[18] Observers were emphatic that those who abstained at this stage were particularly reliable supporters of the court. 'Sir Robert daily loses friends', 'our friends declaring daily against the scheme', 'seeing our friends desert so fast', 'so fast do our friends desert', 'those who had before been . . . fast Friends turned Tail'—such were the expressions used.[19] Many of the deserters were indeed committed friends of the administration who were not likely to be wooed away from it by a sudden access of conscience or pressure of public opinion. Nobody could seriously imagine, for example, that Charles Wills, who sat for the close borough of Totnes, or Thomas Pitt, M.P. for Camelford, or George Treby, M.P. for Dartmouth and Walpole's principal friend among the Cornish boroughmongers, would be very concerned with the public reaction to a vote in favour of the excise. Nor could it be thought that many placemen would willingly court Walpole's disfavour by abstention; yet there were for the first time significant numbers of office-holders among the deserters at this stage. Treby and Wills were respectively Master of the Household and Lieutenant-General of the Ordnance; Sir James Thornhill, M.P. for Weymouth and Melcombe, was also the King's History Painter. Similarly involved were members of the Prince of Wales's household, George Bubb Dodington himself, as well as William Fortescue, M.P. for Newport, Isle of Wight, and the Prince's Attorney-General, and James Lumley, M.P. for Chichester and a Groom of the Bedchamber. There were of course exceptions but, with due allowance for them, the conclusion is irresistible that the defectors at this time included hard-core court supporters who sat for close boroughs and held lucrative places.

[18] *HMC Egmont Diary*, i. 359.
[19] *HMC Carlisle*, pp. 108, 110; *HMC Egmont Diary*, i. 359; *The Projector's Looking-Glass* (London, 1733), p. 10.

Such men, who represented the stripping from Walpole's Court and Treasury party of a further and more central section, were not likely to be moved by the kind of arguments which had influenced many in March. Their parliamentary seats were largely invulnerable to popular opposition and their ministerial places gave them a vested interest in the preservation of the established government. In short, where in March defections from government had been largely unavoidable losses due to the proximity of the general election, those of April were definite declarations of no-confidence by powerful figures in the ruling party. The latter, in the course of the month between 14 March and 10 April, had found reasons for disassociating themselves from Walpole if not actually for engineering his downfall. As the French ambassador pointed out, 'leur absence ou leur retraite marque asses leur repugnance a Courir la meme fortune que M. de Walpole'.[20]

These reasons are probably to be found in the crisis at Court which was developing apace with that in Parliament. This was indeed the one element in the political situation which changed between the division of 14 March and that of 10 April. From the start of the excise crisis it had been apparent that rebellious courtiers would seize the opportunity to make trouble, and the result had been the defection of important political figures like the Earl of Chesterfield, the Earl of Stair and the Duke of Bolton. Still worse than such desertions, however, were the activities of the rebels in the royal closet. Even in February 1733, before the excise had actually come before Parliament, there had been sinister rumours flying about.

I found a current report [Perceval noted,] that the design of the excise is dropped, and that the Queen had told Sir Robert that though she thought his scheme the best in the world, yet seeing the people expressed such a dislike to it, she would not have them displeased, but I believe nothing of the story.[21]

Once the matter was in the Commons the pressures on the King and Queen grew much stronger. Stair, for example, made a direct approach to the Queen to lecture her on the gravity of the situation. According to Hervey he told her, 'in no reign, in no country, was ever any Minister so universally odious as the man you support'. Far worse, this interview was misrepresented in other quarters.

[20] Corr. Pol. Angl., 380, f. 74. [21] *HMC Egmont Diary*, i. 329.

Stair 'boasted much to all his party, who circulated the history, of the bold truths he told the Queen, and the strong effect they seemed to have upon her'.[22] Not surprisingly the rebellion gathered momentum. Two respected court peers, Lords Clinton and Scarbrough, respectively a Lord of the Bedchamber and Master of the Household, declared against the excise, a notable triumph for the opposition. 'The comment that is made on this report', Hervey pointed out to George II, 'is, that if those who have the honour to serve Your Majesty in such near and high stations did not know this declaration would not be displeasing to you, they would certainly not have ventured, so explicitly at least, to have made it'.[23] Even more damaging from this angle was the king's failure to take clear action in favour of his minister and against the rebels. When the possibility of punitive dismissals was raised three prominent court magnates, Wilmington, Dorset and Scarbrough himself, threatened to resign.

this made his Majesty pause, and he ordered a meeting of them all with Sir Robert Walpole to reconcile matters, at which meeting Lord Chesterfield refused to be present, so ill he resented this affair. But the conclusion was that he should not be turned out, and he afterwards declared he would not lay down purely to spite Sir Robert, who wished he would.[24]

To what extent the royal family did waver in its attachment is not easily judged. Generally speaking Walpole's control of the closet was far stronger than most of his opponents liked to think. Moreover, George II had engaged himself very strongly in the fate of the excise: Hervey commented 'that if it had been an act to secure and settle the Crown of England on him and his posterity he could not have been more eager in the measure, more anxious for its fate, or more solicitous for its success'.[25] On the other hand, he did not have quite that degree of pertinacity in defending his ministers which characterized his successor. He had a horror of committing himself to an administration which could not command a continuing majority in Parliament, and certainly Walpole's difficulties in the excise crisis concerned him; again according to Hervey 'Every division showing a decrease in the majority, the King grew, every division, more and more uneasy'.[26] Walpole's offer to resign at this time was rejected,[27]

[22] *Hervey Memoirs*, p. 145.
[23] Ibid., p. 159.
[24] *HMC Egmont Diary*, i. 357.
[25] *Hervey Memoirs*, p. 149.
[26] Ibid., p. 150.
[27] Ibid., pp. 157-8.

but if the situation had continued to deteriorate, both Walpole and Queen Caroline might have had some difficulty in sustaining the king's resolution.

In any case the actual sentiments of the king were in one sense irrelevant; what mattered was the political world's impression of them. It was the general and growing suspicion that Walpole's support in the closet was weakening, which transformed the ministry's position between the first excise division on 14 March and the last on 10 April. The defections of normally very reliable supporters which developed in early April reflected this general belief in a major crisis at court. As Hervey diagnosed, it was from St. James's that the effective political pressures during this phase of the excise crisis came—'the most zealous friends to the excise began to be of opinion that, considering what had happened at this end of the town, the clamour at the other grew too hot to be struggled with'.[28] This is not to underrate the importance of public opinion in the destruction of the excise scheme. The clamour out of doors had created the basic situation and given birth to the crisis, but in the last analysis it was the sudden threat at court which brought it to a climax. No wonder the Queen was informed that many 'are said openly to have declared themselves against this measure, and many more are thought to have taken the quiet part of lying by till things are ripe for a revolution in the ministry'.[29] Moreover, even if by some miracle enough independent support had been secured to carry the excise through the House of Commons, the losses at court would have had a fatal effect elsewhere. Under Walpole the House of Lords was not the safe preserve of government that it was later to become. When Lord Stair held his celebrated audience with the Queen he boasted to her face that 'the defection there will be among the nobility on this point, . . . will be such as will make it impossible for this Bill to pass the Lords, though power and corruption may force it through the Commons'.[30] Quite apart from the rebellious courtiers who had previously voted with administration and were especially well represented in the Upper House, there were the bishops, on whom Walpole could normally rely for support. But the episcopal bench was by no means insensitive to the currents and cross-currents of court. According to Perceval, the Bishop of Lichfield was 'frighted at the universal discontent against the Excise, and I found by him that he and divers other Bishops are like to vote

[28] Ibid., p. 159.   [29] Ibid., p. 161.   [30] Ibid., pp. 140–1.

against it, when it comes into their House'.[31] Horace Walpole himself told Perceval that this had been a factor in his brother's decision to give way. 'He said another reason for giving up the Bill was the falling away of friends in the House of Lords'.[32] It was not merely in the Commons and among the Court and Treasury men that Walpole had to look to his position.

[31] *HMC Egmont Diary*, i. 356.
[32] Ibid., 359.

VII
The Court and the Excise

ALTHOUGH the excise had been defeated it was not to be expected that the parliamentary opposition would rest on their laurels at this point. Their object had been to destroy the ministry, rather than its proposals, though the excise had given them the pretext they needed. However, it was quickly made apparent that their hopes were to be disappointed. Almost as soon as he had announced his decision to drop his project Walpole was gratified to find that his position was recovering fast. Indeed this was clearly demonstrated on 11 April, when in the moment of defeat he also brought off a minor triumph. His announcement in the Commons on that day was merely to the effect that he had decided to abandon his scheme, and that the appropriate mode of doing so would be to postpone its consideration to a day when the Commons would not be sitting. But the opposition was anxious to forestall even this face-saving operation. The excise agitation was still at its height. The City was simmering with excitement, only increased by the Commons' marginal rejection of its petition on 10 April, and on the 11th two further petitions from Coventry and Nottingham were to be laid before the House. The opposition's excuse for continuing to press Walpole was that his suggestion of a postponement of the excise was no more than a ruse. But this was nonsense; nobody could seriously imagine that after his speech of 11 April, which was most specific in renouncing further schemes, Walpole would attempt to revive his excise proposals later in the parliamentary session. The real intention of the opposition was to squeeze the last drop out of the anti-excise agitation and humiliate the minister still further. But in this they failed to carry the Commons with them, and so obvious was the sense of the House in favour of Walpole's manoeuvre, that the administration's motion went unchallenged on division. The following day one observer noted, 'Sir Robert I thought looked melancholy and disappointed the night of the seventeen majority, but yesterday he had recovered very well'.[1]

[1] *HMC Carlisle*, p. 108: Howard to Carlisle, 12 Apr. 1733.

Even so this minor victory for the ministry did no more than provide the briefest of breathing-spaces. The fact that the Commons would not agree to the total humiliation of the ministry on the excise scheme did not prevent the opposition from attempting to drive home its underlying advantage. In fact it manufactured two ideal opportunities to test Walpole's defences after the trauma of the excise defeat. The first was in connection with the old excises on tea, coffee and chocolate, and was thoroughly predictable. Walpole himself had pointed out in the Commons that in principle there was nothing to choose between the excises on wine and tobacco proposed in 1733 and those on tea, coffee and chocolate actually carried in 1723. 'To all these objections one general observation will apply; that if for these reasons this scheme is to be relinquished, the whole system of excise laws ought to be abandoned'.[2] The logic of this was obvious to all parties, not least the opposition, and it surprised nobody that on 20 April, just nine days after Walpole's announcement that he was abandoning his project, the druggists, who were most involved in the grocery excises of 1723, petitioned Parliament for repeal of the duties affecting them. There can be little doubt that the druggists' action was politically inspired. As the government newspaper, the *Daily Courant*, pointed out, the actual petition betrayed considerable divisions even among the druggists themselves. Many of the wealthier dealers declined to become involved in a campaign which was clearly levied more against the court than the excise, and those who did sign were obviously associated with the City agitators.[3] In any event the upshot was to the advantage of the government. The Commons again refused to follow blindly where the opposition and the City led, effectually rejecting the druggists' petition by a handsome majority of 250 to 150.

But this was as nothing to the culminating triumph of the ministry on 24 April. The occasion was the voting of members for a Committee of Frauds, the erection of which had been pressed by the opposition after the collapse of the excise scheme. Walpole, in view of his decision to drop the excise scheme, had no enthusiasm for an independent Commons investigation into the customs administration; it could do no good since the excise was now ruled out, and by prying into the customs it could only uncover the more unsavoury aspects of the administration's control of financial departments. On

[2] Coxe, i. 396.
[3] See *Daily Courant*, 25 Apr. 1733 and *Craftsman*, 19 May 1733.

the other hand, since the alleged object of such a Committee was to root out commercial abuses and frauds—precisely the main object, according to the minister, of the excise scheme—it was impossible for him openly to oppose it. All he could do was to ensure that it was packed with friends of the government, in response to the opposition's efforts to staff it with their own allies. The result was the formation of two lists, one composed entirely of reliable court supporters, the other of committed opponents of government; the Commons was asked on 24 April to choose, individual by individual, between them. Everyone was aware of the significance of this division. Charles Delafaye rightly described it as 'a matter indeed of greater consequence than even the excise bill itself';[4] it was in fact a straight vote of confidence in Walpole and his system, and no less than 503 M.P.s were present, considerably more even than on the original excise division of 14 March, and one of the fullest Houses of the entire century.[5] And yet the result was a gigantic majority for Walpole. A precise statement of the numbers is difficult because votes were registered for each of the names on the lists in such a way as to preclude an overall comparison between government and opposition. However, Walpole himself calculated a majority of 85 or more, an overwhelming victory for administration after the desperate straits of early April.[6]

There were additional circumstances which made it particularly striking. For one thing the packing of an impartial enquiry committee by government servants was bound to irritate many of those who possessed any degree of independence. Lord Charles Cavendish, for example, under great pressure from his brother, the Duke of Devonshire, to vote for Walpole's list, replied that it seemed

'a kind of farce, when the house of commons has ordered a committee to inquire into the frauds and abuses of the Customs, to trust it intirely to those, who have allways had it in their power to make that inquiry without the authority of Parliament; and who cant be supposed to be very desirous

[4] Coxe, iii. 134: Delafaye to Waldegrave, 26 Apr. 1733.
[5] *HMC Egmont Diary*, i. 366; only the division of 21 January 1742, just before Walpole's fall, exceeded this; see P. D. G. Thomas, *The House of Commons in the Eighteenth Century* (Oxford, 1971), pp. 124-5.
[6] For a full list of the votes, see C(H) MSS. 66/8. The average vote cast for government nominees for the Committee amounted to 289, and for opposition nominees 202, a difference of 87. However, the figure of 85 was reached by comparing the highest vote achieved by a government nominee (294) with the highest for an opposition nominee (209).

at present to find out any abuses in the management of the Customs and to point out the remedys for the frauds complained of, after having lost a bill which was founded upon the impossibility of curing those frauds by the laws of the Customs'.[7]

The whole affair was seen by many in this light and the sarcasm of the opposition press was perhaps justified. 'Tremble all you who have long had the Fingering of the publick Money, for the following Gentlemen are chosen of this Committee, who will lay open all Frauds in the Revenues, let the Delinquents be never so great'.[8] In principle the government's part in the voting of the Committee of Frauds was practically indefensible, and yet it still obtained the overwhelming endorsement of the lower House. It was even more astonishing that this majority was obtained on a secret ballot. When the opposition had first proposed an investigation of fraud, it had followed one of the standard procedures of the House in demanding that the membership of the Committee should be selected by secret ballot. But ballots, though not irregular in such cases, were always dangerous to ministers. Where there was no check on the way individuals voted, there was no means of discipline, and members who normally supported the court were unleashed to vote entirely according to their conscience. It was a notorious fact that secret ballots for membership of committees had a way of producing opposition bodies, which the ministry could tolerate only when they did not involve the political interests of administration to a significant degree. This had been demonstrated only recently in the great enquiries into corruption. Of the thirteen members elected to the committee to enquire into the affairs of the York Building Company in February 1733, at least half were either opponents of government or independents; among the twenty-one ballotted for the inquiry into the Charitable Corporation, a year earlier, opposition members took the fifteen first places.[9] It was therefore a great blunder on the part of the ministry, and one for which Henry Pelham was apparently responsible, to accept the opposition's demand for a committee of secrecy.[10] An investigation into frauds was unavoidable but it should not have been beyond the power of government to carry it

---

[7] Devonshire MSS.; the letter is not dated.
[8] *Fog's Weekly Journal*, 5 May 1733.
[9] *Journals of the House of Commons* (London, 1803), xxii. 39; xxi. 795-6.
[10] *Hervey Memoirs*, p. 178.

in the form of a Committee of the Whole House rather than a committee of secrecy. However this circumstance, which could so easily have been disastrous for the court reinforced the significance of the ministry's victory. The friends of Walpole could on that occasion have deserted him with impunity, had they wished; instead, they showed their complete confidence in him in no uncertain terms. So far as the House of Commons was concerned the ballot division set the seal on the administration's recovery from the effects of the excise crisis. Little disturbed the remainder of the session of 1733. The ministry received safe majorities in the questions where its credit was involved, notably in the affairs of the Charitable Corporation,[11] and the Committee of Frauds set up on 25 April made its predictably uncontroversial report without serious difficulty. After the ballot indeed, the opposition admitted their defeat at Walpole's hands. 'Their language', one government supporter noted, 'is very different now, from what it was three weeks ago; then they looked upon him as gone, now they say it is to no purpose to attend, nothing is to be done'.[12]

In retrospect Walpole's recovery is almost as remarkable as his original retreat. In the course of the session of 1733 he passed from total security to imminent collapse and to complete safety again. To some extent this recovery was the result of a sharp reaction in favour of Walpole and against the violence of his opponents. Particularly in the City the riotous atmosphere of March and April had become distinctly alarming. On 11 April, after his announcement that the excise was to be given up, Walpole had to be escorted from the Commons by his friends and some fifty special constables, and narrowly escaped personal injury; the same evening effigies of Walpole and Queen Caroline were burnt in Fleet Street, Smithfield and Bishopsgate Street.[13] 'Such Rejoicings', the *Weekly Register* commented, 'have never been known in this City in the Memory of Man'.[14] The mob's sense of humour took the form of burning Walpole's effigy in company with that of Sarah Malcom, a murderess whose activities had lately enthralled the newspaper readers.[15] Even gentility and sex were not proof against the activities of the city mob.

[11] *Journals of the House of Commons*, xxii. 131, 142.
[12] *HMC Carlisle*, p. 113: Howard to Carlisle, Apr. 1733.
[13] *Hervey Memoirs*, pp. 164–5; *Fog's Weekly Journal*, 14 Apr. 1733.
[14] *Weekly Register*, 14 Apr. 1733.
[15] *HMC Egmont Diary*, i. 362.

I heard this day things that concern me much [Perceval noted on 9 April]. The City is so inflamed that some ladies going in their coach thither were rudely stopped, and the cry was: 'We know this coach, it comes from St. James' end of the town; knock the coachman down'. One of the ladies having presence of mind, saved her servant by calling out: 'Though we live at St. James's end, we are as much against excise as you'. On which the mob said: 'Are you so? Then God bless you. Coachman drive on!'[16]

Such boisterous goings-on were doubtless a normal part of eighteenth-century life, though only up to a point. Bonfires and illuminations were one thing, but the fevered riots which took place in London and actually worsened after the news that the ministry had given way on the excise were scarcely tolerable for long. Moreover, the role of the metropolitan authorities gave particular cause for disquiet. The City's technical breach of privilege in obtaining a copy of the excise bill in order to draw up its petition, and openly discussing it in Common Council before even the Commons had had a proper chance to debate it, had caused sufficient annoyance; but many must have wondered at the affair reported in the newspapers in May. When the Grand Jury of Middlesex considered the excise riots, it was treated to a strong condemnation of the riots from the Recorder and a remarkable reply by Lord Mayor Barber, who shamelessly praised those who had thus expressed their loathing for the excise. The Grand Jury responded by thanking Barber for his 'just Distinction between Publick Rejoycing and Riotous Mobbing'; at this time indeed its main concern was with more important matters, in particular 'loose, idle and disorderly Persons, playing at Cricket, and using many other new invented Ways of Gaming'.[17] Nothing could more clearly have demonstrated the alienation which the government's project had inspired even among the more responsible citizens of the capital. Such episodes were most worrying. Later on men were to grow accustomed, if not reconciled, to the spectacle of the City conducting a vigorous opposition to the government of the day; but in 1733, after years of considerable support for the court in London, it was as novel as it was alarming. Equally disturbing was the complete co-operation which the metropolis drew from the provinces at this time. The news that the excise had been dropped was greeted by the same riotous conduct in the pro-

---

[16] Ibid., i. 357.
[17] B. Berington's Evening Post, 12 May 1733; Craftsman, 14 Apr. 1733.

vinces as in London, particularly in great ports like Bristol and Liverpool, where it was to be expected that the mercantile oligarchies would encourage political demonstrations. In the circumstances it is not surprising that many in the Commons began to feel alarm at the extent of the disorders. Walpole's first levee after his rough handling by the mob was especially well attended, and on 12 April the Commons drew up a set of strong resolutions against the violence outside their walls. How effective this reaction was in a political sense is difficult to estimate. Hervey made much of a 'desire to discountenance tumult',[18] and certainly some M.P.s may have recalled Walpole's warning after the first demonstrations against the excise in February: 'When tumults are once begun, no man knows where they may end'.[19] Even politicians who strongly supported the excise agitation and loathed the Walpole administration were not without anxiety on this point. Thus Lord Berkeley remarked in May 1733, 'Victory is soe new a thing to one side, that I wish they be not too much transported and behave with decency'.[20]

Walpole himself naturally played his part in promoting and exploiting the reaction in his favour. Indeed nothing is more impressive in the history of the excise scheme than Walpole's vigour and determination in this great moment of crisis. Where a Henry Fox or Lord North might have quailed, Walpole threw all his energies into resisting his attackers. His ceaseless lobbying and closeting of doubtful votes, his remorseless pressure on those over whom he could exercise any degree of influence, did much to rally a Court and Treasury party which had been demoralized almost to the point of disintegration. Nothing reveals this more clearly than Walpole's great effort immediately prior to the crucial ballot of 24 April. The evening before, he had arranged for a meeting of all M.P.s who might be regarded in some sense as potential government voters. This great assembly at the Cockpit, which lived long in the minds of those who attended it, was of the utmost significance. It gave Walpole his opportunity for an absolutely characteristic piece of theatre, with an audience of no less than 263 M.P.s, many of whom must have been among the deserters in the crucial excise division of 10 April.[21] It is intriguing that Walpole's appeal was not of the kind

[18] *Hervey Memoirs*, p. 168.
[19] *Parl.Hist.*, viii. 1306: 14 Mar. 1733.
[20] Add. MS. 31142, f. 73: Berkeley to Strafford, 7 May 1733.
[21] *HMC Carlisle*, p. 112: Howard to Carlisle, 24 Apr. 1733.

which might have been expected later in the century. Where the Court and Treasury party in the 1760s would have been rallied only by playing on the plight of the crown, there was sufficient bite left in old rancours in the 1730s to make possible an appeal to party. Walpole's theme was an uncomplicated one: 'as I have always fought on Whig principles, I will never desert them; as I have risen by Whigs, I will stand or fall with them; . . . it is in Whig principles I have lived, and in Whig principles I will die; . . . I am now therefore, Gentlemen, not pleading my own cause, but the cause of the Whig party'. The division scheduled for the next day he interpreted in the crudest party terms: 'the contention of this ballot is in plain and intelligible language for dominion, for dominion between Whigs and Tories'. Predictably, the Revolution of 1688 was dragged in. 'What must become of all the Revolution measures that have been pursued with so much steadiness and maintained with so much glory for above forty years? What must become of this Government and this Family, and the true freedom, liberty, welfare, and prosperity of this country?' Inevitable, too, was the stress on the menace of Jacobitism. The fight, Walpole urged, was against the 'common enemies of this party, this country, and this Establishment'. There were, he was compelled to admit, ex-Whigs in the opposition, but they were 'every day and every hour consulting with Jacobites, taking directions from Jacobites, and promoting Jacobite measures'.[22] Even Walpole's greatest personal enemy was suitably worked into this polemic; 'a push was made at the Administration, to throw the Government into confusion, and my Lord Bolingbroke was at the bottom of it all'.[23]

In retrospect it is easy to stigmatize this great speech as a tissue of lies or misrepresentations. The downfall of the Walpole administration would not in 1733, any more than in 1742, have meant the end of the Whig Protestant establishment. A ministerial reshuffle would have ensued and little else would have altered. 'Revolution measures' were not at issue and not threatened, nor was the opposition's campaign a gigantic Jacobite conspiracy. Whig and Tory, whatever their emotive significance, were coming to mean little that was positive so far as measures or convictions were concerned. Nonetheless, Walpole's remarks went home. Party loyalties had not yet collapsed so completely as to prevent a partial revival of old quarrels. The Jacobite threat was still sufficiently alarming to make for

[22] *Hervey Memoirs*, pp. 179–84.   [23] *HMC Egmont Diary*, i. 365.

cautious treatment of the Tory party. Moreover, there was some superficial colour for Walpole's views. It was undoubtedly the case that, of the twenty opposition names put forward for the Committee of Frauds, precisely half belonged to committed Tories. A government likely to be made up in similar proportions was not a comforting prospect to wavering friends of the ministry, as the opposition Whigs, who vainly urged their Tory colleagues to take a back seat on this occasion, were aware. Moreover, the violence which accompanied public demonstrations against the excise could all too easily be seen as the result of Jacobite agitation. Fortunately for Walpole one of the more spectacular riots associated with the excise had occurred at Oxford, the bastion of Toryism. Of these riots, Richard Meadowcourt, a Whig don, had assured the ministry, 'The Spirit of Jacobitism that for some years has slept at Oxford, has been rouz'd up again on the late foolish occasion'.[24] The qualification which went with this remark—'What was done here, was done by the youth of this Place'—was forgotten, and the obvious truth, the fact that the demonstrations were little more than a mixture of undergraduate wildness and urban mobbing, ignored. Moreover, there was no need to take Walpole's word alone. At the meeting of 23 April there were not merely other ministers present, including the Attorney and Solicitor General, but one of the most respected and independent friends of the establishment, the Speaker of the House of Commons himself, Arthur Onslow. Small wonder then that the occasion made its mark. There is no reason to believe that the example of Sir Philip Parker, who had acquired a diplomatic illness during the excise divisions and was clearly preparing to leave the government camp, and whose mind was apparently changed as a result of going to the Cockpit meeting, was untypical.[25] Hervey was not alone in seeing Walpole's manoeuvre as a remarkable success. 'This speech had so good an effect on those to whom it was addressed, that for two or three days there seemed to be a resurrection of that party spirit which had so long been dormant that most people imagined it was quite extinct'.[26] Not a little of the credit for the government's triumph on the ballot must be given to Walpole himself.

Even so, the general feeling of concern at the violence of the

[24] C(H) MSS. Corr. 2179: Delafaye to Walpole, 5 June, enclosing Meadowcourt's letter of 16 Apr. 1733.
[25] *HMC Egmont Diary*, i. 359, 365.
[26] *Hervey Memoirs*, p. 184.

excise agitation and Walpole's skill in reviving the morale of the Court and Treasury party are scarcely sufficient to explain the dramatic change of political climate which permitted the administration's recovery. In fact the critical development which intervened between 10 April, when the government had come so near to defeat, and the divisions of 20 and 24 April, when it was triumphantly vindicated, was almost certainly the action which George II took on 13 April. On that day he dismissed from his service Lord Chesterfield, the Lord Steward, and Lord Clinton, a Lord of the Bedchamber. Two dismissals may not seem very significant, yet there can be little doubt that they utterly transformed the situation for Walpole. What was essential was to reassure those courtiers who had temporarily deserted the government in the excise divisions. As has been seen, the reason for their defection at that time was not so much a calculation about the merits or demerits of the excise bill as a conviction that the closet itself had declared against the excise. However fallacious this belief, it had been a major factor in the ministry's problems, one which could only be countered by a clear, unequivocal piece of evidence that the court strongly disapproved of the activities of the opposition. Hence the dismissal of two peers peculiarly associated with the rebellion against Walpole at court. Such a measure would have been advantageous even before the excise defeats. But at that time George II was reluctant to take action unless it was demonstrated to be essential, and Walpole himself could not afford to take too much notice of a petty revolt among the court lords. However, once the gravity of the crisis was clear, once George II had been fully apprised of the extent to which the opposition had misrepresented his views, and once Walpole himself had been made aware that he was fighting not for the excise scheme but for his political life, sterner measures were needed. The importance of the resulting dismissals was appreciated at once. The *Craftsman* correctly described Walpole's manoeuvre as 'a politick Step, in order to convince the World that He hath not lost Ground'.[27] On the government side Thomas Pelham rejoiced in 'the king's declared support of the present ministry by the examples his majesty has already made of some who would obstruct their measures',[28] while Charles Delafaye noted that 'The King has very wisely shewn the world that these attempts upon Sr Robert Walpole are vain, by

[27] 12 May 1733.
[28] Coxe, iii. 133: Pelham to Waldegrave, 26 Apr. 1733.

removing Ld Clinton from being a Lord of the Bedchamber, and, if I am rightly informed, the Earl of Chesterfield'.[29]

In a sense it is surprising that such a declaration was necessary at all. As we now know, the King had no real thought of setting up a new ministry or dismissing Walpole; both his and the Queen's faith in Walpole was substantially undamaged. However, it is essential to bear in mind the psychology of eighteenth-century courts and court parties. In the first place government servants were primarily the servants of the King, not of the ministers. Sometimes, it is true, ministers had such a long tenure of office or such a powerful hold on the government machine that they could claim a degree of personal loyalty. There were moments when this loyalty was for exceptional reasons sufficiently strong to turn the balance in politics, notably in the 1740s and 1750s when the Court and Treasury party repeatedly pledged its loyalty to the Pelhams. But generally a large proportion, indeed a majority of government supporters, put the King, from whom all favours ultimately flowed, above his minister. Normally this mattered little, since minister and King usually worked in harmony and did not force their supporters to choose between them. But if such a choice became necessary a very large number were likely to opt for the King—perhaps the oustanding example of this was the emergence of the notorious party of so-called 'King's Friends' in the 1760s. What is truly surprising is not that such situations could arise but that, although the court party was always intensely concerned with the precise wishes and intentions of the King, it was also strangely ignorant of them. This could lead to extraordinary misunderstandings. In 1783, for example, most of the government's friends were for long unaware just how much George III loathed the Fox-North Ministry; it required his drastic action in allowing the use of his name in the House of Lords to make them perceive the true situation. Conversely, in 1766 many refused to believe that George III really supported the policies of his minister, Lord Rockingham, and on this occasion too it took a clear declaration through Lord Rockingham to correct the false impression.[30]

The reason for such ignorance was simple. Although the court was to the modern eye an amazingly open and public place—any gentlemen of substance, and many of none, could meet the King

[29] Add. MS. 23787, f. 99: Delafaye to Robinson, 13 Apr. 1733.
[30] J. Brooke, *King George III* (London, 1972), pp. 253, 130.

without prior appointment at his levee—it was also very formal. Few of the friends of government had not on a number of occasions spoken to George II and Queen Caroline; yet many of them remained completely unaware of their real feelings. In this curious climate of excessive interest in the opinions of monarchy and little knowledge of its actual thoughts, the role of rumour was enormous. It needed very little to set off a report that the minister was losing ground in the closet. Usually such reports were in time discredited or forgotten. But in moments of crisis they leapt into alarming significance. This was especially so in the case of George II, ironically in view of what he once told Hervey: 'A prince who will be well served in this country, must free his minister from all apprehensions at Court, that the minister may give all his attention to the affairs of his master; which, with all the support that master can give him, are still liable, from the nature of this Government and the capriciousness of the people, to ten thousand accidents and difficulties unknown in other countries'.[31] In practice he was not quite as good as his word.

Rather paradoxically in the light of their respective historical reputations, George II was far less frank and plain in his ways than George III. Where the latter was accustomed to exert himself in support at least of those ministers of whom he approved, George II was made of different metal. For example, he was vain and capricious. He disliked being taken for granted and was shy of playing a leading role in support of his ministers. He did not enjoy dismissing courtiers from office without good cause, and he did not like losing what he chose to think of as his freedom of action. In the end he could generally be brought around to what was needed, but only with the expenditure of much time and patience. The fact that Walpole and Queen Caroline, and later Lady Yarmouth and the Pelhams, proved so successful at flattering his vanities and obtaining his support is apt to obscure the problems his personality created. The excise crisis was typical. Powerful court rebels tried to exploit the King's uncertainties, not altogether unsuccessfully, and the result was growing uneasiness in the court party. Eventually he was bound to take the necessary action and dismiss the offenders. Hervey's comment on this was exaggerated but also penetrating: 'It was indeed full time for Sir Robert Walpole, if he had power, to make more examples among those who distressed and opposed him at Court in order to show it. For hitherto, in this reign, all his known ill-wishers faring as

[31] *Hervey Memoirs*, p. 151.

well as his friends, it became the interest of everyone to be thought his foe, since without losing them anything in present, that character secured them a reversionary interest in case of a change with those who should succeed'.[32] It was the resulting action, the dismissals of 13 April, which, coming as it did before the critical divisions on the druggists' petition and the frauds ballot, dramatically improved the ministry's position. 'We have been all put to our stumps', wrote Henry Pelham, 'but by the steadiness of the Party which appeared in a Ballott in the house of Commons, and the firmness of our master in the main point, we are now gott pretty firm in our seats again, and I doubt not in the least but we shall continue so'.[33] Later on the King's support for his ministry at this juncture could be seen as the decisive factor in the opposition's failure to drive home its advantage. In that other great explosion of popular rage, the Sacheverell affair, the event had been quite different. 'As I have Likend this to Dr. Sacheverell Tryall', one Tory diarist remarked of the excise crisis, 'So I must Persew It with this differance, that northing could allay what was Rais'd at the Dr Tryall, in the Brest of Good Queen Ann. Who soon After Chang'd Her Ministry'.[34]

In view of the importance of the court at a crucial stage in the excise crisis, it was fitting that the final phase of the session of 1733 should have been a renewed and extended rebellion among the court peers. This phase was essentially a footnote to the major crisis of 1733. Once Walpole had reimposed his control of the Court and Treasury party and triumphed in the Commons he was to all intents and purposes secure for the immediate future. Unfortunately the House of Lords chose this moment to erupt. Previously the excise crisis had been seen by the opposition peers as the ideal opportunity to launch a full-scale attack. However, when the excise was dropped without coming to the upper House, a new target had to be selected. The result was a motion for an enquiry into the murky affairs of the South Sea Company which Walpole was sufficiently ill advised to oppose. In the event the government was actually defeated on one division and eventually scraped home by only a narrow majority.[35] As Hervey claimed, Walpole was himself responsible at least in part for this sudden and unexpected renewal of the crisis.[36] He could

[32] Ibid., p. 173.   [33] Add. MS. 27732, f. 170: Pelham to Essex, 17 May 1733.
[34] Bodleian Library, MS. Film 740, Mrs. Caesar's Diary.
[35] For the best account of the crisis in the Lords, see J. H. Plumb, *Sir Robert Walpole: The King's Minister*, pp. 274–9.
[36] *Hervey Memoirs*, pp. 197–8.

have ridden out the storm without panicking; other eighteenth-century governments were defeated in the House of Lords and had the wisdom not to treat such defeats as matters of confidence. However, since Walpole chose to take the crisis more seriously than he need have, the consequences were bound to involve more purging at court, to destroy this 'most violent and peevish plot'.[37] Just two dismissals had been sufficient to convince the Court and Treasury party in the Commons that all was well with the Walpole establishment; partly because, in the House of Lords, the role of a few aristocratic courtiers was so much more influential than in the Commons, partly because intense excitement, repressed while the Commons and the public raged in March and April, had to be released, more was needed in the Lords. As a result there was much closeting of peers by the King and Queen, and in the end a whole series of dismissals had to be made. The Dukes of Montrose and Bolton, the Earls of Stair and Marchmont, Lord Cobham and his clan, all were rooted out, before the crisis in Parliament could finally be regarded as at an end. 'There is no fighting', remarked Henry Pelham, 'without troops that acknowledge their general'.[38]

[37] Add. MS. 27732, f. 188: Pelham to Essex, 9 July 1733.
[38] Ibid.

VIII
The Electorate and the Excise

IN theory the end of the parliamentary session of 1733 should also have meant the end of the excise crisis. 'The storms that lately threaten'd Ruin and Desolation, are quite blown over', it was announced.[1] The opposition rightly expressed doubts on this point. 'It appears by Accounts from all Parts of the Kingdom, that the People are very far from having *done with it*', the author of one pamphlet insisted.[2] In fact most on both sides were well aware that the approaching general election would prevent the peaceable interment of the excise scheme. As early as July the gravity of the situation was revealed at court when the King and Queen themselves closeted peers and M.P.s before they left London for the summer in order to show them 'how desirous they are of a Whigg parliament'.[3] Indeed it is not too much to claim that after the rising of Parliament the political excitement positively intensified. From June 1733 until April 1734 there was only one topic of political conversation—the general election and with it the problem of the excise and its effect. This was demonstrated very forcibly, for example, by the final session of the 1727 Parliament which began in January 1734. Throughout that session the opposition kept up a bitter onslaught on the government's position, with a long series of divisions in the Commons. On 23 January Walpole had to defend himself against charges of undue pusillanimity in his relations with the Spanish court, on 4 February the opposition spirited up renewed petitions from the grocers in favour of abolishing existing excises, and on 13 February there was a move to make army commissions irrevocable by the crown, a reaction to Walpole's dismissals of politically insubordinate officers the previous year; there followed motions in favour of a new qualifications bill, a place bill, a bill to repeal the Septennial Act and various schemes for financial retrenchment. In none of these divisions, which represent one of the most uninhibited

[1] Add. MS. 22222, f. 148: Orrery to Strafford, 8 May 1733.
[2] *A Review of the Excise Scheme*, p. 3.
[3] *HMC Lonsdale*, p. 125: Newcastle to Lonsdale, 21 July 1733.

of all parliamentary campaigns by eighteenth-century opposition, was the administration really in great danger. The lowest ebb to which the government sank was a majority of 39 in a house of 431 on the place bill; for the rest its majority hovered satisfactorily between 60 and 120. The most important division of the session, that on which the opposition pinned most hope, took place on the motion of 13 March to repeal the Septennial Act, and then the ministry had a secure if unspectacular majority of 63 in a crowded house. 'For sure', one rather despondent opposition peer commented, 'the damnd majority was not near so great in either House last year as it is in this'.[4]

However, the ministerial superiority in Parliament was almost irrelevant since the opposition's prime concern was not at this point to obtain an actual victory at Westminster. As one government supporter had forecast earlier, 'there is no doubt of carrying matters thro' the next Session: the great Struggle will be on the Elections'.[5] The object of the opposition's campaign was not so much to sway M.P.s as to sway voters, a preoccupation which is apt to be forgotten of a period often treated as if extra-parliamentary politics had no role to play. Everyone was well aware that the government was being subjected to a propaganda exercise rather than a frontal attack, and the essential fact was that the administration was powerless to counter this campaign. Its own ploy for obtaining electoral popularity, the excise scheme, had turned sour, and its only course in 1734 was to defeat each measure proposed by the opposition by sheer weight of numbers; about the impression outside Parliament it could do little. The King's Speech had warned rather fruitlessly at the commencement of the session against 'unnecessary Delays, when the whole Kingdom seems prepared for the Election of a new Parliament, an Event which employs the Attention of all *Europe*'.[6] Understandably, the opposition ignored this plea and took every opportunity of embarrassing the ministers. In particular, the revived grocers' petition in favour of revoking the excises laid in 1723, which had been rejected the previous year, was thrown out again, and as Walpole pointed out, 'the rejecting of it may perhaps be made use of by some gentlemen to raise new clamours, and to increase the number of

---

[4] *HMC Polworth*, v. 83: Haddington to Marchmont, 4 Mar. 1734.
[5] Add. MS. 27732, f. 206: Delafaye to Essex, 24 July 1733.
[6] *Journals of the House of Commons*, xxii. 206.

cockades, with the fine motto of "Liberty, Property and no Excise".[7]

The motion to repeal the Septennial Act was similarly calculated to appeal to public opinion, though, perhaps rather surprisingly in view of the general dislike of septennial parliaments out of doors, the opposition's efforts to whip up an agitation like that of the previous year misfired. Apparently only Warwick and Coventry responded to the call for instructions.[8] Even so the lesson went home; typical was the complaint voiced by one government supporter that 'the motion seems calculated for no other end but to continue that ferment and that spirit of division and disaffection which was so artfully raised in the nation, upon a late memorable occasion'.[9] The qualifications bill, the place bill, the military commissions motion, were all similar measures, designed to appeal to traditional country ideas of restricting the crown's influence and asserting parliamentary independence. Dodington's comment could not have been more apt: 'The Opposition in general seem to design through this session to throw out points only that may look well in print and hurt the popularity of those who oppose them, without any hopes of carrying them, possibly without the wish of doing it'.[10]

This is not to say that Pulteney and his colleagues had no hopes of embarrassing the government more directly. It was naturally one of their intentions to force the more independent M.P.s away from the ministry and out into the open. As Lord Marchmont remarked, 'It will be most advisable to propose easy Whig points to bring off honest well meaning people, and render others inexcusable',[11] and this clearly had its effect; one independent, for example, confessed that he voted for the qualification bill 'because I would have the Parliament do something popular to please the nation, and not give a handle to the discontented party to confirm them in the scandal they have thrown upon us, which they will assuredly do'.[12] At the very least such tactics would swell the opposition vote and harass the government. Even so this was clearly a subordinate consideration. The object was primarily electoral, as Sir William Yonge pointed out in the debate on the repeal of the Septennial Act; 'it is now the last

---

[7] *Parl. Hist.*, ix. 256: 4 Feb. 1734.
[8] *London Evening Post*, 23–25 Apr. 1734.
[9] *Parl. Hist.*, ix. 424: Hon. J. Cornwallis, 13 Mar. 1734.
[10] *HMC Stopford-Sackville*, i. 155: Dodington to Dorset, 17 Feb. 1734.
[11] *A Selection from the Papers of the Earls of Marchmont* (London, 1831), ii. 14: Memorandum, 3 Jan. 1734.
[12] *HMC Egmont Diary*, ii. 31.

session of a Parliament, a new election must soon come on, and as this motion has an appearance of popularity among the meaner sort of electors, it may be of service to some gentlemen at the next elections'.[13] All eighteenth-century oppositions seized the opportunity of a final parliamentary session to appeal to the people. If this is sometimes forgotten, it is doubtless because most administrations avoided giving their opponents a handle at such moments; Walpole miscalculated over the excise and, later, Henry Pelham stumbled in the Jew Bill affair, but normally ministers trod more carefully at such moments. Later in the century too, as political conflicts both at local and national level simmered down, as the boroughs came increasingly under the control of oligarchy, and as the gentry united to kill dissensions in the county community, in short as the entire electoral process came to be little more than an appendage to the rule of Parliament and property, such national appeals became more difficult. Opposition in the late eighteenth century achieved little electorally, and was forced to evolve new weapons—notably the petitioning and association movements of George III's reign. But in the age of Walpole this was not at all the case. Nothing is clearer evidence of the great importance attributed at that time to the electorate than the parliamentary session of 1734.

However, manoeuvrings in Parliament were only a small part of the election campaign. Though the general election itself did not get under way until April 1734, the preparations began much earlier. The customary practice in eighteenth-century elections was for the candidates to start campaigning in earnest even before the final session of the old Parliament. It was in the summer that the fashionable world returned from London to the country, in the summer that the events of any importance in the country community—the local races, the assizes—took place, and in the summer that the local political world came to life. Nothing could be done during the session itself, and the interval between the dissolution of Parliament and the holding of elections was quite insufficient to permit the assiduous courting essential for eighteenth-century electors. In 1734, for example, Parliament was dissolved on 18 April, and the first result, that for Westminster, was declared only four days later. So there could be no question but that the important period was between the rising of Parliament in 1733 and its reassembly in 1734.

In terms of organization the scope of both sides was extremely

[13] *Parl. Hist.*, ix. 452: 13 Mar. 1734.

limited. There was after all practically no national machinery, and at election time the loose party groupings which operated at Westminster were apt to dissolve. Apart from the administration's direction of electoral policy in a handful of Treasury and Admiralty boroughs, the government itself was rather an amalgam of magnates, gentry and carpet-baggers than a true party. The opposition was even less united; at this stage it scarcely had an adequate whipping system, let alone really effective machinery for elections. The Tory Williams Wynn talked rather vaguely of 'an association or confederacy between twenty-four or thirty very great men . . . to exert all their interest and power in all parts of the kingdom to get a majority if possible against that villain Walpole', but this was scarcely more than a pious hope.[14] Only in one respect could politics be organized effectively from the centre, and that a very restricted one. The power of the press at least was considerable, and the propaganda of Grub Street was required to do what in other times party machinery would be expected to achieve. In this area at least both sides demonstrated their intention to develop the election campaign on clear and co-ordinated lines.

Two points in particular the government's enemies set out to drive home. Firstly, the central issue was to be the excise; secondly, the opposition was to appear not as a loose coalition of Whigs or Tories but as a genuine country party. In one sense the success of this strategy is surprising. Eighteenth-century elections, as historians of the period have pointed out, rarely centred on national issues.[15] After 1734 only the general election of 1784, with its polarization of the political world into two great camps behind the Fox-North Coalition on the one hand and George III and the Younger Pitt on the other, was to provide an example of local elections significantly affected by the debate at the centre. However, in the age of Walpole it was still possible for the electorate to take a stance on a national scale provided a clear issue of principle was involved, and the excise crisis offered just such an issue. It was excellent electoral tactics on the part of the opposition to squeeze the last drop of juice out of this topic. Throughout the summer, winter and spring of 1733-4 the opposition press thundered against the excise. Pamphlet after

[14] Diary of W. Bulkeley, 30 Apr. 1734, quoted in A. N. Newman, 'Elections in Kent and its Parliamentary Representation, 1715-1754', p. 93.
[15] See, for example, Sir L. Namier and J. Brooke, eds. *History of Parliament: House of Commons, 1754-1790* (London, 1964), i. 86.

pamphlet, newspaper after newspaper, showed why the excise had been an appallingly sinister and irresponsible scheme and why its projector must be instantly unseated. Far more was indeed published in relation to the excise scheme in the year following its withdrawal than in the months preceding its defeat. 'When one of this Party sets down to write a libel,' the *Daily Courant* complained, '*Excise* is so naturally at the End of his Pen, that there is no keeping it from slipping in'.[16] Nor was all this intended merely as polemic. Particularly significant was the opposition's tactic of publishing incriminating lists of those who had voted for the excise scheme in Parliament. It is no coincidence that there are more published lists extant for the excise division than for any other in the eighteenth century. The monthlies and collections printed lists as a matter of common information, but the anxiety of the *Craftsman*, *Fog's Weekly Journal* and the other newspapers to publish an 'accurate' list testified to something less disinterested.[17] Even more strikingly, the provincial press took either to advertising one or other of these lists for local sale, as in the case of the *Gloucester Journal* which charged 2*d*., or simply to including a list as part of the newspaper itself, a major concession in journals as short of space, for example, as the *Suffolk Mercury*.[18] The *Craftsman* justified this campaign and the lists 'that are now spread through most Parts of the Kingdom', on the grounds that some M.P.s were falsely denying that they had in fact supported the excise, and that others were printing inaccurate lists in order to mislead their constituents.[19] In any event the publication of these lists represented the most determined and effective attempt by any eighteenth-century opposition to attract electoral support on a national basis.

The excise as an issue greatly assisted the opposition's second tactic in the general election, the assertion that 'Court and Country' was the rivalry currently at work. Though this claim has traditionally been associated with Bolingbroke, such a connection is scarcely necessary. Rather it was a logical development of the growing pressure for a united party to oppose Walpole's government, which reflected the gradual defusing of old Whig and Tory animosities. Fortunately excises were not as such either Whig or Tory measures, a fact which the opposition was for ever stressing. 'This is no Party

---

[16] 27 Apr. 1734.   [17] See Appendix B.
[18] *Gloucester Journal*, 28 Aug. 1733; *Suffolk Mercury*, 16 July 1733.
[19] 14 July 1733.

Cause: It is no Dispute betwixt *Whig* and *Tory*, or Contention, whether this or that Set of Men are to have the Administration of publick Affairs'.[20] At a time when the ministry's opponents were anxious to bury party feuds and unite the mixed forces in opposition to the court, nothing was better calculated than a straightforward Court and Country issue like the excise to reinforce its strategy. Certainly a steady stream of propaganda assured the voters with more confidence than was altogether justified, but nonetheless significantly, that there was no longer any need to take note of ancient party divisions. The remarks in *Fog's Weekly Journal* may stand for all:

If any one had told me in Queen *Anne*'s Reign, that some time about the Year 1732 the invidious Names of *Whig* and *Tory*, of *High Church* and *Low Church*, should be utterly abolish'd and forgot, I should have consider'd him as a false Prophet, or a Dreamer of Dreams. And yet this Thing is actually come to pass, entirely owing to the excellent Management of our Great Man. There are indeed a Set of Wretches unworthy to bear the Names of *Englishmen*, who very awkwardly attempt to revive the old Party Distinctions, and would fain disunite us again. But let them be branded with the Marks of Infamy! Let them be proscribed as Conspirators against the Commonwealth, who blindly follow the Dictates of a *Vasconcellos*, and have nothing in View but to build their Fortunes on the Ruins of their Country![21]

The government naturally responded with a campaign of its own. In a host of pamphlets, newspapers and even sermons, ministerial agents rehearsed the party line. The excise had been meant well and would, if carried out, have been proved beneficial; the details of the excise made public by the opposition were inaccurate and would in any case have been materially altered if the excise had been placed on the statute book; above all, those who had voted for the excise had voted only to have the scheme investigated in the Commons' Committee, not necessarily to turn it into legislation. Moreover, 'the Parliament agreed to let the Bill drop. And now, where is the Injury done our Country, and why is this Ferment kept up? Why must those Gentlemen who were disposed to *examine* that Project be accounted Betrayers of their Country's Liberties'.[22] The very

[20] *Fog's Weekly Journal*, 13 Jan. 1733. [21] 10 Mar. 1733.
[22] Viscount Perceval, *The Thoughts of an Impartial Man upon the Present Temper of the Nation; Offer'd to the Consideration of the Freeholders of Great-Britain* (London, 1733), pp. 23–4.

defensiveness of these arguments reflects the extent of the ministry's fears. There was little or no attempt openly to champion the excise in the way that had been tried the previous year. All too clearly the administration and its friends were conducting a full-scale retreat so far as the excise was concerned. More convincing was the assault on the notion of a Court and Country dichotomy. Walpole had ever been an adept exponent of party, had always recognized the dangers for his own regime of a genuine Country opposition and had invariably sought to forestall it by appealing to traditional enmities. The excise crisis had produced one of his most spectacular performances in this respect, and it was predictable that the election campaign should feature the same theme. The arguments advanced by the ministerial press in this context are particularly interesting. In the first place it was asserted that the distinction between Court and Country was basically an unfair and improper one. The two interests, it was claimed, were identical under a benevolent regime like the Hanoverian monarchy. 'To set up a *Country Interest* against the *Court*, at a time when there is not *one Act* of the *Court* against the *Country*, or the *least Appearance* of any Design against *General Good*, is a Crime of the highest Nature'.[23] More important still was the unconcealed appeal to the ancient party distinctions. The *Norwich Mercury* declared that 'none but professed Jacobites will alledge, that the King's and Country's Interest is not one and the same'.[24] Above all, the propagandists warned particularly against the dangers of Whigs co-operating with Tories in a so-called Country cause. 'If a Parliament be obtain'd by the Union of *some of the Whigs*, with the *Jacobite* and *Tory* Interests, it cannot be a *Whig Parliament*'.[25] This was the crucial point. The nightmare for the court was a mass desertion by normally friendly Whigs as a result of disillusion with the excise scheme. 'Now is the Crisis', declared the *Free Briton*; 'The Constitution is saved or lost by the Choice of a *House of Commons* . . . Whoever hath been made angry by any Whigg whatever, let him not avenge his Quarrel on A L L the *Whiggs* in *England*; but let him remember, he owes it to himself and his Country, to preserve the Power of the Publick in the *Hands* of the *Whiggs*, though his Private Resentments might induce him to avert it from any particular *Whigg*'.[26]

Whatever the intensity of the battle in the press, the ultimate

[23] *London Journal*, 1 Dec. 1733.   [24] 15 Dec. 1733.
[25] *London Journal*, 2 June 1733.   [26] 25 Apr. 1733.

testing-ground for the different arguments put forward by opposition and government was the general election. There can, of course, be no complete certainty in any election as to the considerations which guide electoral behaviour, let alone in an eighteenth-century election, with its complex diversity of franchises, constituencies and interests. Even so it is clear that the excise crisis dominated the general election in a way that was most unusual. This is not to say that in every constituency, in every area, it was the only topic of political conversation. On the contrary the electoral system was such that in a large number of constituencies this could simply not be so. In Scotland, for example, the opposition's campaign to make the excise a real issue never got off the ground. The Scottish constituencies were tiny by English standards and scarcely allowed for the concept of public opinion at all; in addition the whole question of the excise was far removed from the problems of North Britain. 'They have endeavoured', Islay reported to Newcastle in September 1733, 'to talk the fashionable language of their accomplices in England, relating to the Excise, but that is so cold a scent here, that I doubt very much whether it has any influence at all'.[27] Even one of Walpole's bitterest enemies in Scotland was put to some difficulty to find grounds for optimism in December 1733:

The spirit is certainly rising in this country and will rise if due care, and dilligence be used. It will be cruell if a good cause suffer for want of these. That of the Excyse but begins to be known among most of our people.[28]

In England too in the small, corrupt boroughs, nobody expected the excise to be a significant issue. In close constituencies, elections were too beneficial to the local economy in general and the pockets of the electors in particular for any serious consideration of constitutional issues to be an appropriate exercise. Thus it need not be surprising that, at Malmesbury in Wiltshire, the healths of those who had voted for the excise were drunk after the sitting M.P.s had contributed generously to the comforts of the corporation; similarly the inhabitants of the corrupt Cornish borough of Penryn had every incentive for wishing 'the utter Confusion of *Fog*, *The Craftsman*, and such like Incendiaries'.[29] These, however, were scarcely typical of the

[27] Add. MS. 32688, f. 291: 8 Sept. 1733.
[28] *HMC Polworth*, v. 72: Grange to Marchmont, 10 Dec. 1733.
[29] *Gloucester Journal*, 6 Nov. 1733; *St. James's Evening Post*, 7-9 May 1734.

general public reaction in the elections. What mattered so far as the government's public credit was concerned were the larger open boroughs, where the power of vested interests was limited, and the counties, the most authentic arena of public debate in electoral politics. Here there can be no question that the excise was the only significant issue and that it forced the nation's politics into a new and, for the administration, extremely awkward mould.

That the candidates themselves considered the excise to be the crucial issue is amply revealed by the care they took to make plain their sentiments with regard to it. The opposition candidates in Kent, for example, described themselves as 'zealous Opposers of the late Excise Scheme'; those in Gloucestershire issued a circular letter in which they promised 'to oppose all unnecessary Taxes in Time of Peace, and any further Extension of the Excise-Laws, etc.'; in Leicestershire they declared themselves to be 'Gentlemen of known Inclinations to oppose all Excise and other Schemes, which may tend to the Destruction of the Liberty of the Subject', and in Bedfordshire the sitting member simply announced that he had voted against the excise.[30] Such advertisements were repeated up and down the country on a vast scale. In the larger constituencies, especially the counties, wherever opposition candidates advertised themselves, they chose to draw the attention of the electors to their credentials as enemies of excise.

The same concentration on the excise was made apparent in the general campaigning and demonstrating which was a normal part of eighteenth-century elections. For such demonstrations there were a number of possible occasions. These included the assizes when the propertied classes of the countryside met and, for example in the case of Derbyshire, ostentatiously thanked the county's parliamentary representatives for opposing the excise in 1733, and the races which took place normally in the summer and, for instance in Shropshire, provoked massive electoral demonstrations with much placarding and chanting of anti-excise slogans, not to say violence.[31] Above all there were the great electoral progresses which were the only effective means of contact between electors and candidates and formed the mainstay of the campaigns in the counties. In the more keenly contested counties, for example Norfolk, Sussex, Hampshire

[30] *St. James's Evening Post*, 14–16 Aug. 1733, 11–14 Aug. 1733; *Northampton Mercury*, 31 Dec. 1733, 18 Feb. 1734.
[31] *Craftsman*, 4 Aug. 1733; *St. James's Evening Post*, 13–15 Sept. 1733.

and Kent, these were one long riot of mobbing and parading. In each case the pattern was the same; the paired candidates on either side would proceed about the county from parish to parish, accompanied throughout by their particular friends and agents, and also picking up local supporters at various points. At every stop there was at least a small treat, and more generally a great banquet or dinner; for the candidates the result was an appalling bout of festivities which was likely to be as damaging to their digestions as to their pockets. These progresses were eagerly reported not merely in the provincial papers but also in the London journals, and the avidity with which the press recounted the stories of drunken celebrations and riotous demonstrations was inexhaustible.

Where there were competing local papers the results were bizarre. In Norfolk, for example, the Jacobite *Norwich Gazette* and the Whig *Norwich Mercury* disputed every inch of the ground. Their reports of the same event often bore little resemblance to each other, and neither could make a claim as to the political disposition of any locality without being flatly contradicted. At King's Lynn, for example, Crossgrove of the *Gazette* claimed that one of the Tory candidates for the county was met on his entry into the town by 100 freeholders; but according to the *Mercury*, which not only reduced the number to 24, but actually named them, the demonstration was less impressive.[32] The consequence was a heated controversy which died down only when new and equally contentious material was reported from other parts of the county. In any event the one fact which clearly emerged from all such accounts was the undoubted hostility of the great mass of voters to the excise scheme. The poor communications of the countryside together with the less sophisticated political attitude of the rural freeholders meant that the excise as an issue had been slow to sink in but, once absorbed, became difficult to eradicate. The clearest evidence on this comes from Sussex, not because that county was exceptional in this respect, but because the Duke of Newcastle left an enormous mass of material relating to it.[33] Report after report testified to the extent of the

[32] *Norwich Mercury*, 29 Sept. 1733. In this case the *Mercury* was commendably accurate. The Norfolk poll book for 1734 shows that in Lynn, which was of course very much under Walpole influence, 25 electors cast their vote for the opposition candidates (against 209 on the other side). *A Copy of the Poll for the Knights of the Shire for the County of Norfolk, Taken at Norwich, May 22, 1734* (1734).

[33] Much of this material is used in B. Williams, 'The Duke of Newcastle and the General Election of 1734', *Eng. Hist. Rev.*, xii (1897), 448–88.

reaction against the excise and Whigs associated with it. The voters in Rye, for example, promised to 'be at Mr. Pelham's and Mr. Butler's service provided they cou'd have a Letter from them with assurances that they will oppose the Excise for the future'.[34] In the parish of Isfield one freeholder 'did not like that an Exciseman should take an account of his Park', and another 'said he would kill any Excise man that offered to come into his house'.[35] That the rural populace was extremely vulnerable to the opposition's alarms on this score was confirmed by the Bishop of Chichester:

I coud wish something were writ in the way of Dialogue between 2 farmers or persons of that size, in a natural easy familiar way, so as to be intelligible to the meanest capacities, in which the nature of the excise might be thoroughly explained, and the objections fairly discussed and answered, such objections as the Country people are taught to make and in fact do make. Something of this kind, I am apt to think, would be much more read and have a greater effect than the finest writ papers in the way of a continued argument, which is necessarily above vulgar capacities; for such things must be minced and cutt into small pieces, since they can take in but a little at a time.[36]

The ministry's unpopularity among these classes of the community was general. In Kent, for example, 'a merry passage happened at Rochester, where some apothecaries were botanizing, and the country routed them, alarmed by a Joke of a Gent. who told the Louts they came to measure their lands in order to excise them. So dreadful is the word and idea fixed to it'.[37] Shropshire was reported to be 'mighty zealously against the excise scheme', as were Derbyshire, Cheshire, Northamptonshire, Surrey, Sussex and Yorkshire.[38] Even the political power of the landlord was challenged by the excise issue. In Cambridgeshire, for example, where the Whig candidates were Henry Bromley and Samuel Shepheard, Lord Lincoln's tenants agreed to support Shepheard, who had voted against the excise bill,

---

[34] Add. MS. 32688, f. 113: Col. J. Pelham to Newcastle, 16 Aug. 1733.
[35] Ibid., f. 121: W. Hay to Newcastle, 16 Aug. 1733.
[36] Ibid., f. 136: Bishop of Chichester to Newcastle, 18 Aug. 1733.
[37] *Remarks and Collections of Thomas Hearne*, xi. 244: Rawlinson to Hearne, 20 Aug. 1733.
[38] Add. MS. 32688, f. 187: W. Jessop to Newcastle, 26 Aug. 1733; E. G. Forrester, *Northamptonshire County Elections and Electioneering, 1695-1832* (Oxford, 1941), p. 54; *Universal Spectator*, 25 Aug. 1733; J. Cartwright, ed., *Wentworth Papers, 1705-1739* (London, 1882), p. 494.

but proved 'a little reserv'd as to Mr. Bromley on the Account of the Excise Bill'.[39] Equally conclusive was the fact that the government's pamphleteers themselves were unable to deny the extent of the disaffection. Thus the *Hyp-Doctor* freely, if contemptuously, conceded the existence of 'our NEW ENGLISH FEVER, unlike those which have reign'd in former Years. To trace the Topography thereof would be to go over most of the Counties of *England*'.[40]

Nor was this pattern one which applied only in the counties. In the towns too there can be no question that the government suffered seriously as a result of its excise scheme. Not surprisingly the trading community was slow to forget its experience of the excise affair. From Nottingham, for example, Newcastle's friend, John Plumptre, reported that the likely government candidate, George Gregory, was in serious trouble for voting for the excise. 'Here are several of the more considering Traders who would pass by his having voted for the Excise and be for him in Adherence to their old Principles, but with the rest, and especially the young Ones (who should be our Champions at a Poll) his Sin is still unpardon'd'.[41] In Bristol, the country's second city, the wrath of the commercial community against John Scrope, Walpole's Secretary to the Treasury and one of those most involved in the initiation of the excise scheme, was unquenchable. Even Scrope himself was reduced to pleading penitence before his electors: 'he had taken all due Care to observe the Dictates and Directions of his County; and if he had been short in any respect, he hoped they had Goodness enough in them to excuse him'.[42] No less striking was the threatened revolt of a small country town like Lewes against the traditional influence of the local magnate, the Duke of Newcastle. The sitting members, Thomas Pelham of Stanmer and Thomas Pelham of Lewes, were closely related to Newcastle; both had voted for the excise and both were standing for reelection. But according to Newcastle's local agent, the town's community of small tradesmen and retailers, who had traditionally supported the Whigs, were now turning to a renegade dissenter called Garland. One merchant named Whitfield, 'says you set out in the World with good Principles, and have acted upon them till the last affair: he says, that he and all considerable Merchants have great

---

[39] Add. MS. 32689, f. 55: T. Moore to Newcastle, 27 Nov. 1733.
[40] 14 Aug. 1733.
[41] Add. MS. 32688, f. 31: 21 July 1733.
[42] *Daily Post-Boy*, 11 Sept. 1733.

Obligations to those Gentlemen, that relieved them against a Scheme, which would have proved their Ruin: and that they sought to express their Gratitude to them: that he would shew that he had some Interest in Lewes; and he thought Mr Garland a proper Person to represent it, because he understood Trade'.[43] These three towns were very different. Bristol was a great commercial port, Nottingham a substantial trading and manufacturing town, Lewes a small county market town; but all were united in the extreme disillusionment of the mercantile community with the government, and despite the fact that business was traditionally a Whig preserve.

If the administration could derive little comfort from the election campaign so far as the excise was concerned, the picture was less black in relation to its attempt to resist the growth of a Court-and-Country dichotomy. It is difficult to be precise in this area because the newspapers in the opposition interest took to labelling all their candidates 'Country party' men. Their grounds for so doing were often very slight, and more frequently than not the new term signified not a novel party grouping but an old one. In Tory-dominated boroughs and counties, for example, the Tories who described themselves or were described as being 'in the country interest' would not seriously have contemplated alliance with opposition Whigs. Throughout the West Country, Wales and much of the Midlands, the county seats were controlled by the Anglican country gentry; Whiggism was practically non-existent, so that the introduction of the new party pattern was largely irrelevant. On the other hand, in parts of the country the old Whig and Tory division was so deep that there could be no question of burying the hatchet. In the north, for example, the Jacobite crises had left a legacy too bitter for any compromises, and nothing would have induced the Whig families of Northumberland, Cumberland and Westmorland to join their traditional enemies, though many of them were far from being friends of Walpole. In one county, Norfolk, the power of the Walpole family had so united local Whiggism that a cleavage was inconceivable. Indeed the government's supporters there felt able to describe the Whig candidates as 'the County Candidates for the Court and Country Interest (which happily for us, are now the same)'.[44] The only areas where the new doctrines made some progress were the economically more advanced, and therefore politically more so-

---

[43] Add. MS. 32688, f. 379: W. Hay to Newcastle, 24 Sept. 1733.
[44] *General Evening Post*, 15-18 Dec. 1733.

phisticated, parts of the country, around London and in the southeast generally and to some extent in Yorkshire.

Not surprisingly, it was in Middlesex that the clearest lead was given for coalition. There the sitting members were two Tories, James Bertie and Sir Francis Child; Bertie did not stand again, but his place was taken by none other than the leading opposition Whig, William Pulteney. For the first time a Whig and a Tory genuinely stood on the same platform, both having voted against the excise, both in the country interest. Though the *Free Briton* fulminated that Pulteney's object was to 'gain that Power by the Strength of a *Tory-Faction*, which he could not obtain from the Grace of a *Whigg-Prince*', the resulting combination was so strong that, despite one or two abortive attempts to produce a government candidate, the election proved a walk-over.[45] Middlesex was not the only example. In the neighbouring county of Kent, the Whig interest split down the middle. The excise scheme, the overweening aristocratic influence of the Dorset family which provoked considerable resentment among the smaller landowners, and serious personal disputes between the two government candidates, Lord Middlesex and Sir George Oxenden, combined to shatter the Whig interest in the county and drove many Whigs to join with the Tories. There emerged a genuine country alliance between Sir Edward Dering, the sitting member and a Tory of an ancient Kentish family, and William Vane, a Whig. In Sussex too the opposition candidates were respectively a rebel Whig, Sir Cecil Bishopp, and a Tory, John Fuller.

In Yorkshire the picture was confused. There the fight was three-cornered, with two Whigs, Cholmley Turner and Sir Rowland Winn, standing on a joint interest against one Tory, Sir Miles Stapylton. But the Whigs were bitterly divided, not least because of the excise crisis, and although Stapylton did not attract an avowed Whig ally (Yorkshire was still too rent by old political conflicts to stomach the new creed in its entirety), he was enormously assisted by the intervention of a rebel Whig candidate, Edward Wortley Montagu, who stood with no hope of obtaining a seat himself but every hope of assisting the Tory camp. Even in those areas where a 'Country' alliance was a possibility there were none the less considerable obstacles. Some opposition Whigs, for example, found the prospect of increased Tory representation in Parliament alarming. In Gloucestershire Lord Berkeley admitted, 'tho' I would not have the Court,

[45] 25 Apr. 1734.

and Sir Robert, have just such a Parliament as they please, I am very far from desiring there should be a Tory Parliament'.[46] Similarly Lord Stair remarked in March 1734, 'Our Tories seem now disposed to draw together with us, and we are labouring with some of our friends to join with them in matters of elections to oppose the Court. The doing otherwise has been a considerable disadvantage to the common cause. Our friends complain of it in one another, and yet do it themselves. Such inconsequential ways of action are most destructive'.[47]

On the Tory side there was equal difficulty. Even those Tories who were prepared to work for a 'Country' coalition did so only in the most reserved spirit and with every intention of deserting at the appropriate moment. Lord Bruce, for example, revealed that in Hampshire he was working with the Whig Lord Carteret only as a second best. 'I have writ to Lord C[arteret] to propose a coalition, which would, I believe, make the thing sure; but should that not be entered into, Mr. Lisle would be joined by Sir S. Stuart, or some other of his own sort. I wish two such could be, but when one cannot do as one would do, one must do as one can do.' In Hampshire this scheme indeed failed thanks to mutual suspicion, and the result was to aid the government and damage the opposition. Similarly Bruce explained that in Yorkshire the Tory Stapylton was to stand without a running partner in order to reassure rebel Whigs, but the Tories had 'fixed Sir Myles Stapylton's being chosen with a good prospect of having the two of our own sort another time'.[48]

One particularly awkward problem in this context was religion, which was still capable of arousing considerable political tension. Walpole's propaganda machine played most effectively, for instance, on the anxieties of the dissenters with regard to Tory High Church views. The government press was for ever recalling the Occasional Conformity and Schism Bills, both Tory measures repealed by the Whigs, and to great effect.[49] This was important because in many cases the dissenters were among those who had traditionally supported the Whig establishment and were now beginning to have doubts. The repeated failure of the dissenting pressure groups to

[46] Gloucestershire Record Office, Sherborne Muniments, Berkeley to Dutton, 18 Sept. 1733.
[47] J. M. Graham, ed., *Annals and Correspondence of the Viscount and the first and second Earls of Stair* (London, 1875), ii. 208: Stair to Grange, 2 Mar. 1734.
[48] *HMC Dartmouth*, iii. 153, 154: Bruce to Dartmouth, 1 Apr. 1732, 1 Jan. 1734.
[49] See, for example, *Flying Post*, 28 Aug. 1733, 11 Sept. 1733.

extract real measures of reform, particularly the repeal of the Test and Corporation Acts, was already putting the Whiggism of the nonconformists under considerable pressure. Moreover, the dissenters were especially strong among precisely those elements most discontented with the excise scheme, the small traders and businessmen in the towns. Consequently any argument which would arrest the mass desertion of government dissenters was particularly welcome to the ministry, and in this respect at least the rebel Whigs' stress on the importance of a new Whig-Tory coalition under the name of the Country interest did not a little to help it. 'It is this jealousy', William Pulteney confessed, 'that makes the well-meaning dissenters fearful that what we are doing may establish their enemies the Torys in power, and they are told by some of their corrupted leaders and some of their clergy that the discontented Whigs are little better than Jacobites. However it is certain that the dissenters are far from being unanimous, for I am assured in several countrys we shall have their assistance'.[50] In fact Pulteney's qualification was unduly optimistic. The government's campaign was rammed ruthlessly home. In Sussex, for example, Newcastle's agents made effective use of the Schism Act, and in London the government press declared, 'the Mask is now taken off, it is no longer Whig and Tory, Court or Country, that is now the Question; but the Church of England or Dissenters'.[51] By the time of the general election some dissenting communities were ready to declare for their traditional alliance with orthodox Whiggism. The dissenters of Devon and Cornwall announced their desire 'to undeceive such as may flatter themselves with Hopes that in the ensuing Election we should act a different Part from what we have always acted'.[52] Similar declarations were made by the dissenters of Shrewsbury, Chester, Bristol and Gloucestershire, Monmouth, Lancaster and elsewhere, while those of Northamptonshire were reputed to 'have the common sense to see that it were madness to throw our selves into the hands of the tories, and to seek our further establishment from those who are united in thirsting for our ruin'.[53] No doubt there were some who voted against government candidates in the subsequent elections, but generally it

[50] *HMC Mar and Kellie*, p. 536: Pulteney to Grange, 22 Mar. 1734.
[51] Add. MS. 32688, f. 121; *Daily Post-Boy*, 6 May 1734.
[52] *Read's Weekly Journal*, 6 Apr. 1734.
[53] *St. James's Evening Post*, 26–29 Jan. 1734; *Gentleman's Magazine*, 1734, p. 217; J. D. Humphreys, ed. *The Correspondence and Diary of Philip Doddridge, D.D.* (London, 1829–31, 5 vols.), iii. 125.

can scarcely be doubted that the dissenters remained loyal. Scrope was not the only M.P. who was later to vote in Parliament for religious reforms on account of 'the obligation they had to the Dissenters in their elections'.[54]

In one way or another the excise crisis had the effect of making the general election of 1734 arguably the most bitter, and for government the most dangerous, election between 1714 and 1830. This is the impression whatever yardstick is used. For example, there were many contested elections, more than in any subsequent eighteenth-century election. The number — 136 — was indeed exceeded only by two earlier general elections, 156 in 1722, and 143 in 1710.[55] But this is only a rough guide. In the elections of 1734 some constituencies failed to go to the polls not because there was no real conflict or electoral anxiety, but rather because the swing against administration was so strong that candidates could not be found to stand in the ministerial interest. In Middlesex, for example, where political excitement was high, the want of a contest was no indication at all that the electors of that county were uninterested in the issue of the day; quite the contrary was the case. Moreover, where there were contests, the voting turn-out was exceptionally high. In Gloucestershire it was noted that there was 'of Freeholders the greatest Number that ever was known',[56] and in a number of counties the polling in 1734 was the highest in the entire period 1715-1790. This was the case, for example, in five large and important counties, Essex, Kent, Norfolk, Sussex and Yorkshire, where the election was described as 'the strongest Contest that ever was known in Yorkshire', and even as 'the hotest Election that ever was in England'.[57] Particularly striking was the example of Hertfordshire, the most frequently contested of all English counties in this period, which achieved its highest turn-out in 1734. Again, in Cheshire both the county and the county town were contested at every general election

---

[54] *HMC Egmont Diary*, ii. 243-4; on the dissenters' relations with the government in this period, see N. C. Hunt, *Two Early Political Associations* (Oxford, 1961).

[55] See J. Cannon, *Parliamentary Reform, 1640-1832* (Cambridge, 1973), p. 277; the statistics on this subject are necessarily imprecise since there is no absolutely reliable record of contested elections. However the above work contains the most useful set (pp. 278-89), which have to be supplemented, so far as Scottish and Welsh elections are concerned from the *History of Parliament: 1715-1754* and *1754-1790*, and from W. Speck, *Tory and Whig* (London, 1970), pp. 124-31.

[56] *Gloucester Journal*, 14 May 1734.

[57] Add. MS. 40748 (Bowes Papers), f. 67: unidentified, 25 Jan. 1734; Add. MS. 31142, f. 151: R. Wardman to Strafford, 22 May 1734.

from 1715 to 1734. In both, the 1734 poll was substantially higher than on the previous occasions.[58] Nothing could more clearly demonstrate the extraordinary interest of the electorate in the elections which followed the defeat of the excise.

In terms of expenditure too the general election of 1734 was a spectacular one. In theory it should not have been, since in 1729 Parliament had passed an act providing severe penalties for cases of bribery and corruption. The newspapers made a point of printing the oath required by the act and warning of its consequences, and at least a few politicians apparently anticipated some difficulties as a result of it.[59] But in the event the act seems to have had almost practically no effect on the normal methods of electioneering. All the usual varieties of bribery went on. Easily the commonest, particularly in the counties, was the feasting and treating which the eighteenth-century electorate regarded as an indispensable part of campaigning. Perhaps less frequent but still by no means unusual was the payment in cash or kind to electors which the bribery act had particularly been levelled against. In Worcester, for example, tickets worth 2s. 6d. were given out to enable voters to make purchases from tradesmen.[60] Less crude were the public benefactions from which so many boroughs with declining economies and inflating political assets benefited in the eighteenth century. In Coventry in 1734 the sitting member settled an endowment of £50 for poor freemen and offered several hundred pounds towards the corporation's purchase of common lands outside the city.[61] Again, Tewkesbury, regarded as a peculiarly corrupt corporation, might have surprised many by treating its sitting member and candidate, Lord Gage, to an election dinner 'shewing their Abhorrence of Bribery, and Disregard for selfish Interest: A noble Example worthy of all true Britons', had it not been the case that the borough had already received the douceur of 'a very handsome Fire-Engine' from Gage.[62]

Just how expensive the election was in general is impossible to estimate. Normally it was the bigger constituencies with their very large electorates and endless campaigning which put a strain on the

---

[58] These conclusions are based on the voting figures given in the *History of Parliament: 1715-1754* and *1754-1790*.
[59] E. Hughes, *North Country Life in the Eighteenth Century: The North-East, 1700-1750* (London, 1952), p. 277.
[60] *Whitehall Evening Post*, 8-11 June 1734.
[61] *General Evening Post*, 12-14 Mar. 1734.
[62] *Gloucester Journal*, 8 Jan. 1734, 11 Dec. 1733.

candidate's purse, and in 1734 there were thirteen counties which went to the poll as well as fifty boroughs with electorates of more than 500. This meant a great deal of expenditure. In Kent it was reported as early as September 1733 that 'The Expences have been greater than ever were known so long before an Election', while in Norfolk Walpole's share alone was some £10,000, and in Cheshire one of the candidates spent £13,000.[63] However, perhaps the most significant statistic was the amount of government money spent in 1734. Secret service expenditure for that year was very much higher at £117,000 than in any other year between the Revolution of 1688 and Burke's civil list reform of 1782.[64] Nothing could more clearly indicate the desperate plight of the government and the resources it poured into the election campaign of 1733-4.

The election was a violent as well as an expensive one. The *Craftsman*, anxious to stress the moderation of those who opposed the ministry, claimed that 'There never was a *general Election* in this Kingdom attended with less *Rioting* than That, which is lately over'.[65] But this was not the general impression. No doubt much of the violence was of the ephemeral kind naturally associated with Georgian electioneering, but it was considerable nonetheless. Certainly the supporters of government were concerned. 'Unless some proper Measures are taken, to crush these mad Riots', one Sussex man declared, 'They may produce downright Insurrections in many Parts of the kingdom: for the Frenzy is not less than in Sacheverel's Time'.[66] In Yorkshire too there was violence, said to be particularly strong in the countryside. 'People of all denominations are heated, some by drink, others by zeal, and the Test of the latter with many is most commonly violence; a more determind sett of Gentry, are for leading on to Slaughter, whereas the Burgesses amongst themselves give one another a broken-head and go off satisfy'd, and shake hands again next morning'.[67] Another county badly affected in this respect was Norfolk, where the election campaign was particularly bitter. For some reason Great Yarmouth was the worst offender.

[63] *Whitehall Evening Post*, 25–27 Sept. 1733; Coxe, i. 456; P.R.O., S.P. 36/32, f. 4: Cholmondeley to ?, 20 May 1734. See also *Suffolk Mercury*, 27 Aug. 1733.
[64] For civil list expenditure annually under George II, see L. B. Namier, *The Structure of Politics at the Accession of George III* (London, 1961, 2nd edn.), p. 195. Figures for the rest of the period are not readily available in published form and have to be abstracted from the Treasury papers.
[65] 13 July 1734.
[66] Add. MS. 32688, f. 336: Curteis to Newcastle, 15 Sept. 1733.
[67] P.R.O., S.P. 36/31, f. 149: W. Chetwynd to Newcastle, 13 Apr. 1734.

When the Tory candidates visited the town in September the Tory mob went on a rampage, and again when the Whig candidates arrived in December there was something like a full-scale riot.[68] Nor was the violence all on one side. The retaliation of the Yarmouth authorities was so savage that it led to a suit in the courts, after the Mayor had allegedly maltreated one offender who had broken the windows in Lord Hobart's coach, whipping him 'very severe, as if he would cut him asunder'.[69] The result was a judgement against the Mayor and an award of £15 damages. More good-humoured and perhaps more typical were the activities of the mob in Harleston, where the Whig cavalcade of carriages found itself in a parlous plight. 'The Populace bereav'd them of their Coach Wheels, and having roll'd them about half a Mile out of Town, receiv'd a Crown apiece for bringing them back again.'[70]

Good humour was, however, altogether lacking in the one great band of really serious violence which spread along the Welsh marches, on both sides of the Dee and Severn, from Cheshire in the north to Gloucestershire in the south. It is not easy to explain these disturbances, though there are at least some clues. For example, in the southern part of the area the issue was only partly political. In Worcestershire, in Herefordshire and in Gloucestershire, the riots were ostensibly against the new turnpikes. But politics was at least involved since Tory turnpikes were noticeably less affected than their Whig counterparts.

There is great reason to suspect that there is something ugly at the bottom of this [one citizen of Gloucester claimed]. For the Cry of these Rioters has all along been Bathurst and Chester, and no Turnpikes. But it is particularly remarkable that here, where the Money, which has been lent upon the Turnpikes, has been lent by Gentlemen who are well affected to the Government, no Turnpike has been spar'd, but that at Cirencester, where the Money which has been lent upon the Turnpikes has been lent by Gentlemen who are thought to be not well affected to the Government, no Turnpike has been touch'd.[71]

Further north there was not even the issue of turnpikes to muddy the

[68] See the *Norwich Mercury* for these months.
[69] G. Harris, ed., *The Life of Lord Chancellor Hardwicke* (London, 1847), i. 287.
[70] *London Evening Post*, 4–6 Dec. 1733.
[71] C(H) MSS., Corr. 2283: Dr. H. Galley to ?, 21 July 1734. On the turnpike riots, see D. G. D. Isaac, 'A Study of Popular Disturbances in Britain, 1714–1754' (Ph.D. thesis, Edinburgh Univ., 1953), chap. v.

waters. In North Wales and the neighbouring English counties the violence was purely political. The language of the mob there, while clearly exaggerated and not to be taken at its face value, was certainly not of the stylized and ritualized kind which characterized the usual popular slogans. In Newcastle-under-Lyme, for example, the government candidate, John Lawton, was physically assaulted by the local colliers, 'vowing to wash their Hands in Mr. Lawton's Heart's Blood, and to make the Channels run with the Blood of his Burgesses'.[72] In Flint the Riot Act had to be read when the mob attacked the local bailiffs and declared 'That the Sun should shine through them; that they should be pinn'd to the Wainscot, etc.'.[73] In fact one of the bailiffs was lucky to escape with his life, being 'held by the Throat and Beat by three Persons, under which Charge, being a Corpulent Man, he fell into a Swoon and with much ado was convey'd out of the Hall, and carried to his own Home, where he was attended by a Chirurgeon, who declar'd that without his immediate bleeding of him, he must have been a dead Man'. In Radnor, where the account of the campaign reads like that of a Tudor election, there was also excessive violence.[74] Indeed the situation was so serious in the marches that the army had to be employed, a measure to which government resorted only with the greatest reluctance. In Knighton it was insisted that the 'true friends of the administration, must positively quit their homes, or be murderd or ruind', and troops were quartered in the town.[75] Similarly in Shropshire the violence was so intolerable that troops had to be despatched to Bridgnorth.[76]

It is not easy to account for this regional outburst of violence, though sheer epidemic infectiousness was obviously a factor. The key was probably one town, Chester, and one fanatic, Watkin Williams Wynn. Wynn alone, one of the ministry's most bitter and unrelenting enemies, was quite capable of provoking the violence of the North Welsh elections. As a great Welsh magnate, whose influence ran right across North Wales and into the neighbouring counties of Cheshire and Shropshire, and as one of the leaders of the Tory gentry who were so strong a force both in Wales and the marches, he was in a position to cause considerable trouble. Certainly he used his Welsh tenantry, a force much feared both in

[72] *St. James's Evening Post*, 7–9 May 1734.
[73] *General Evening Post*, 11–13 June 1734.
[74] Ibid., 4–7 May 1734; *London Evening Post*, 7–9 May 1734.
[75] C(H) MSS. Corr. 2205: H. Howarth to Walpole, 11 June 1734.
[76] P.R.O., S.P. 36/30, ff. 148–64.

Cheshire and Shropshire, more in the style of a feudal lord than a Georgian landowner. Still more important, however, was probably the incidental build-up to the elections of 1734. Quite by coincidence Chester had been the scene of two separate by-elections in 1733, precisely at the moment the excise crisis came to a head. There were other complicating considerations at work; in the early 1730s a powerful mercantile interest which owed a good deal to its Liverpool connections was attempting to wrest control of Chester from the traditional hold of the Tory gentry, particularly the Grosvenor family. Similarly there were the varied and involved schemes for reviving the port of Chester by cleaning the Dee, a project which became hopelessly entangled in local politics. The result of this combination of factors was that in 1733 Chester and the neighbouring countryside were in a constant turmoil. It needed only the general setting of the 1734 general election with the issue of the excise and the resurgence of Country Toryism to spread this excitement south, east and west into neighbouring and in terms of political, social and economic character, very similar counties. In any event the disturbances of the border country helped not a little to make the general election of 1734 one of the most ferocious elections to the unreformed Parliament.

IX

The Impact of the Excise

THE government was well aware by the time that Parliament was dissolved in April 1734 that it had on its hands a contest of the utmost gravity. And so it proved. The polls themselves were spread over two months, the first result, that at Westminster, being declared on 22 April and the writs for every constituency being returned at the latest by 13 June. In fact right up to this date polls were being held, especially in Scotland and Wales and in the English counties, where the elections came relatively late. Understandably, though the press reported the results in general, most of the attention was concentrated on the large constituencies, the open boroughs, and above all the counties, where the electorate could be numbered in thousands instead of tens or hundreds, and where the public attitude to the administration would be registered far more clearly than in the smaller constituencies. As the results in these polls came in it grew increasingly apparent that the ministry was facing a defeat of considerable magnitude. This was particularly marked in the counties around London, most of them marginal seats with a Whig bias in recent years. In Kent, for example, the court candidates, Sir George Oxenden and the Duke of Dorset's son, Lord Middlesex, were forced to throw up the poll after 8,000 votes had been cast and showed a clear superiority for their opponents Vane and Dering—an 'almost incredible Majority', the *Craftsman* called it.[1] Dorset subsequently had no hesitation in imputing 'every miscarriage of the Court candidates to the excise scheme'.[2] In Essex, another large county, two Tories were returned where previously the representation had been shared by a Tory and a government Whig. The ministerial candidate who stood on this occasion, Lord Castlemaine, was overwhelmingly defeated on the poll. In Hampshire the government also suffered a severe shock. There the forces of Whiggism were sufficiently divided to produce a close contest between two

---

[1] 25 May 1734. The figures were as follows: Sir E. Dering 4441, Viscount Vane 4252, Earl of Middlesex 3569, Sir G. Oxenden 3450.

[2] *Hervey Memoirs*, p. 295.

Tories and two government supporters. Largely by reason of the Duke of Bolton's desertion from the Whig camp after being proscribed by Walpole for his part in the revolt of 1733, the first Tory candidate led the poll with 2,669 votes. Though the other seat went to a ministerial supporter, Lord Harry Powlett, it did so by an extraordinarily narrow margin. Powlett's vote was 2,575, that of Sir Simeon Stuart (the other Tory) 2,573. The opposition press had every justification for seeing this as a famous victory in a county where the government, partly as a result of influence in the ports and partly on account of traditionally strong local Whiggism, was normally secure.

Still more sensational was the opposition's success in Gloucestershire. There again it was the combination of the excise and a country party coalition that transformed local politics. In the preceding Parliament the county had been represented by two government Whigs, Henry Berkeley and Sir John Dutton. Yet so demoralized was the Whig establishment in 1734 that at the polls only one Whig candidate, John Stephens, could be prevailed upon to stand at all, and even he fared astonishingly badly. The two Tories, Benjamin Bathurst and Thomas Chester, were returned with great majorities. Lord Bathurst consequently had some reason to boast of an almost unprecedented triumph in a county normally dominated by the Whig families. 'We are very proud of our Victory', he declared, 'it being to be observ'd that there have not been two Torys sent out of this County not once since the Revolution, and only 2 or 3 instances that one has got in'.[3] In other counties too the Tory cause prospered. In Yorkshire the Tory Sir Miles Stapylton was returned in an exceptionally bitter contest, while in both Leicestershire and in Rutland the Tories acquired their second seat. In some places it was not merely the division and demoralisation of the Whig cause which helped to bring the administration into difficulties, but simply the reaction of freeholders against the excise, though the ministerial interests were reluctant to admit this basic truth. In Cheshire, for example, the representation was divided before the general election. In 1727 a government Whig, Sir Robert Cotton, and a Tory, Charles Cholmondeley, had been placed above another Tory, John Crewe. The same trio stood as candidates in 1734 with the difference that Cotton was severely beaten, a clear 700 votes behind the man he had

---

[3] Add. MS. 22221, f. 129: Bathurst to Strafford, 13 May 1734.

easily defeated in 1727. Walpole's son-in-law, the Earl of Cholmondeley, who had played a prominent part in the contest, blamed this failure on the villainy of Tory opponents who were alleged to be creating freeholds illegally by 'Erecting new Inclosures in all parts of the County on all the Waste Grounds—where they happened to be Lords of the Manners'.[4] Yet even Cholmondeley had to admit that feeling among the freeholders was running so high that normally loyal Whig supporters who had cast their votes solidly for Cotton in 1727 had become totally unreliable. No less than half of his brother's tenants, for example, had switched to the Tory side. Such volatility, not often credited to the aristocratically dominated electorates of the eighteenth century, can only be accounted for by Cotton's sudden unpopularity. It was well known that he had voted for the excise. In the summer of 1733 the county meeting had unanimously agreed to vote him out of his parliamentary seat for this offence, and with the excise a constant issue in the ensuing campaign it was not surprising that Cotton lost.[5]

However, all these reverses for the ministry paled into insignificance by comparison with its disaster in Norfolk, the most spectacular result of the election. Norfolk was traditionally content to divide its representation between Whigs and Tories, partly because the two interests were of reasonably comparable strength, and partly because the Whigs had sufficient control of most of the county's boroughs to feel able and even anxious to avoid contests in the county. However, in 1734 both sides were committed to a full-scale contest, with two local country gentlemen, Sir Edmund Bacon the sitting member, and William Wodehouse, representing the Tories, and for the Whigs William Morden, a wealthy associate of Walpole's, and Robert Coke, of one of Norfolk's premier families, who had been reluctantly drawn to fight a seat for which, in the heady days before the agitation against the excise, Walpole had probably intended to stand himself. Though the excise embittered local politics to the highest degree, the entrenched strength of the Whig families was so great and the finance, prestige and organization committed by the Walpoles so enormous, that both sides expected Walpole to get his way. Walpole himself was extremely optimistic as late as 15 May 1734, and the Tories were so certain that he would carry

[4] P.R.O., S.P. 36/32, f. 4: Cholmondeley to ?, 20 May 1734.
[5] *Gentleman's Magazine*, 1733, p. 379; Add. MS. 32688, f. 187: W. Jessop to Newcastle, 26 Aug. 1733.

at least one of his candidates that they were busy preparing a safe seat at Cirencester for William Wodehouse in the event of his defeat.[6] Yet the result in a close contest eagerly followed by the national press was a great victory for the Tories and the utter humiliation of Walpole in his own county. Nothing could more clearly have demonstrated the revolt of nominally dependable electors against the government in the aftermath of the excise.

The pattern in the counties was repeated in the other significant constituencies, the large boroughs with electorates of more than 1000. At Bristol, where the electorate of between four and five thousand was larger than in many counties, John Scrope, Walpole's Secretary of the Treasury, was predictably defeated and had to seek refuge in the close borough of Lyme Regis. Henceforward Bristol was represented by one rebel Whig and one Tory. At Canterbury the sitting government member, Sir Thomas Hales, who had voted for the excise, was easily turned out by two Tories in a violent election fought entirely on the issue of the excise. Hales himself informed the Duke of Dorset as early as October 1733, 'If there were two able bodied men I don't think but they may have a good chance if not concerned in the Excise'.[7] Not surprisingly Hales was compelled to fight on his own in the event; nobody was prepared to stand in harness with an avowed supporter of the excise. In the Welsh marches Hereford elected two Tories against a government Whig where previously it had permitted an equal share; at Worcester the sitting members were Samuel Sandys, one of the opposition Whig leaders, and a government Whig, Sir Richard Lane. But Lane had long before warned Walpole that a vote for the excise would mean the loss of his seat, and indeed he did not attempt to stand again.[8] Instead his substitute, John Willes, threw up the poll when he had gained 609 votes against 1,628 for Sandys and 1,094 for a Tory, Richard Lockwood. At Coventry it came as no surprise that one of the sitting members, John Neale, was overwhelmingly defeated by a local merchant named John Bird. Neale had not merely voted for the excise, but had gone to the length of declaring in the Commons that his constituency's instructions against the excise were not representative of its true sentiments. Such folly could only produce

[6] Add. MS. 32689, f. 241: Walpole to Newcastle, 15 May 1734.
[7] Quoted in A. N. Newman, 'Elections in Kent and its Parliamentary Representation, 1715–1754', p. 204.
[8] See above p. 68.

one result, and Neale's lavish spending during the election made little difference. In Coventry indeed the moral of the excise affair was all too plain. The other sitting member was Sir Adolphus Oughton who had wisely absented himself from the excise divisions in Parliament. Oughton was as much a government man as Neale, but his prudent refusal to support the excise stood him in good stead at the polls. His own vote was 820 and Neale's only 405, 383 behind the new member, John Bird. Other boroughs in a similar position were Newcastle and Lancaster. In both the previous representation had been shared. In each case the government member had blotted his copy-book by voting for the excise and in each case he paid for it at the polls. At Newcastle indignation at the excise ran particularly high. There the local corporation had gone out of its way ostentatiously to bestow its freedom on a local magnate, the Earl of Scarbrough, who, though a courtier, had shown signs of uneasiness during the excise affair. One alderman 'being in Liquor sd my Ld deserved it, for he had opposed the Excise with Zeale', a slip which sent Scarbrough scurrying to the King and Queen to explain himself and caused intense embarrassment among northern Whigs.[9] At Lancaster too feeling was strong. In October the *Corn-Cutter's Journal*, one of Walpole's hack newspapers, had optimistically announced that 'The Freemen begin to open their Eyes in relation to the Excise Scheme, believeing it not so bad as has been represented by the Enemies of the Government'.[10] Local Whigs, however, did not take the same view, and the sitting government member put up no fight against an interloping Tory.

The fact that there was no contest at Lancaster or indeed at some other of the larger constituencies which changed their members in the general election of 1734 is important. Understandably, contested elections attracted the most interest, but in their way the uncontested elections could be as significant. As has been seen in the case of Middlesex, the want of a contest was frequently not evidence that the political climate was too cool to raise a poll, but on the contrary that the tide was running so fast against the government that a poll was not worth its trouble. Eighteenth-century elections were too expensive for candidates to fight hopeless battles in the way that is expected of aspiring party hopefuls in the modern system. In many counties and many large boroughs government candidates were so

[9] C(H) MSS., Corr. 2012: G. Liddell to Walpole, 10 July 1733.
[10] 23 Oct. 1733.

appalled by the violence of the reaction against Walpole and his excise scheme that they declined to take the financial and indeed physical risks inseparable from a poll. Almost all the counties which were already represented by two Tories, for example, were allowed to re-elect them without opposition. In counties like Lancashire ('this disaffected Country' as one local Whig called it),[11] Staffordshire, Warwickshire, Herefordshire, Oxfordshire, Berkshire and Northamptonshire, there was scarcely the pretence of Whig competition. In the great belt of western counties, where Toryism was always strong, this was particularly true. In Somerset there was a feeble attempt by the government's supporter, Lord Hinton, to work up some Whig opposition, but there was never the possibility of a poll. In Cornwall, Devon, Dorset and Wiltshire, even this limited measure of opposition was not essayed. Moreover, in this area even the last remnants of Whiggism were rooted out without a contest. Worcestershire had one staunch government supporter as a knight of the shire, Sir Thomas Lyttelton, who had loyally voted for the excise; in December he published a grovelling letter in which he apologized for doing so.[12] However, as the polls approached he recognized the utter hopelessness of his cause and withdrew to the safety of a Cornish borough, Camelford.

A comparable experience was that of government supporters in the metropolitan constituencies. London and its environs had been so violently involved in the excise that the very notion of anyone who had supported the excise even contemplating a fight there was ludicrous. In Middlesex the Country pairing of Pulteney and Child carried all before it, and though the government tried to find respectable candidates, none were forthcoming. In London itself there was a contest, but it was scarcely between those for and against either the excise or the government. It was taken as read that the candidates would be thoroughly opposed to both; the struggle at the polls was merely a personal one between the existing opposition members and the rising star of Lord Mayor Barber. In the event Barber, despite his attempt to claim that his own opposition to the excise had been even more zealous than that of Sir John Barnard and Micajah Perry, was defeated by the power of better-organized politicians.[13] One of

---

[11] C(H) MSS., Corr. 2146: Sir H. Hoghton to Walpole, 2 Apr. 1734.
[12] *General Evening Post*, 18–20 Dec. 1733.
[13] *Daily Post-Boy*, 30 Apr. 1734. The M.P.s returned were Humphrey Parsons, Barnard, Perry and Robert Willimot.

the sitting members had been Sir John Eyles. Eyles had actually voted against the excise on grounds of political expediency; any other conduct would have been dangerous in the extreme. Even so the fact that he was associated both with Walpole personally and with the court was sufficient to damn him. Wisely he retreated, though in his case the borough which he selected as a safer option, Chippenham, proved an injudicious choice. His brother, Joseph, who also sat for a great metropolitan constituency, Southwark, and had also voted against the excise out of prudence, similarly retreated, in his case more successfully to the family borough of Devizes in Wiltshire. In any event, if there were any doubts about feelings in London they were resolved in the purely local elections of 1734 for a city chamberlain. It happened that one of the candidates for this lucrative office was John Bosworth, a tobacconist prominent in the excise campaign, and that his opponent, John Selwyn, was a Whig with some connections at court. On this slender foundation it was put about that Selwyn supported the excise whereas Bosworth was advertised as 'a strenuous Opposer of the Excise Scheme'.[14] Selwyn found himself in the unfortunate position of having to deny his connection with the ministry or forfeit his election, which he eventually did. Where in the counties the cry was of court versus country, in London it was court verses city—'a wicked Artifice' the ministerial press called it, but an immensely potent one.[15] In other local elections, for example that of a sheriff of London, the excise was also raised.[16] If any government supporters felt interested in standing for the parliamentary elections in London these examples were sufficient to deter them.

The government's reverses in the open constituencies were from Walpole's point of view extremely serious. The counties and boroughs with electorates of over 1000 formed a vast majority of the total property-owning electorate, and that electorate clearly cast its vote overwhelmingly against the court even in places which had previously supported it. In all, the ministry lost twenty-one seats in the great open constituencies. This alone would in theory have reduced Walpole's majority by forty-two in the Commons and brought him to the verge of disaster. It also demonstrated very clearly that public opinion was very heavily against him at this moment. There was of course considerable dispute to be expected on this point in the press. Nonetheless, the argument went very

[14] *Daily Journal*, 25 Mar. 1734.   [15] *Daily Courant*, 5 Apr. 1734.
[16] *Daily Post*, 11 July 1733.

much with the opposition, who fairly claimed that it was the testimony of the counties and large boroughs that constituted the sense of the nation. 'I hope', the *Craftsman* remarked, 'the *Court-Writers* will be so modest, for the future, as not to insist on the *general Sense of the People*; nor to say *that every Body, except the* Craftsman, *hath done with the* Excise; for the late Elections are sufficient to convince Them that it is neither forgot nor forgiven by the Body of the Nation, who have hollowed it down in such a Manner through the whole Kingdom'.[17]

In particular the counties were selected as the significant battleground. According to the *Craftsman*, the sense of the people 'is to be seen best in the *Elections for Knights of the Shire*; for though there is not one County in *England*, where the same *ministerial Influence* does not prevail in some Degree; . . . yet as the Body of the Inhabitants, in every Shire, is generally assembled upon these Occasions, We may easily judge from the *Voice of the People* what are the *genuine Sentiments of the People*; and if those *modest Writers*, who boast so much of their Success, will be pleased to look over the list of *Knights of the Shire*, I believe they will find at least *Three to One* chosen against Them'.[18] In fact the evidence of the open constituencies was so overwhelming that not even the ministerial press could reasonably claim to have the public on its side. The court's journalists resorted to strange arguments in response to the opposition's assault on this point. Some of them simply denied that the public mattered at all. 'Supposing it true', the *London Journal* commented, 'that *the Majority* of the People are against the Ministry, what doth that prove? The People are sometimes *right*, and sometimes *wrong*'.[19] The *Free Briton* was more subtle—'The People must be distinguished from themselves', it declared.[20] Various ploys were used in aid of this distinction. For one thing the public was usually against the court. 'To put an End to this Boasting of the Sense of the People, let it be observed, that the deluded Multitude have ever been ungrateful to their best Governours'.[21] Moreover, the population of the countryside, which represented the great majority both of property and the electorate, were not entitled to play an important part in the nation's affair, or equipped to do so. The freeholders were 'as unable to express the *Sense* of the Nation about the Conduct of the Ministry, as the *Beasts* they ride on to give their Votes'.[22] Even

[17] 25 May 1734.   [18] Ibid.   [19] 22 June 1734.   [20] 20 June 1734.
[21] *Norwich Mercury*, 1 June 1734.   [22] *London Journal*, 15 June 1734.

their social superiors were little better. The country gentlemen and country clergy were veritable Squire Westerns, 'gaping Country Fellows', 'Minds *absolutely unimproved* by Study and Conversation', and moreover ideologically unsound, having 'not yet shaken off their *old Prejudices* against a *Whig-Administration*; nor are they entirely come into the Principles of the *Revolution*'.[23] The final argument was equally unimpressive. The government might not have a majority of the country's landowners with it, but it did have wealth, at least according to the *London Journal*. Half the court M.P.s had personal fortunes in excess of £2,000 per annum, and a quarter more than £3,000, figures with which the opposition's forces could allegedly not compare.[24] To such arguments was the Whig oligarchy reduced at the point of maximum alienation from the society it ruled.

Though the general election of 1734 registered the clearest electoral rejection of any administration in the eighteenth century, it did not produce a change of ministry. The eighteenth-century system was of course too fluid and its party configurations too confused to permit a simple calculation of government and opposition forces. What is clear is that despite the significant opposition gains in the large constituencies the government's majority in the Commons was not reduced sufficiently to endanger its position.[25] Newcastle's careful statement to Horace Walpole about the complexion of the new Parliament was probably accurate: 'Our parliament is, I think, a good one; but by no means such a one, as the queen and your brother imagine. It will require great care, attention, and management to sett out right, and keep people in good humour'.[26] The opposition was compelled to admit that in the Commons its triumph was limited. Carteret put the situation no better than a 'reasonable hope of a very strong party in the House of Commons', and even the irrepressible Duchess of Marlborough had to content herself by

---

[23] Ibid., 15 June, 6 July, 27 July 1734.   [24] 6 July 1734.
[25] R. Sedgwick, ed., *History of Parliament: The House of Commons, 1715–1754*, i. 42–3, gives a government majority of 126 (342 to 216) at the dissolution of 1734, and of 102 (330 to 228) in the first session of the new Parliament in 1735. At the time the opposition press calculated a ministerial majority after the general election of 57 (*London Evening Post*, 27–29 June 1734), though this did not take account of changes made by the decision of election disputes in 1735. The government press declined to venture any precise figures, perhaps wisely. In an age when many M.P.s were independent or neutral and when those who were not were apt to vary their voting loyalties a great deal, precise totals were of doubtful value. In this case the truth may be assumed to be somewhere between the figures given by Sedgwick and the *London Evening Post*.
[26] Coxe, iii. 168: Newcastle to Horace Walpole, 24 May 1734.

assuring all her friends that she had it on excellent authority that 'this parliament will begin with a greater opposition than has been known these many years'.[27] In fact the divisions in the Commons demonstrated that, while the government was weaker, there was no real danger at least in the short term. Admittedly on 27 January 1735 the ministry secured a majority of only 265 to 185 in a minor debate on foreign policy. 'It was surprising', Perceval recorded, 'to the Court that in the beginning of the Parliament, and when the affair was only to address his Majesty, the minority should be within 16 of the number that approved the Excise Scheme'.[28] Moreover, on the army estimates the ministry was alarmed to see its opponents break 200 once again to reach 208, though its own figure of 261 was sufficient to beat off this assault. Generally the minority reached the 180s on really important divisions, enough to exceed its average totals in the preceding Parliament but not to present any immediate prospect of bringing down the regime. This, for the opposition, relatively depressing state of affairs needs some explanation. Why, after a general election in which the court suffered such humiliation, did Parliament not adequately reflect the changed electoral climate? How is it possible to reconcile the violently hostile mood of the electorate with a secure if not quiescent House of Commons?

The answer to this question lies in a combination of factors. For example, Walpole was able for various reasons to modify the electoral effects of the public hostility against him. Even in the open constituencies the court scored some minor triumphs. In one or two cases the opposition did its worst and failed. In Sussex, for example, where the county election was one of the most bitterly contested, the government candidates got home, and by a reasonable margin.[29] But this was a Pyrrhic victory; it resulted not from any enthusiasm either for the court or the excise among the freeholders, but rather from the almost frighteningly thorough commitment of the Duke of Newcastle to the government cause. No eighteenth-century electioneer fought with more intensity than Newcastle and nowhere was he more jealous of his influence than in his own county. His triumph

---

[27] *Marchmont Papers*, ii. 28: Carteret to Marchmont, 15 June 1734; G. Scott Thompson, ed., *Letters of a Grandmother, 1732–1735* (London, 1943), p. 118: to Duchess of Bedford, 7 June 1734; *Stair Annals*, ii. 224: to Stair, 15 June 1734.
[28] *HMC Egmont Diary*, ii. 146.
[29] The voting was as follows: H. Pelham, 2271; J. Butler, 2053; Sir C. Bishopp, 1704; J. Fuller, 1581.

over those who sought, as he himself put it, 'to drive me out of the County',[30] was private, not ministerial, as his brother (and one of the returned members), Henry Pelham, had foreseen. 'We shall carry it, I verily believe', Pelham had prophesied even in September 1733, 'by a great majority, but it is more up-hill work than ever I expected to see in this county. The whole county is poison'd, very little regard in the common people for the king or Royal family, less for the Ministry, in short it is personal interest must carry this election, nothing else will or can'.[31] Another notable victory was that of the Whig interest in Norwich. This success particularly irritated the opposition since the Norwich merchants, one of the most important business communities in the kingdom, had instructed their M.P.s against the excise and were expected to throw out the Whigs in the general election.[32] But the pollbook makes clear just why Norwich adhered to the Walpole interest. Well over a third of the electorate of some 3,300 were worsted weavers, and Walpole left no doubt in their minds as to the government's power to influence the cloth trade. 'The supporting the Woollen Manufacture', he personally assured them at a special reception in July 1733, 'was what he ever had at Heart'.[33] This proved to be decisive. Only two hundred votes separated all four candidates in the election, and had the weavers divided in the same proportion as all other categories of voters (with the exception of the wealthy oligarchs of the city), the result would have been a severe defeat for the Whig candidates. Instead, the weavers cast 841 votes for Horace Walpole, 793 for his running-mate Waller Bacon, and only 546 and 516 respectively for their opponents, Ward and Branthwaite.[34] In Norwich as in Sussex some considerations were proof against national issues and opposition propaganda.

In other large constituencies the government hung on for a particularly important reason. Back in 1733 it had infuriated Walpole that so many independent Whigs had thought it necessary to oppose the excise. But in 1734 their wisdom in doing so was amply vindi-

---

[30] Add. MS. 32688, f. 510: Newcastle's circular, 16 Oct. 1733.
[31] Ibid., f. 423: H. Pelham to Newcastle, 29 Sept. 1733.
[32] *A Word to the Freeholders and Burgesses of Great Britain* (London, 1733), pp. 45–6.
[33] *Universal Spectator*, 21 July 1733.
[34] These figures are derived from *An Alphabetical draught of the Polls of Sir Edward Ward, Bart., Miles Branthwayt, Esq.; and of Horatio Walpole, Waller Bacon Esq.s for Members of Parliament for the City of Norwich, Taken May the 15th 1734, and of Miles Branthwayt, Esq., and Thomas Vere Esq., taken February the 19th, 1734, Incorporated in one list* (Norwich, 1735).

cated. In the north independent friends of the court were able to resist the general tide against the government precisely because they too could claim to have opposed the excise. In Derbyshire, for example, even the ministry's agents admitted that the excise was the great issue.[35] But the Cavendishes, who had deserted the ministry in the later excise divisions, did not suffer by it. They were thanked by the assizes with the other Derbyshire M.P.s who had voted against the excise, and still more significantly they not only retained one of the seats at Derby, but also gained a seat from the Tories in the county, a major victory which represented the court's only new success in the counties, and was to give the Cavendish family a knight of the shire for more than a century. In one sense of course this success was the result of a most impressive display of aristocratic power. County communities were always very jealous of aristocratic influence, and most noble families had to tread carefully in relation to them. But in Derbyshire the Cavendishes had been building up a political base with which to defeat the Tory country gentlemen. By their ruthless exploitation of seigneurial power they secured almost the entire vote in the hundred of High Peak, which contained the ducal seat of Chatsworth, and a dominating position in the neighbouring hundred of Scarsdale—sufficient to defeat the Tory control of the rest of the county.[36] But they were able to carry through this manoeuvre only because their declining to associate themselves with Walpole's excise neutralized the issue which caused so much difficulty for Whigs elsewhere. This spectacular stroke for the ministry was unique, but there were other examples at least of holding the line. In Northumberland, for example, there took place a particularly bitter contest between the two sitting members, Ralph Jenison and Sir William Middleton, both independent government supporters and friends of Walpole and Newcastle, and two Tory challengers. As it was, only forty votes separated Middleton from one of his opponents, and but for the fact that both Whig candidates

---

[35] Add. MS. 32688, f. 187: W. Jessop to Newcastle, 26 Aug. 1733.
[36] In High Peak Lord Charles Cavendish secured 769 votes against 195 for Sir Nathaniel Curzon and 164 for Henry Harpur. In Scarsdale the corresponding figures were 518 against 311 and 254. These Cavendish enclaves were strong enough to neutralize and indeed surpass the safe Tory majorities in the hundreds of Appletree, Mareleston and Litchurch, Repton and Griesley, and Wirksworth Wappentake. These figures are calculated from *A Copy of a Poll Taken for the County of Derby, The 16, 17 and 19 Days of April, Anno Dom, 1734, before George Moore, Esq; High-Sheriff for the said County* (Nottingham, n.d.).

had voted against the excise in defiance of their normal loyalties, this too would surely have been a Tory victory.[37] Such instances were extremely significant. The crucial criterion in the general election of 1734 was not so much support for government as support for the excise scheme. Just as the friends of the court who had openly supported the excise, like Lyttelton, Lane and Neale, were unseated for their fidelity, those who had defected on the excise, like the Cavendishes, Jenison and Middleton, remained secure. This was an important lesson; while it did little to encourage loyalty it did much to reinforce the vulnerability of those who sat for open constituencies.

A further device which helped to stave off total defeat for government in the open constituencies was that of the compromise. Partisan passions ran high in the general election of 1734, but in some places men nonetheless thought of their pockets before embarking on a violent and possibly futile contest. At Gloucester, for example, the situation was particularly difficult. There the existing representation was divided between two local families, the Whig Selwyns and the Tory Bathursts, and the city itself was similarly split. But the preceding general elections had witnessed violent and costly contests, and, as it was, the county election for Gloucester threatened to be a difficult one. In these circumstances it was not surprising that both sides agreed to compromise on the sitting members, 'the Interests uniting in these Two Gentlemen for the Sake of the Peace and Good of this City, which has been much sacrificed by the Violence of former Elections'.[38] This irritated many of the more extreme opponents of government who felt, probably rightly, that this was the ideal opportunity to exploit the hostility towards the excise and achieve a great Country victory. In London the freemen who were entitled to vote in Gloucester met 'to oppose all Compromises and Excise', and in the election itself such was the rebellious feeling that there was indeed a contest with a 'pure' Tory setting up against the establishment.[39] Though this candidate managed to gain 434 votes, a pointer to the way a free election would have gone, there was little real danger with the party leaders firm for the compromise. A comparable case was that of Nottingham. There too a compromise al-

---

[37] The figures were as follows: R. Jenison, 1,189; Sir W. Middleton, 1,092; John Fenwick, 1,052; William Bacon, 153.

[38] *Gloucester Journal*, 9 Oct. 1733.

[39] *London Evening Post*, 27–30 Apr. 1733; the voting was as follows: J. Selwyn, 1,155; B. Bathurst, 905; N. Hyett, 434.

ready existed and was seriously threatened by the excise, a significant issue in a trading town so large and important. The Whig candidate, John Plumptre, and his Tory opponent, Borlase Warren, were both 'for the Peace and quiet of the Town', but the compromise was cautiously arranged and 'kept secret as long as possible to prevent the Mutiny of the generality of the Freeman who are always averse to such peaceable doings'.[40] Again, in both these cases compromise was made possible because the excise issue was neutralized. At Nottingham, Plumptre had judiciously opposed the excise, and in Gloucester Selwyn, a placeman for whom outright rebellion was dangerous, had at least managed to absent himself in the vital division. No less striking was the example of Wigan. There one of the sitting members was Sir Roger Bradshaigh, a powerful influence in the town but also a government supporter who had cast his vote for the excise, despite his constituents' instructions. Moreover, there was a strong anti-Bradshaigh party in the town which was already in control of one seat and anxious to obtain the other, not to say a state of intense excitement over the excise in Lancashire generally. In the circumstances it was not to be expected that Bradshaigh would easily retain his seat at the general election. However, the other candidate in 1734 was the Tory Lord Barrymore, and Barrymore was reluctant to face an expensive contest especially if as was the case, Bradshaigh was prepared to compromise. As a result what Barrymore himself called 'this hurly burly about the Excise' was sidestepped; not only did he preserve his alliance with Bradshaigh, but his friend Williams Wynn, the most violent Tory in the northwest, was asked to become a burgess at Wigan, in order, as Barrymore himself informed Bradshaigh, to influence 'the hott men that noe opposition might bee given at Wigan. . . . I am positive he would come and vote for you and mee, and by that he might prevent the ill designs off others who would not differr with him in an affairr off that nature'.[41] Evidently, for Barrymore, a cheap bird in the hand was preferable to two expensive ones in the bush.

Though the neutralization of the excise issue enabled Walpole to lessen the impact of the tide against government in the constituencies

---

[40] Add. MS. 32688, f. 30: Plumptre to Newcastle, 21 July 1733; see also J. H. Moses, 'Elections and Electioneering in the Constituencies of Nottinghamshire, 1702–1832' (Nottingham Univ. Ph. D. thesis, 1965), pp. 129 et seq.

[41] M. Cox, 'Sir Roger Bradshaigh, and the Electoral Management of Wigan, 1695–1747', pp. 157–8.

where public opinion was a really influential force, it scarcely did more. Had the fate of the Walpole administration depended on these constituencies it would have been unseated in Parliament by a considerable majority. What prevented this, the factor which largely accounts for the court's success in defying a public heavily opposed to it, was the picture in the smaller, close constituencies. It was a basic fact of eighteenth-century politics that in the great majority of constituencies public opinion could play either a very limited role or no role at all. Of 558 M.P.s only 143 were sent to Parliament by the seventy-seven constituencies with over 1,000 voters. These constituencies were all of them in England and Wales, and most of them counties. Moreover, only a further sixty-four M.P.s were sent by constituencies with electorates of between 500 and 1,000, the medium-sized boroughs, and so barely two hundred M.P.s, less than two-fifths of the House of Commons, could fairly claim to represent substantial constituencies. A further 163 came from smaller boroughs with voting populations of less than 500 but more than 100, and precisely 200 from those with less than 100. In few of these boroughs with less than 500 voters could public opinion as such be a really effective force. The smaller the constituency, the greater the influence of particular and personal interests, and generally the years of the early Georgian period were years when the power of interests, the power of oligarchy, was steadily increasing at the expense of local liberties.[42] No generalization is altogether safe in such a diverse pattern, but for many constituencies the story of this period is one of dwindling electorates, decaying corporations, and increasing concentrations of power. By 1734 this process was by no means complete, but it had unquestionably gone far enough to preserve Walpole from disaster in the general election of that year.

This is demonstrated very forcibly by the statistics of the election. There is no precise way of estimating government and opposition strength before and after the general election because the political position of many M.P.s returned cannot be judged with sufficient accuracy. One simple test, however, is to compare the number of M.P.s involved on either side in the excise divisions, before and after the election, and to do so in terms of the classification of constituencies above. The results are shown in tabular form below.

---

[42] On this theme, see J. H. Plumb, *The Growth of Political Stability in England, 1675–1725*, chap. iii.

The effect of the General Election of 1734 on M.P.s who had voted against the excise in 1733

Categories of constituencies	Before 1734	After 1734	Reduction as percentage
Over 1,000 votes:	88	77	12½%
500–1,000 votes:	30	21	30 %
100–500 votes:	66	36	36 %
Under 100 votes:	40	26	35 %

The effect of the General Election of 1734 on M.P.s who had voted for the excise in 1733

Categories of constituencies	Before 1734	After 1734	Reduction as percentage
Over 1,000 votes:	37	19	49%
500–1,000 votes:	27	16	41%
100–500 votes:	71	60	13%
Under 100 votes:	121	92	24%

The correlation between size and constituency, voting on the excise, and election results is perfectly clear from these figures. In the larger, more open constituencies opponents of the excise fared well, such losses as did take place being the result largely of death or retirement rather than defeat in the polls. By contrast, supporters of the excise suffered severely; those who hung on did so only as a result of compromised elections or untypical polling. However, the boot was very much on the other foot in the smaller, close constituencies. There the supporters of the excise who stood for re-election were generally successful. The opponents on the other hand found it much more difficult to maintain themselves in their old constituencies. The disparity between the pattern in the large constituencies and that in the small was of critical importance for the ministry. So successful was the government in the close boroughs that in the new Parliament those who had voted for the excise were actually better represented than those who had voted against. The overall reduction of the former in the election as a whole was from 256 to 187, or 27%, and of the latter 224 to 160, or 28.5%. Nothing could more clearly demonstrate the built-in advantage for government and the built-in disadvantage for public opinion in the electoral system.

In detail this theme could be illustrated from many small constituencies up and down the country. However, it was particularly marked in two regions. In Scotland the excise had never really got off the ground. The largest of its constituencies, Ayrshire, had an electorate of just 153, and most others much less. Consequently the election campaign functioned as little more than a well-oiled piece of machinery, operated by the Earl of Islay. The ludicrous example of the election at Stirling Burghs may stand for all. There the sitting M.P., Thomas Erskine, had actually voted for the excise but had deserted to the opposition in 1734, and so compelled the court to put up a new candidate, Peter Halkett. The electorate consisted of ninety-eight voters who were responsible for choosing five electoral commissioners. Though the ground was well prepared by the ministry, the result was a minority of 2 to 3 of these commissioners for Halkett. Yet this did not deter the government. Pressure was put on the local magnates to 'make the return not according to plurality of votes but as the person to be returned was agreeable or not'.[43] As the *London Evening Post* pointed out, 'The Question is short, viz. Whether the Case is to be determin'd by *political* or *common* Arithmetick'.[44] Inevitably the ministerial candidate, an army officer who had not thought it necessary to show his face in the constituency before the election, was returned.

The pattern in Cornwall, that other great preserve of the court, was similar. Fortunately for Walpole, the Prince of Wales, who as Duke of Cornwall had considerable local influence, threw his weight behind the administration. Throughout the excise crisis the Prince, under the guidance of the devious Dodington, had played a mysterious role. On the one hand he had constantly declared his dislike of the ministers, talking 'violently and publicly against Sir Robert'.[45] On the other hand he seemed reluctant to burn his boats behind him. He went to court for a 'reconciliation' with his mother and father in January 1734 and generally infuriated the opposition by his enigmatic conduct, 'ni chair ni poisson', as Chesterfield remarked.[46] In fact he was clearly not ready to break with the court yet, and this was fortunate for Walpole. Later on, in the general election of 1741, the Prince's activities against the ministry in the Cornish elections were

---

[43] *HMC Polwarth*, v. 71: Elphinstone to Col. J. Campbell, 7 Dec. 1733.
[44] 30 May–1 June 1734.
[45] *HMC Stopford-Sackville*, i. 157: Lady Betty Germain to Dorset, Jan.–Feb. 1734.
[46] *Hervey Memoirs*, p. 233; *Stair Annals*, ii. 218: Chesterfield to Stair, 15 June 1734.

to play a crucial part in Walpole's ultimate downfall. His refusal in 1734 to anticipate this event enabled Walpole to exploit the government's advantage in the West Country to the full. The result was predictable. As the *London Evening Post* remarked, 'It's thought the Cornish Boroughs will all re-elect the same Members for the very same Reason that they first chose them'.[47] The *Craftsman* exaggerated when it commented on 'the antient Dukedom of *Cornwall*, which was reserved, . . . as an Asylum for those *worthy Gentlemen*, who have been *excis'd* out of their own Counties and Boroughs by the Pievishness of the People',[48] but certainly there was no shortage of government M.P.s sitting for Cornish boroughs after 1734. Generally it is clear enough why the administration actually increased its membership in close constituencies, instead of merely holding its own. Many of those who formed the parliamentary opposition at the close of the Parliament of 1727 had started it as loyal supporters of the court. The Whig element in that opposition had indeed to a considerable extent been built up in the years after 1730. Consequently there were a number who sat for close government constituencies and who could hardly expect to remain in them under changed circumstances. Two of Lord Stair's relatives, Sir James and John Dalrymple, were ejected from their close boroughs, respectively Haddington Burghs and Wigtown Burghs in 1734. Significantly, the third member of the connection, William Dalrymple, who sat for the county of Wigtownshire where the family interest was strong, was able to retain his seat despite government opposition. A similar case was that of the two M.P.s from Lymington, Lord Nassau Powlett and William Powlett. Both were related to the Duke of Bolton who had gone into opposition during the excise crisis, like Stair, and both suffered for their conduct in 1734. Lymington was to some extent influenced by the Bolton family, but not sufficiently to prevent the administration firmly expelling the sitting members without even a contest. It was not surprising, then, that in the close constituencies the opposition's cause suffered almost as much as it prospered in the open. According to Perceval even unimpeachably independent M.P.s were affected. 'They say', he remarked, 'that it is not enough that independent gentlemen vote with the Court out of a principle, for if they have no other attachment than their judgment, they may be happy to be of a different judgment from the Court measures in a following Parliament.'[49] This remark was founded largely on

[47] 2–5 Feb. 1734.   [48] 25 May 1734.   [49] *HMC Egmont Diary*, ii. 96.

Perceval's own experience at Harwich, where his undoubtedly opposition-minded son was allegedly betrayed by Walpole in favour of a government supporter, but there was nonetheless something in it. Walpole was not squeamish in such matters and doubtless he had little to thank the more independent court Whigs for. Certainly there can be little question that in the general election of 1734 he was even more careful than usual to check the credentials of those who requested his support in close boroughs.

The way in which the close constituencies reinforced the security of Walpole's regime is clear. Long before the general election, George Bubb Dodington had pointed out the paradox involved. In the same letter to the Duke of Dorset, he first remarked that Walpole was unpopular, 'for the nation is certainly in a great ferment, and in general not favourably disposed towards him', and then went on to comment that nonetheless there was no real danger. 'That there will be a Whigg Parliament there is no doubt, and I think, considering the reall weight that the families, fortunes, and interests of those in the King's service naturally give us, separate from the vast influence of the power and very great revenue of the Crown (if either should be made use of), I say I think that there is no room to doubt but that it will be a Court Parliament'.[50] However, that this was so was not solely the result of the deployment of oligarchical and monarchical influence in the general election. Even after the election it became clear in various ways that the government's majority would be bigger than was initially apparent. For one thing not all M.P.s returned on the opposition interest were equally dangerous to Walpole. For example, despite Walpole's constant inveighing against Jacobitism, in some respects his Tory opponents were much less of a threat than Whigs, if only because Tories were almost by definition country gentlemen, who attended the House of Commons much less assiduously than their Whig comrades. Certainly their parliamentary record was a great deal poorer in this respect. Even in the excise crisis, with a call of the House and tremendous opposition pressure, many had failed to turn up for the main division and had had to be whipped in for subsequent divisions, by which time, of course, many of those voting earlier had vanished. Moreover, it was a fact that this element in the parliamentary opposition was disproportionately increased by the elections of 1734. Those returned in the great contests in the larger constituencies tended to be Tories; those squeezed out by Walpole

[50] *HMC Stopford-Sackville*, i. 151: 15 Jan. 1734.

in the smaller ones tended to be rebel Whigs. The *London Journal* even claimed that 'near *four Fifths* of the *Minority* are *determined Tories*, and that there is near *one Third* more in Number than were chosen into the Old House'.[51] Indeed the general election was the only one between 1713 and 1760 in which the Tories actually increased their number, the high point of Georgian Toryism.[52] However, the Tories scarcely made the best use of their fortune, and from Walpole's standpoint opposition Whigs would have been a greater threat in debate and division.

Another point in Walpole's favour is particularly intriguing. Many of those who defeated government candidates in 1734 did so by exploiting the excise issue. But it did not necessarily follow that such newcomers would automatically vote with the opposition. 'Nothing can be more absurd', the *Norwich Mercury* pointed out, 'than the Stress which seemeth to be laid upon the great Number of New Members. Is there any Colour for the Consequence, that they generally differ in their way of thinking, with regard to the Administration, from those in whose Room they succeed?'[53] This was doubtless exaggerating the position, but there is clear evidence at least in one case. One of the most striking 'excise' elections had been at Coventry, where John Neale's injudicious association with the tobacco bill had brought him defeat at the hands of another Coventry man, John Bird. It might have been supposed that such a bitter opponent of the excise would not hesitate to take his place in the opposition camp. But Bird made it known that this was not the case. Almost as soon as the election was over he wrote an extraordinary letter to Walpole in which he expressed 'my Great Concern at hearing by various means, that I am represented to you, as a person disaffected to his majesty and his government', and with a touch of menace added his hope that he would not 'find myself, forcibly driven by any personal Ill usage into measures of acting as disagreeable to my Inclinations, as against the tenor and Constant practice of my whole Life'.[54] No less striking is the fact that eventually Bird was given a place which compelled him to vacate his seat, and was replaced 'for the Peace and Quiet of the City of Coventry' by Neale

[51] 6 July 1734.
[52] The numbers of Tories returned at the various general elections were as follows: 1713: 358; 1715: 217; 1722: 178; 1727: 130; 1734: 149; 1741: 135; 1747: 117; 1754: 109 (the statistics come from the *History of Parliament: House of Commons, 1715–1754* and *1754–1790*).
[53] 11 May 1734.   [54] C(H) MSS., Corr. 2204: 11 June 1734.

himself—one of the more bizarre examples of the way in which Walpole gradually overcame the problems bequeathed by the excise scheme.[55]

A more conventional means of recovery was manipulation of election disputes. The process by which such disputes were decided was one of the least attractive aspects of the eighteenth-century system, an acknowledged scandal even at the time. Petitions were brought before the House of Commons itself as the final arbiter in matters of its own privilege, which included elections, and were apt to be decided with a view more to politics than to justice. Walpole's own practice was particularly notorious in this respect. He was, as Lord Hardwicke remarked with some understatement, 'not delicate about the decision of Elections',[56] and in 1728, for example, at the opening of the new Parliament had shocked even the complacent and well-disposed Lord Hervey. 'I believe the manifest injustice and glaring violation of all truth in the decisions of this Parliament surpass even the most flagrant and infamous instances of any of their predecessors.'[57] Consequently few on either side had doubts as to the importance of this matter in 1734. The opposition press anticipated 'weeding the House' and a 'general Weeding',[58] and friends of government who had failed in the election prepared for battle in another arena. From Hampshire it was reported, 'The people in employments in this neighbourhood talk of weeding the House of Commons of many they dislike as soon as the parliament meets; particularly that there is to be a petition for Hampshire, where the court met with an unexpected defeat'.[59] At New Shoreham the Duke of Richmond, who had seen his candidates there defeated in a constituency which he had himself described as 'a new Whore, that is any bodys for their money', begged Walpole for his assistance, assuring him simultaneously, 'Our cause is really and truely one of the fairest that will appear before the house of commons' and 'if you seem indifferent, it will be the same as if you declar'd against us'.[60]

---

[55] *A Letter from John Bird, Esq.; To the Right Honourable the Lord Sydney Beauclerc, ... concerning Mr. Bird's Election for the City of Coventry* (London, 1741), p. 28; T. W. Whitley, *The Parliamentary Representation of the City of Coventry From the Earliest Times to the Present Date* (Coventry, 1892), pp. 151–3.

[56] Hardwicke, *Walpoliana*, p. 9.   [57] *Hervey Memoirs*, pp. 75–6.

[58] *Craftsman*, 25 May 1734; *London Evening Post*, 27–29 June 1734.

[59] *Stair Annals*, ii. 436: Shaftesbury to Stair, 29 July 1734.

[60] Add. MS. 32688, f. 46: Richmond to Newcastle, 5 Aug. 1733; C(H) MSS., Corr. 2396a: Richmond to Walpole, n.d.

Unfortunately it is not easy to calculate precisely what difference the ministry's weight in election petitions made to Walpole's majority, since many opposition candidates who might otherwise have petitioned presumably did not bother to do so in view of Walpole's reputation. Moreover, in practice relatively few petitions ever got to a decision. Even with the ministry's support they were apt to be long-dragged-out affairs with expensive and lengthy accumulation of evidence. No less than seventy-three petitions were presented at the commencement of the new Parliament in 1735, and of these only twelve actually proceeded to a decision; even then several were not determined until late in the 1736 session—two years after the general election itself. On most the government took a positive stance. At Canterbury the M.P. who had championed the excise and been thrown out for doing so, Sir Thomas Hales, was seated when the Commons gratuitously gave him 159 votes which it was alleged had been 'prevented by the Crowd, and Insolence of the Mob'.[61] At Shaftesbury, too, Stephen Fox, a close friend of Walpole, was seated on petition, and for this, the very first decision of the Parliament, there was little debate and a majority of 203 to 88. At Warwick two Tories were ejected in favour of two government men as the result of a massive disqualification of votes, while at Southampton, Anthony Henley, one of those who had deserted Walpole in 1733, was rejected in favour of a craven placeman, John Conduitt. At Stirling the extraordinary action of the government's agents in returning a M.P. clearly not elected, was confirmed in the Commons by a majority of 101 to 75, and at Lewes an assault on Newcastle's relations, the Thomas Pelhams, was firmly rebuffed.

Even so it is possible to exaggerate the effect of these gains. Most observers thought that Walpole had achieved relatively little by his activities. William Pulteney, for example, claimed that 'The Ministers have been defeated in their Expectations of weeding the House, and upon the whole we stand stronger in Numbers than we did at first setting out'.[62] Pulteney was doubtless exaggerating, but even Lord Hervey thought that Walpole overreached himself in the matter of election petitions.[63] The crucial case in this respect was Wells, where two government supporters, William Piers and George Speke, had been defeated by a small majority in an admittedly very corrupt

---

[61] *Journals of the House of Commons*, xxii. 456.
[62] *Swift Correspondence*, iv. 327: Pulteney to Swift, 29 Apr. 1735.
[63] *Hervey Memoirs*, p. 417.

borough. Piers was a particular friend of Walpole's and had already been seated in the 1727 Parliament after a similar petition. However, in the initial divisions in 1735 the ministers were actually defeated and 'were so angry', that 'they summoned their whole force and all their troops, being resolved to carry their Members though they had lost that city'; the result eventually on 25 March 1735 was a decision for Piers and Speke by 193 to 175 votes.[64] But this was a Pyrrhic victory, and on other petitions many placemen began to have doubts. Dodington, for example, declined to respond to the whip in the case of the Marlborough election. 'I have assisted our Friends Elections to the best of my little Power hitherto, notwithstanding my sickness, witness both the Southampton and the Wells Elections, and shall never make any Comparisons between their Principles, and those of their Opponents'.[65] Dodington was evidently not alone, since the Marlborough decision went against Walpole. 'This must be a great mortification', Perceval noted, 'to him, who had (as I have heard) declared before the Parliament met that no members of Lord Bruce's recommending, if returned, should keep their seats'. In the Wendover decision, too, the opposition got its way 'notwithstanding the Ministry made it their affair'.[66] The result of these reverses was to reduce Walpole's enthusiasm for pressing the government's case in the more spectacular and controversial disputes. In Yorkshire and Norfolk the Whigs had launched costly campaigns to secure evidence for their petitions, yet in the Commons their proceedings were quietly dropped. The same happened in the Bristol case, though the petitioning candidate, John Scrope, was 'very angry with Sir Robert for making him give up . . . which he was forced to do, Sir Robert saying he would not espouse his cause. Sir Robert's friends say that the mob are so exasperated against Mr. Scrope for having voted for the excise that they are resolved not to have him there and if he carried his petition were determined to rise and stone his friends'.[67] No doubt Walpole benefited to some extent from the election disputes. The twelve decisions made by the Commons produced eleven

[64] The early divisions were as follows: 11 Mar. 1735: 144 to 141 and 125 to 112 against government; 18 Mar. 1735: 115 to 113 for government. The quotation is from Edward Harley's diary, quoted in R. Sedgwick, ed., *History of Parliament, House of Commons, 1715–1754*, i. 318.

[65] C(H) MSS., Corr. 2396 c: Dodington to Walpole, n.d.

[66] *HMC Egmont Diary*, ii. 167, 166.

[67] Hertfordshire Record Office, Cowper (Panshanger) MSS., Lady Cowper's Diary, 24 Apr. 1735, quoted in R. Sedgwick, ed., *History of Parliament, House of Commons, 1715–1754*, i. 245.

M.P.s for government and four for opposition. Had the M.P.s originally returned for the constituencies concerned been left undisturbed, the corresponding figures would probably have been six for government and nine for opposition.[68] This meant a distinct gain for the Walpole regime, but scarcely one to compare with the wild predictions made beforehand.

Whatever the qualifications about Walpole's recovery from the worst effects of the general election of 1734, there was no getting away from the fact that the opposition's hopes, raised so high by the excise crisis, had been shattered. Even so those who despaired were not entirely justified in doing so. In several respects the excise crisis and the subsequent general election permanently weakened the Walpole regime and did much to prepare the way for his downfall in 1742. In terms of policy, the defeat of the excise had a particularly dramatic effect on Walpole. For one thing, the programme initiated in 1723 would never be resumed; the reform of the customs system was at an end. 'If I fail in this proposal', Walpole had declared at a time when he did not expect to do so, 'it will be the last attempt of the kind I shall ever make'; again, in 1734 in response to opposition claims that the excise was to be renewed, he insisted 'I, for my own part, can assure this House, I am not so mad as ever again to engage in any thing that looks like an excise'.[69] He was indeed as good as his word, and this was of especial significance, as Hervey pointed out, because Walpole was scarcely a great reformer anyway. In all but financial matters he was a thoroughgoing conservative. 'His great maxim in policy was to keep everything else as undisturbed as he could, to bear with some abuses rather than risk reformations, and submit to old inconveniences rather than encourage innovations.'[70] The effect of the loss of the excise was to complete Walpole's conversion into a mere powermonger. 'From this period', Lord Hardwicke later commented, 'his administration was rather passive, and he undertook little; contenting himself to repel attacks, watch opportunities, and preserve tranquillity'.[71]

Still more important was the directly political legacy of the excise. In a general sense it did much to weaken Walpole's machine, the system he had built up so successfully in the preceding years.

[68] R. Sedgwick, ed., *History of Parliament, House of Commons, 1715–1754*, i. 43, gives a net gain of four seats for the government. It is of course extremely difficult to be very precise about the political loyalty of those involved.
[69] *Parl. Hist.*, viii. 1270: 14 Mar. 1733; ix. 254: 4 Feb. 1734.
[70] *Hervey Memoirs*, p. 364. [71] Hardwicke, *Walpoliana*, p. 12.

Sections of the community which had previously supported that system, particularly under the stress of the dynastic issue, now began to waver, and so set a new pattern which was long to outlive Walpole himself. The City of London, for example, had always been a natural centre for opposition, but Walpole's alliance with the City Whigs, with the moneyed interests and with the great merchants, had effectively neutralized metropolitan hostility in the 1720s. However from 1733 London was unequivocally in opposition. Though Henry Pelham was partially to regain the confidence at least of wealthier Londoners, not until the Gordon Riots in 1780 was the pattern initiated by the excise crisis fully reversed.[72] Related to this was the growing alienation of the business community in general. After 1733 the traditional alliance between mainstream Whiggism and commerce was decidedly shaky. Businessmen who had supported Walpole as the promoter of peace, stability and commercial prosperity in the 1720s were in the following decade beginning to have doubts, and such doubts were not dispelled by the excise crisis. The Spanish war agitation a few years later was to show again how powerful the new partnership between the merchants and opposition politicians could be. In this area the initiative was shifting decisively from the discredited appeasement associated with Walpole to the new commercial aggressiveness championed by the elder Pitt.

In Parliament, too, the excise took its toll. The Court and Treasury party, though it had rallied to its leaders at the moment of crisis in 1733, did not readily recover from the psychological shock which it had suffered. Henceforward the ministry had to live with the memory of a humiliating defeat. 'It may be foretold', Perceval had declared in 1733 after the excise divisions, 'that Sir Robert Walpole's influence in this House will never be again so great as it has been'.[73] The opposition, too, was raised to new heights of bitterness. In particular Walpole's action in dismissing a considerable number of peers and their followers from places at court was much resented. 'Turning people of quality and fortune out of the army', as one enraged aristocrat put it,[74] was not the way to the hearts of the English peerage, and the enmities engendered in 1733 were not to be cooled until the days of the Pelham regime.

[72] In this connection, see L. S. Sutherland, 'The City of London in Eighteenth Century Politics' in R. Pares and A. J. P. Taylor, eds., *Essays presented to Sir Lewis Namier* (London, 1956).
[73] *HMC Egmont Diary*, i. 361.
[74] C(H) MSS., Corr. 2008: Montagu to ?, 5 July 1733.

Even in terms of numbers the excise crisis was not without its effects. It is true that the Walpole administration survived the general election of 1734 with its majority substantially intact. Nonetheless, the election consolidated and welded the parliamentary opposition into a potentially powerful body. Instead of reducing Walpole's opponents to something like their strength in the sessions immediately after the general election of 1727, the elections of 1734, thanks largely to the repercussions of the excise crisis, produced a minority in every way comparable to that which had emerged in the last sessions of the old Parliament. As a result the 1734 Parliament was never as complacent as its predecessor in the years before the excise crisis. No longer could the court be certain of majorities in excess of 100; indeed on occasion it came perilously close to defeat in the mid-thirties.[75] Some of the more curious features of the period only make sense against this background. The reforming church measures of 1736, for example, were a result of Walpole's need to conciliate the more radical Whig independents, whom he had been strong enough to hold in check in earlier years.[76] Just as the alliance of commerce and government was breaking down, so there were developing tensions in relations between church and state. Difficulties of a different kind arose in 1737, when a sensible scheme for reducing interest on the national debt had to be abandoned out of 'fear of disobliging the moneyed men in the House of Commons by giving into a scheme that was at once to lop off a fourth part of their income'.[77] Not even the smallest displeasure on the part of those whose support might be essential could be risked by the Walpole regime. It need not be surprising, then, that by the late 1730s, when awkward questions involving the position of the Prince of Wales and the threatening Anglo-Spanish war arose, the ministry was to find itself in severe difficulties.

No less significant was Walpole's electoral situation. On the face of things in 1734 the electorate had done its worst and failed, thanks to the court's success in maintaining a large measure of control in the close constituencies. Even so the general election had substantially narrowed the ministry's base in the country. In some sense, it is true, public opinion was almost consistently hostile to the established

[75] See R. Sedgwick, ed., *History of Parliament, House of Commons, 1715–1754*, i. 43–4.
[76] See T. F. J. Kendrick, 'Sir Robert Walpole, the Old Whigs and the Bishops, 1732–1736: A Study in Eighteenth-Century Parliamentary Politics', *Hist. Jnl.*, xi (1968), 421–45.
[77] *Hervey Memoirs*, p. 726.

government under George I and George II. Nonetheless, in the 1720s Walpole, assisted by the divisions and disarray of his opponents, had done much to secure an element of general support for his system. At the beginning of the 1727 Parliament, government Whiggism had been practically as strong as Toryism in the more open constituencies, and the general elections of 1715, 1722 and 1727 had all witnessed a steady lessening of Tory influence. However, after 1734 the government's support in such constituencies was reduced to a mere rump. In many counties Tory country gentlemen were established for the foreseeable future by the general election, and it is no coincidence that the number of contested elections in subsequent elections was absurdly low.[78] The importance of this in the short term was that Walpole's room for manoeuvre was henceforth extremely limited, his margin for error dangerously close to vanishing-point. It needed only a change of circumstances in a few of the close constituencies on which he was now almost totally dependent to weaken the ministry still further and even disastrously. This of course was precisely what was to happen later. Walpole went into the general election of 1741 with his majority diminished by desertions and his credibility staked on a war for which he had no enthusiasm. Significantly, the damage which that election inflicted on the ministry was entirely restricted to the small boroughs. It was in Scotland and Cornwall, secure ministerial refuges in 1734, that the court suffered in 1741. In Scotland the defection of the Duke of Argyll and in Cornwall that of the Prince of Wales were responsible for the loss of vital seats. Ironically, in so far as there was a clear trend in the open constituencies it went with rather than against government, though the number of contests in this category was too few to permit safe generalizations.[79] In any event Walpole must bitterly have regretted at this moment the losses which he had suffered at the hands of public opinion in 1734, which in retrospect had sapped the foundations of ministerial security and had been directly attributable to the unpopularity of his excise scheme.

[78] In 1734 there had been thirteen contested county elections in England; this figure was never again attained under the unreformed system, and in the mid-century contests were particularly rare. In 1741 there were only four, in 1747 three, in 1754 five and in 1761 four. As a result the pattern set in 1734 in the politics of the counties was substantially undisturbed in many cases for decades. For the figures cited above, see J. Cannon, *Parliamentary Reform, 1640–1832*, pp. 278–9.
[79] See J. B. Owen, *The Rise of the Pelhams*, p. 7, for details of the general election of 1741.

X
Public Opinion and the Excise Crisis

WHATEVER its impact on Walpole's subsequent career, the excise crisis is primarily interesting for the light it casts on the role of public opinion in Georgian politics. As has been seen, there were other factors at work even in this, one of the most spectacular triumphs of extra-parliamentary forces. Initially the agitation against the excise was to a considerable degree a contrivance of the commercially interested parties, and when the excise was actually defeated it was not least as a result of the activities of Walpole's enemies at court. Again, the power of public opinion was shown to be limited in the general election of 1734, when a savage and widespread electoral reaction against the government failed to unseat it. On the other hand it would be foolish to ignore the role of the public. Without the agitation out of doors, without the general response of the political nation, there would have been no crisis at all, and Walpole would have met a new Parliament stronger than ever. A comparison with other instances of public opinion at work in the eighteenth century drives the point home. The anti-Spanish agitation of the late thirties, the outcry against the Jew Bill in 1753, the reaction to the loss of Minorca in 1756 and the dismissal of the Pitt-Devonshire Ministry in 1757, the Wilkesite outbursts of the 1760s, the reform agitation of 1779–80, none of them quite compare with the excise crisis. Few were genuinely on a national basis—the agitations of the 1760s, for example, were primarily metropolitan or regional in character[1]— and those that were, were scarcely comparable in scale or significance to the excise crisis. The Jew Bill affair was the subject of a campaign in the press, and only a handful of authentic protests, the Pittite agitations of the 1750s, owed as much to interest and artifice as to spontaneity.[2] Moreover, in none of these examples was a general

[1] See G. Rudé, *Wilkes and Liberty*, and L. S. Sutherland, *The City of London and the Opposition to Government, 1768–74* (Creighton Lecture, 1958).
[2] See T. W. Perry, *Public Opinion, Propaganda and Politics in Eighteenth Century England*, L. S. Sutherland, *The City of London and the Devonshire-Pitt Administration* (Raleigh Lecture, 1960), P. Langford, 'William Pitt and Public Opinion, 1757', *Eng. Hist. Rev.*, lxxxviii (1973), 54–80.

election dramatically affected as in 1734. Perhaps only the economical reform campaign of 1779–80 vied with the excise crisis in its intensity and breadth; yet even this achieved little that was concrete, and certainly it failed significantly to affect the subsequent general election.[3] If any comparison can be made at all, 1733–4 smacks more of the reign of Queen Anne than of the reign of George III. It was much compared with Sacheverell's affair by contemporaries, and certainly the combination of extreme rage out of doors followed by a massive electoral reaction was similar.[4] In any event the excise crisis is an outstanding example of the whole political nation at work. As such it raises a number of questions about the nature of out-of-doors politics at this time.

In the first place it is important to identify the precise section of public opinion which operated to most effect in the excise crisis. In the early stages the position was clear enough. The pressure brought to bear on the Commons in the parliamentary session of 1733 was that of the business community. Walpole's proposals remarkably succeeded in uniting the diverse elements in the commercial world, the great merchants of London, Bristol and Liverpool on the one hand and the tradesmen and retailers of the small towns on the other. However, in retrospect this is neither surprising nor obscure. Much more intriguing is the gradual build-up of pressure, particularly after the dropping of the excise, which in a sense represents a far more widespread and authentic expression of public opposition and accounts for the anti-ministerial character of the 1734 general election. All the evidence of that election points to a marked reaction against the government not merely among the commercial classes, but also in the countryside. It has been seen that in 1734 the opposition did spectacularly well in the counties; however, the pollbooks which survive[5] reveal more specifically to what an extent that election

[3] See H. Butterfield, *George III, Lord North and the People*, for the perhaps rather implausible view that the agitation of 1779–80 was a revolution manqué, and I. R. Christie, *The End of North's Ministry, 1780–1782* (London, 1958), for its impact on the government.

[4] See G. Holmes, *The Trial of Doctor Sacheverell* (London, 1973).

[5] It must be stressed that the statements which follow are offered tentatively on the basis of limited evidence. The sources for a really detailed analysis of political loyalties among the electorate are necessarily exiguous for this period. Voting records naturally occur only where contests went to a completed poll. Even then in some cases the pollbooks were not preserved for posterity. Assuming the existence of pollbooks, there still remain problems. The amount of information recorded regarding social background and status is usually minimal. Fortunately such records as are available relate mainly to the

was essentially a rural protest, a movement of the backwoods. The simplest test lies in a comparison between small rural parishes with few voters and larger municipal ones with substantial electorates. On this analysis the evidence is clear. In Norfolk, for example, the Tory candidates, Bacon and Wodehouse, would have lost if they had depended on the conduct of the electors in large parishes containing more than fifty votes, where their rivals, Coke and Morden, had almost half as many votes again as them. But in the remaining, smaller parishes they had a decisive advantage.[6] In Essex, where two Tory runners faced a lone Whig challenger, the pattern was similar. Castlemaine, the Whig, would have gained a seat in Parliament on the vote of the Essex towns, but in the rural parishes he was utterly crushed. In particular, in the really small parishes with less than twenty-five votes his oppoents achieved almost double Castlemaine's total.[7] In Sussex too, though the government nominees of the Duke of Newcastle, Pelham and Butler, actually won, their position was very much stronger in the towns than in the countryside.[8] In Kent the opposition candidates were hugely successful, winning by a substantial margin. Yet in the towns and larger parishes they were overwhelmed. Apart from Maidstone, the county town, where Country politics were especially strong, and Tonbridge and Westerham, both in close proximity to the estates of opposition supporters, the urban vote was cast largely for the government candidates.[9]

Almost as interesting as the breakdown of the crucial polls in terms of town and country is that in terms of social class. It emerges strongly that the gentry, and clergy, were in most cases rabidly anti-government. In Derbyshire, for example, the Tory candidates Curzon and Harpur did substantially better among those described in the pollbook as 'Esquire', 'Gentleman' or 'Clerk', than did their opponent Cavendish, even though Cavendish came at the top of the poll overall.[10] In Essex this feature was still more striking. The Whig Candidate, Castlemaine, obtained only one third of the vote which his opponent Abdy achieved among these categories, though he scored more than two thirds overall.[11] More curious was the position

---

crucial county contests in the south-east, where the battle between court and country was at its most intense, where electors were given a real opportunity to make plain their views, and where the government suffered some severe reverses after many years of relatively secure tenure. Even so the conclusions revealed must be treated as pointers only.

[6-11] See pp. 169-70 below for these footnotes.

in Norfolk and Sussex. In these counties the clergy tended to vote on the government side, a direct reflection no doubt of the fountain of ecclesiastical patronage on tap in two counties where Sir Robert Walpole and the Duke of Newcastle were respectively powerful. In addition the categories labelled 'Esquire' and 'Gentleman' in these counties behaved rather differently. In Norfolk the 'Esquires' were evenly divided between the two sides, but the 'Gentlemen' were overwhelmingly Tory, a discrepancy which was mirrored in the case of Sussex.[12] The terms 'Esquire' and 'Gentleman' are not sufficiently clear to permit altogether watertight generalizations about such statistics. Nonetheless, they do correspond very broadly to a distinction between the better-off landowners with the status of 'Esquire' and the smaller farmers with that of 'Gentleman', and the significance of this in 1734 was obvious. The government fared badly among landowners in general, but among the smaller gentry it did disastrously. In so far as it is possible to separate voters who were accorded no particular social status, it seems that this trend was reversed again below the rank of the small gentleman. As the social scale descended further aristocratic influence grew stronger and the government's hold firmer. This is a tentative generalization since it was a fact that the court had relatively little support of any kind in the countryside. Nonetheless, there is a moral to be drawn. In the great county elections where the government faced such a serious threat, the archetypal opposition voter was the small gentleman or yeoman farmer, and the characteristic government voter either an urban businessman or wealthy landowner at one end of the scale or a small and easily influenced tenant farmer at the other.

These conclusions, such as they are, are confirmed by the impressionistic evidence of contemporary comment. It has been seen that the government press sought the explanation for the ministry's difficulties in the election of 1734 in the bovine prejudices and ignorance of the backwoods gentry and freeholders.[13] The country gentlemen, small squires and J.P.s, the natural leaders of the countryside, were certainly crucial. One of the Whigs most involved in the Norfolk election, for example, had no hesitation in attributing the Whig defeat there to what he called 'the county power (by which they carried it) I mean the Justices of peace'.[14] On the other side of

[12] See below, p. 171.   [13] See above, pp. 131–2.
[14] C(H) MSS., Corr. 2196: Lovell to Walpole, 9 June 1734. On the political significance of J.P.s, and particularly the tendency of opposition-minded justices to remain in

the country also the same factor was stressed. In the Forest of Dean there were complaints of 'the power of the Magistrates in those parts having for many Years past been in the hands of the Tories, which must always be attended with great influence in Elections'.[15] A symptom of positive resurgence on the part of the gentry at this time is the way in which they appear to have made a deliberate attempt to influence many of the corporations during the election campaign. At Canterbury, for example, the gentry and small farmers played a vital part in a constituency which traditionally acted as a safety valve for local electors who had been prevented from following their inclinations in the county.[16] In Berkshire the local gentry, who had no need to fear a contest in their own county, nonetheless met to put pressure on the boroughs of Abingdon and Wallingford and even proposed economic sanctions unless these constituencies returned opposition members. They pledged themselves 'to purchase in London such Commodities as they now usually buy in that Town (Abingdon), to be brought to them by Water or Land Carriage, which they can with great Conveniency do'.[17] In the event this ploy did not succeed but the example is interesting as an illustration of the forwardness of the countryside in 1734. Moreover, it is clear that in the elections of 1734 it was indeed the countryside rather than the towns that made all the difference. In the case of Essex, for example, it is possible to compare in detail the situation in the 1734 election, a great Tory victory, with that in 1710, another Tory triumph, and with that in 1715, a marginal Tory win.[18] These elections are particularly interesting in that the elections of 1734 and 1710 were both preceded by major crises (the Sacheverell and excise affairs) which worked to the advantage of Tories, and that of 1715 by another one (the succession) which divided and demoralized them. So far as the Essex towns were concerned, voting along party lines was very similar on each occasion. But it was the countryside that decided the

---

substantial numbers despite ministerial purges, see L. K. J. Glassey, 'The Commission of the Peace, 1675-1720', Oxford Univ. D. Phil. thesis, 1972.

[15] Sherborne Muniments, 219: Dutton to Westfaling, 9 Apr. 1740.

[16] A. N. Newman, 'Elections in Kent and its Parliamentary Representation', p. 217.

[17] *London Evening Post*, 26-28 Feb. 1734.

[18] This comparison is not easily made in most cases, because it requires not merely three comparable contested elections in the early Hanoverian period, but also the survival of pollbooks in each case. This coincidence does not occur in the other cases relevant in 1734. However, there is no reason to believe that Essex was in any way uncharacteristic in this context.

matter. In 1734, as in 1710, the country vote was strongly Tory; however, in 1715 it had been so nicely balanced as to produce a very close result and a successful Whig petition to Parliament subsequently. Moreover in 1734, again as in 1710, the gentry—the 'Esquires' and 'Gentlemen'—voted heavily against Whiggism. Yet in 1715 they had preferred the Tory by only a small margin.[19] In short, in 1715 when Toryism was suffering from the effects of the succession crisis the countryside in general and the landowning class in particular had held back from their traditional loyalties. But in 1734 with the excise affair in their minds they had no doubts about returning to their allegiances in great strength. The towns on the other hand were similarly divided on each occasion. The excise, though it had infuriated the business classes in 1733, had not led many of them to change their vote in the counties when they were faced by diehard Tories.

The curious feature in this analysis is the partial reversal of the predictable roles. It might have been expected that in urban communities the excise would considerably reduce Walpole's electoral base. This indeed it did in substantial measure, particularly in towns which were themselves represented in Parliament. But in the counties the damage to the government was much more pronounced among the voters of the countryside than among those of the towns. This, perhaps, is the greatest mystery of all in the excise crisis. Why did precisely those sections of the community which Walpole had surely expected to support his great excise reform turn out to be its bitterest opponents? The fundamental fact about the excise was that it involved two great advantages for the landed classes; relief for those

[19] *Essex voting in 1710, 1715 and 1734 compared*

Voting in towns (more than fifty voters)

	Whig candidates		Tory candidates	
1710 (3 candidates)	Masham	941	Child	1,074
	Middleton	1,058		
1715 (2 candidates)	Honeywood	652	Harvey	778
1734 (3 candidates)	Castlemaine	689	Abdy	728
			Bramston	658

Voting in country parishes (less than fifty voters)

	Whig candidates		Tory candidates	
1710 (3 candidates)	Masham	1,706	Child	2,194
	Middleton	1,620		
1715 (2 candidates)	Honeywood	1,739	Harvey	1,889
1734 (3 candidates)	Castlemaine	1,457	Abdy	2,650
			Bramston	2,398

PUBLIC OPINION AND THE EXCISE CRISIS 157

who paid the land tax, and effective taxation of the businessman. Yet there was little evidence either at the time of the excise bill itself or in the subsequent general election that the countryside interpreted its own interest in the obvious way. The letter from Wellingborough in Northamptonshire which castigated the 'proud Tobacconist and Saucy Vintners'[20] was almost unique. This was despite the fact that the court spared no effort to remind the landed classes of ancient prejudices at this time. 'By having unequal Advantages against the *Landed Interest*', it was pointed out, 'the monied Men devour the Country Gentlemen, and work the most antient Families out of their *Inheritances*'.[21] Particularly strong attempts were made to inflame the resentments of the small freeholders in the countryside. The ballad used by the Whigs in Norfolk, and entitled 'The honest Freeholders Resolution, to the tune of Tobacco is an Indian Weed or any other that will fitt it', may stand for all:

> Next year evr'y Man that has ground
> Four Shillings must pay in the pound.
>   All this must be done,
>   That knaves may cheat on
> Think of this when ye Smoak Tobacco.
>
> We farmers must Toil, and must Sweat,
> And the hard Bread of Carefullness eat,
>   That Smuglers may thrive,
>   Nay in Luxury live,
> Think of this, etc.
>
> Brave Boys there's but this to be done,
> And thats at the next Election
>   We must choose men of Land,
>   Who by Farmers will Stand,
> Think of this, etc.[22]

This was not the most inspired of lyrics, but it reflected, and very typically, the anxiety of government candidates to make the electorate aware of the nature of the issue before them. Even so such tactics

---

[20] E. G. Forrester, *Northamptonshire County Elections and Electioneering, 1695–1832*, p. 56.
[21] *London Magazine*, 1732, p. 56.
[22] Norfolk and Norwich Record Office, Hobart Papers, NRS 13688.

made little impact, as the election results, not least in Norfolk itself, attested. The ministerial press, with little else by way of consolation, savoured the irony of country gentlemen and their followers co-operating with their traditional enemies the merchants against a scheme avowedly designed to help them, and thereby maintaining the land tax at an unnecessarily high level. The *Daily Courant*, for instance, mocked 'the ever glorious 205 . . . who signalised themselves so lately, in endeavouring to lay *Two Shillings* upon the *Land* and have the *Modesty* to call themselves the *Country-Interest*'.[23] This strange paradox, which runs so strongly through both the excise crisis and the general election, was certainly not concealed by the gentry themselves. Lord Berkeley, himself a Country peer, had prophesied as early as February 1733 that 'The noise made about the excises will I fear bring the load again upon Land'.[24] Some of the opposition even claimed that a land tax of 10s. in the £ would be preferable to excises.[25] It could not be said that those who opposed the excise were not aware of what they were doing.

There is no simple explanation of this problem, apparently a clear case of entire classes taking a political attitude which conflicted directly with both their traditional prejudices and their obvious financial interests. The most ingenious hypothesis offered is that the opposition to the excise was in fact a peculiarly elaborate form of self-interest. According to this argument the prospect of the land tax vanishing altogether was such as to induce fears that at some future time ministers would introduce a new and really effective property tax which would far outdo the existing land tax in severity. In short, the excise failed as the result of 'the lukewarm support of many wealthy landowners who were in favour of seeing the land tax reduced to one shilling, but were very much against its abolition'.[26] This is scarcely a very convincing argument; in the first place the opposition did not consist merely of a few wealthy landowners; in the second it was by no means clear that the land tax would in fact disappear altogether if the excise bill were passed; and in the third it may be doubted whether the rejection of immediate gain out of fear of future loss is a plausible element in the tax-payer's psychology. Equally unlikely was the argument which the *Craftsman* suggested

[23] 26 Sept. 1733.
[24] Add. MS. 31142, f. 61: Berkeley to Strafford, 3 Feb. 1733.
[25] W. R. Ward, *The English Land Tax in the Eighteenth Century* (London, 1953), p. 72.
[26] N. A. Brisco, *The Economic Policy of Robert Walpole*, p. 119; see too S. Dowell, *A History of Taxation and Taxes in England*, ii. 102.

at the time, drawn from conventional theories of taxation. Locke was much quoted for his view that in the last analysis all taxes of whatever kind fell on land, which bore the strain ultimately even of customs and excise duties. 'Struggle and contrive as you will', the country gentlemen were told, 'lay your *Taxes* as you please; the *Traders* will shift it off from their *own Gain*; the *Merchants* will bear the least Part of it, and grow poor last'.[27] It is not easy to accept that landowners, who knew well the difference between a 1*s*. and a 4*s*. land tax, would be convinced either by lengthy quotations from Locke and Temple or by demonstrably absurd reasoning about the effects of indirect taxation.

A more plausible explanation is suggested by the way in which the excise was described by so many contemporaries, that is simply the phrase 'general excise'. As early as October 1732 the *Craftsman* asked 'whether the Practice of turning one Duty after another into *Excises* hath no Tendency to a *general Excise*',[28] and thereafter this appellation was used without restraint or scruple. Even when it was made clear after Parliament met in January 1733 that only two commodities, wine and tobacco, were to be affected by Walpole's proposals, the opposition strove to broaden the argument. Pulteney, for example, insisted that 'one may clearly see a design of subjecting every branch of the public revenue to those arbitrary laws; only the gentleman has a mind, it seems, to be a little cunning, and to do it by piece-meal'.[29] This caught on, and in many of the instructions which were sent to M.P.s the 'general excise' was presented as the great enemy. Beaumaris, for example, protested at 'the terrible Prospect of a general Excise', while Westminster firmly predicted 'a General Excise on all Commodities whatsoever'.[30]

The beauty of this description from the opposition's point of view was that the term 'general excise' was a magnificent catch-all. When dealing with the relatively sophisticated, in Parliament or in the press, the opposition could claim that the danger was the conversion of every customs duty into an excise. This was alarming enough and certainly found its mark. Sir Paul Methuen, for example, one of the independents who opposed the excise, declared in the Commons, 'I cannot but think that it is a wide step towards establishing a general excise, and therefore I must be excused assenting

[27] 9 Dec. 1732. [28] 28 Oct. 1732.
[29] *Parl. Hist.*, viii. 1298: 14 Mar. 1733.
[30] *Craftsman*, 31 Mar. 1733; *B. Berington's Evening Post*, 20 Mar. 1733.

to it'.[31] Far more important than this, when the subject was aired among those whose political education was less extensive, the charge of a general excise took on a whole new set of objections which would not seriously have occurred to most M.P.s. These involved the belief, potentially devastating, that a general excise meant an excise levied on foodstuffs generally. The unpopularity of the excise in the mid-seventeenth century had had much to do with this belief, and in 1733 and 1734 it was again the crucial consideration in the nation at large. In the county which has left the clearest evidence about the election campaign, Sussex, its importance was obvious. One of the Pelham tenants at Hellingly, for example, was reported as saying that 'he believed most in Hellingly and Haylsham would go the other way, that they liked your Grace very well, but were very much dissatisfied with what had lately happened; for that he and his neighbours had heard, that Bread and Meat would have been taxed if it had not been for a Petition from Bristol'.[32] Similarly, in Isfield the freeholders specifically declared that it was not the excise on wine and tobacco to which they objected but rather its expected sequel. 'They said they did not value a tax on Wine and Tobacco, but did not like their victuals should be taxed.'[33] At the other end of the country William Stout, a loyal Whig quaker and a businessman to boot, diagnosed this as the Achilles heel of the government. The excise, he insisted was 'represented to the people as if they were about to excise all eatables and cloths'.[34] The point was rammed home by the press: 'What is meant by a *general Excise* is a new Tax upon all such common Conveniencies of Life, as the Poor and laborious Part of the Nation cannot subsist without'.[35]

That this consideration was decisive in the agitation against the excise can scarcely be doubted. As one pamphleteer remarked, 'The great Outcry against that Bill was, because (as they say) It tended to induce a General Excise'.[36] The more acute ministerial observers had no doubts on this score. 'The world', Charles Delafaye remarked, 'were made to believe, that next sessions of parliament something else would be excised, and so on till we should have a general excise

[31] *Parl. Hist.*, viii. 1285: 14 Mar. 1733.
[32] Add. MS. 32688, f. 98: W. Hay to Newcastle, 14 Aug. 1733.
[33] Ibid., f. 121: W. Hay to Newcastle, 16 Aug. 1733.
[34] *Autobiography of William Stout*, p. 212.
[35] *Englishmen's Eyes Open'd*, p. 15.
[36] C(H) MSS. 73/20a: MS. of 'A Letter to —— concerning his Voting at the next Election for Parliament Men'.

upon everything useful or necessary for life'.[37] Hervey agreed: 'There was hardly a town in England, great or small, where nine parts in ten of the inhabitants did not believe that this project was to establish a general excise, and that everything they eat or wore was to be taxed'.[38] This, perhaps, was the crucial factor in the excise crisis, one that explains why a scheme to which succeeding generations could conceive of no reasonable objection met with such an outcry at the time. Without it, neither the merchants and tradesmen on the one hand nor the opposition politicians on the other would have been able to fire the resentment of the nation and bring Walpole almost to his knees. Faction may have exploited the excise crisis, but Adam Smith was quite wrong to impute its outcome to this alone.[39] Involved were real fears, however chimerical they might seem in retrospect. It is, of course, easy enough to scoff at the credulity of those who believed that Walpole was about to tax even their bread.

Yet they had some colour for their fears. Tobacco, after all, was part of the common man's fare. True, it was already subject to customs duty. But the distinction between excises which were merely recasts of customs duties and those which were entirely novel imposts was not altogether obvious to the public in 1733. For one thing, there was the unfortunate affair of the salt tax in 1732. Here was a tax which had never been anything but an excise, an inland duty on basic foodstuffs produced at home. Salt was a staple food, an essential item in everybody's larder. The opposition naturally made the most of this argument. The press stressed the dangers in 'laying Duties on the Consumption of the Growth of the Country'.[40] In Parliament Sir William Wyndham also pointed the moral of the salt duty. 'From this, which is really an excise upon salt, we may come to have an excise laid upon everything we can either eat or drink'.[41] The projected excises of 1733 merely added fuel to this fire. If salt in 1732 and tobacco and wine in 1733, why not bread in 1734 and meat in 1735?

The logic, to a population readily supplied with horrific tales of excises on every imaginable commodity in Holland and France, was compelling. No doubt Walpole did not conceive of anything as drastic as the Sussex peasantry feared. But the alarm of even the country gentry that large-scale excises of one kind or another were

[37] Coxe, iii. 134–5: Delafaye to Waldegrave, 18 June 1733.
[38] *Hervey Memoirs*, p. 145.   [39] See above, pp. 2–3.
[40] *Flying Post*, 8 June 1732.   [41] *Parl. Hist.*, viii. 953: 9 Feb. 1732.

on the way is more difficult to laugh out of court. Not least suggestive was the language of the government itself. In 1732, before the excise agitation made such comments imprudent, the Walpole brothers had not hesitated to applaud the principle involved in excise extensions. 'If all or most part of our customs were converted into excises', Sir Robert had declared, 'I am persuaded it would be beneficial'.[42] In their private correspondence ministerialists maintained this belief even after the excise crisis. Typical was the view expressed by Charles Delafaye. 'I was always of opinion, that even if it went so far as a general excise, and few or no customs, as it is in Holland, we should by this means become a wealthy nation.'[43] It was not merely rural ignorance, political skulduggery and commercial cunning that turned the political nation against what appeared to be its own interest. The picture presented by interested parties, of 'this overgrown Monster, this great Leviathan the EXCISE', was accepted by the country at large because it seemed to suit existing realities and future dangers as well as ancient prejudices.[44]

One problem remains. If anything was clear in the excise crisis it was the total hostility which the excise provoked among the landed classes. In theory if not altogether in practice the political nation was indistinguishable from these classes. 'The Owners of the Land', as one government pamphleteer admitted, 'are properly the *Body* of the Nation. These, in this Island, are strictly the *People* of *Great Britain*'.[45] In the general election of 1734 it was of course precisely this section of the public which was strongly represented in the electorates of the open constituencies, and precisely this section which cast its vote so unequivocally against the government. Not since 1710 had there been such a dramatic and concerted movement on the part of voters. Yet, as has been seen, this made little difference to Walpole's majority in Parliament. It weakened him, in some respects at least in the light of later events, critically; but for the moment it left him clearly in power. Some of those most opposed to Walpole were infinitely depressed by what seemed the futility of their opposition. All eighteenth-century oppositions went through bad patches, but in most cases they were compelled to admit that the reason was their failure to enlist the public on their side. Indeed

[42] Ibid., viii. 961: 9 Feb. 1732.
[43] Coxe, iii. 135: Delafaye to Waldegrave, 18 June 1733.
[44] *Craftsman*, 20 Jan. 1733.
[45] C(H) MSS. 73/21: untitled MS. pamphlet.

the Rockinghams in the 1770s and the Foxites in the 1790s were even reduced to contemplating secession from Parliament in preference to continued campaigning. However, the odd fact about the 1730s was that most contemporaries would have agreed that the public, in so far as its voice could be ascertained, was actually with the opposition, despite the latter's impotence. 'The opposition, I believe', Lord Grange wrote, 'is stronger to the ministry than ever it was since the Revolution'.[46] Yet in Parliament this scarcely diminished the ministry's security.

I am convinced [wrote William Pulteney in 1735] that our constitution is already gone, and we are idly struggling to maintain, what in truth has long been lost. . . . If this was not our case, and that the people are already in effect slaves, would it have been possible for the same Minister, who had projected the excise scheme (before the heats it had occasioned in the nation were well laid) to have chosen a new parliament again exactly to his mind? and though perhaps not altogether so strong in numbers, yet as well disposed in general to his purposes as he could wish? . . . the minister, I am sure, is as much hated and detested as ever a man was, and yet, I say, a new parliament was chosen of the stamp that was desired, just after having failed in the most odious scheme that ever was projected. After this, what hopes can there ever possibly be of success?[47]

This *cri de coeur* raises in an extreme form one of the most puzzling questions in eighteenth-century politics. Why did the political nation, in the sense that the eighteenth century itself interpreted that concept, put up with a system which it so clearly loathed? In this respect there were significant differences between the reigns of George II and George III. There are grounds for suggesting that from the time of the Seven Years War a large proportion of the propertied classes, admittedly with exceptions, supported the court, though there were moments, for example in the closing stages of the American War, when particular events produced a violent reaction against government. In the first half of the century, however, out-of-doors opinion was consistently more against government than for it, and at moments of crisis, for example the Sacheverell trial, and the excise crisis itself, overwhelmingly so. Yet it scarcely appeared to resent its impotence even though, in parliamentary reform, there was an obvious remedy at hand. Basically Walpole was able to ride the storm which his measures had raised up in the counties and

---

[46] *Spalding Club Miscellany*, iii. 55: Grange to Erskine, 1 Dec. 1733.
[47] *Swift Correspondence*, iv. 436: Pulteney to Swift, 22 Nov. 1735.

large boroughs, because he succeeded in maintaining and even strengthening his position in countless small boroughs. Had some of the more corrupt borough seats been distributed among the counties, the result would have been a Parliament of very different political complexion and certainly one much more representative of public opinion. A reform like that which had been briefly executed in 1653 or that which was to be introduced in 1832, or indeed one much less thoroughgoing than these, would have been quite sufficient to unseat the administration. Contemporaries were well aware that the Walpole regime, and perhaps the Hanoverian establishment, rested on a system of parliamentary representation which was not easily defended by reference to any clear constitutional principle. To those who were in power no such defence was necessary, of course. 'The Body of the People in general', they could declare, 'as well as from the natural Prejudices of the lower Sort, the Thirst of Popularity in the higher, and the incessant Intrigues and Projects of the Factious and *Disaffected*, will indiscriminately be opposite to all Governments'.[48]

Those on the other side could not be expected to sympathize with this view. 'People without Doors', the *Flying Post* replied, 'have most certainly resign'd all their Powers to those within'.[49] Yet the opposition proved strangely reluctant to adopt the obvious strategy. Nowhere was there a serious demand for parliamentary reform, despite the clear arguments for it. The paradox was perfectly expressed in the issue of the *Craftsman* for 27 July 1734, which came soon after the results of the general election had been calculated and its failure to destroy the ministry made clear. In this issue there was presented a table of constituencies and M.P.s which demonstrated the absurdity of the existing system against the yardstick of property. As the writer pointed out, if parliamentary seats were redistributed on the basis of contributions to the land tax, the result would be radically different. Gone would be the heavy over-representation of the West Country, while the South-east and parts of the Midlands and North would receive their just deserts. Moreover, if wealth was to be the criterion, large numbers of small boroughs would need to be disfranchised in favour of much increased county representation. Even so the obvious moral was not drawn. The *Craftsman* confined

[48] *The Freeholder's Alarm to his Brethren; or, the Fate of Britain Determin'd by the Ensuing Election* (London, 1734), pp. 52–3.
[49] 16 Mar. 1732.

itself to a cautious wish that the Cromwellian constitution of Parliament had been retained in 1660, but declined to go further.

I am very far from designing to propose any such Alteration at present, when the Power of the People is not in their own Hands, and the very Attempt might give our Enemies an Advantage over us. It would now be called a Design to remove *Foundations*, to subvert the *Constitution*, and introduce a *new Form of Govt*; as We have lately seen in some other Attempts of the same kind, to secure the *Friends to the Independency of Parliament*, both within Doors and without.

The *Craftsman* was not alone in renouncing what was scarcely a radical or democratic measure. An extreme case of the anxiety to avoid advocating a major reform was the Jacobite 'Scheme for the Counties' proposed about a decade later than the excise crisis.[50] The point made was familiar.

It will appear in succeeding years a just subject of wonder, that such a number of Gentlemen considerable for their Estates, their Parts, Capacity and Reputation, as have for many years appeared in the Cause of their Country, and opposed the Corrupt and Destructive measures of Ministers, should not, though supported by nine parts in ten of the Nation, be able in so long a time to carry their point, and on more than one Occasion, when they had a new prospect of succeeding, still be defeated.

The remedy suggested for this state of affairs was quaint—a committee to represent the different regions which could organize pressure on the establishment. Scotland and Wales were to have one representative each, Mercia and Wessex two, Northumbria, East Anglia, Essex, Kent and Sussex one, and London and the other towns together four. Even an extra-parliamentary committee, it seemed, was preferable to a campaign for parliamentary reform.

The reasons for this caution are not obvious, though in them lies the key to the establishment of oligarchy in eighteenth-century England. One obvious factor was the astonishing impracticability of the classes who were held to represent the political nation. The landowning population was chiefly represented in Parliament by its natural leaders, the wealthier squirearchy. These men tended almost by definition to be unpractical politicians, largely uninterested in office and rarely capable of giving effect even to their own deep prejudices. The political record of the country gentlemen in the

[50] R. W. Greaves, 'A Scheme for the Counties', *Eng. Hist. Rev.*, xlviii (1933), 630–8.

eighteenth century is not an impressive one.[51] Typical was the complaint of Lord Chesterfield in 1741: 'fox-hunting, gardening, planting, or indifference, have always kept our people in the country, till the very day before the meeting of the parliament'.[52] After the excise crisis itself Pulteney had been similarly stung into protest by the inactivity of his more independent friends. 'What excuse can any Gentleman make to Those, whom He represents, if a Point of the utmost Consequence to the Nation should happen to be lost by a *single Voice*, whilst He was in Pursuit of a Fox in the Country, or perhaps loitering away his Time in Town?'[53]

Connected with this was the rigid control which the country gentlemen exercised over the counties. As squires and J.P.s they naturally controlled the countryside, and unless they took a firm lead the opinions of their social inferiors were unlikely to be expressed with any force or effect. It was very rare in the first half of the eighteenth century for the countryside to have political business to deal with as a normal part of its affairs, a situation which contrasts with the 1760s and 1770s when many areas responded to the metropolitan lead in the petitioning movements with considerable independence. But between 1710, the year of the great campaign of addresses which ushered in the new Tory ministry of Harley, and 1756 when the counties resorted to petitions on the loss of Minorca, there was relatively little in the way of addressing and petitioning. As has been seen, the instructions against the excise came almost entirely from the boroughs, and the same was true of subsequent campaigns against the Spanish policy of Walpole, the Jew Bill of 1753 and the dismissal of William Pitt in 1757. For most of this period, of course, general elections were relatively frequent and hotly contested, though after 1734 elections lost much of their significance. In any event, outside the electoral sphere there was no obvious mechanism by which pressures in favour of reform could build up unless at least a sizeable portion of the gentry gave it their willing support. This of course merely strengthens the original paradox. The leaders of the countryside were generally more hostile to government even than their social inferiors, yet they made no

[51] See Sir L. Namier, 'Country Gentlemen in Parliament, 1750–84', in *Crossroads of Power* (London, 1962).
[52] Coxe, iii. 580–1: Chesterfield to Dodington, 8 Sept. 1741.
[53] *An Humble Address to the Knights, Citizens, and Burgesses, Elected to represent the Commons of Great Britain in the Ensuing Parliament* (London, 1734), p. 17.

move in the direction of reform. Consequently, the answer to this problem can only be sought in the political psychology of the English gentry at this time.

Perhaps the most important factor was the crippling conservatism which was part of the political tradition of the Augustan age. In recent years it has become fashionable to emphasize the survival into the eighteenth century of that popular, radical tradition which had been so marked a novelty in the mid-seventeenth century and was to re-emerge so shatteringly in the nineteenth.[54] Yet in some ways the most significant fact about the eighteenth-century commonwealthman is his utter insignificance in the practical politics of the age of Walpole. The arguments no doubt existed, but they existed in a vacuum, and certainly anything as fundamental as parliamentary reform was out of the question. It is significant that those reforms which did attract support from respectable elements in the first half of the eighteenth century were precisely those which were intended to restore the old constitution. A Triennial Act would undo the work of Stanhope and help to restore independent parliaments of the kind which had threatened exclusion in 1679, and attempted the impeachment of the junto in 1699. Similarly, place acts would wreck the government machine and reduce the Court and Treasury party to its relative impotence before Walpole's day, if not before that of Sunderland or Danby. Parliamentary reform, to the modern eyes an obvious answer to the influence of the Crown, would not have been in this sense truly conservative. Once again this demonstrates how deep and how damaging was the effect of the Civil Wars. In the mid-seventeenth century the idea of parliamentary reform had not been particularly frightful. James I had advocated it, and Clarendon thought it reasonable. But its association in particular with Cromwell and his works, and in general with the 'levelling' of the Interregnum, wrecked any chance of its adoption subsequently. The English ruling class had a long memory in such matters, and in questions of political reform nothing had scarred its corporate mind more deeply than the experience of the Great Rebellion. Presbyterians, Roundheads and Commonwealthmen were still part of everyday political vocabulary even in the 1730s. Nothing was more deplored than 'new-fangled', or 'new-modelling' measures, and only authentically reactionary reforms, those designed to restore the

[54] See C. Robbins, *The Eighteenth Century Commonwealthman* (Cambridge, Mass., 1959).

half-mythical, half-real constitution of earlier times could be tolerated. Even the Walpole system, with all its horrors, was preferable to the return of the Levellers.

Finally, it is possible that while the public out of doors did not have a truly representative Parliament, in a sense it did have what it wanted. After all, the lesson of 1733 is that public opinion was not without influence. If the excise on wine and tobacco had been pushed through after the general election of 1734, the pessimistic tone of Pulteney would have been justified, but of course the fact was that it was not. According to one government pamphleteer the ministry's sacrifice of the excise scheme 'proved to the People of *England*, that it is their *firm* Resolution to do *nothing* against the *general Bent* of the Nation'.[55] However, the truth was that the bent of the nation had given them no option. And this in a sense was sufficient. It is worth remembering that not everyone assumed that it was for the public to dictate who should govern the country. The government was hated; but many of those who hated it would have denied their own constitutional right to bring it down either by winning elections or by more direct action. It is easy to forget this simply because both opposition and government often talked most misleadingly as if the prime object of the general election in the eighteenth century was to select a government. In the nineteenth century this was to be so, but in the eighteenth it was still sound constitutional theory, and up to a point practice, that the king chose his ministers without reference to the public. Measures were naturally a different matter, one which was legitimately of interest both to Parliament and people. Moreover, the excise crisis demonstrated that when a crucial measure came up, one on which both important pressure groups and the public at large had strong feelings, ministers did not automatically get their way. Perhaps this is the ultimate lesson of the excise crisis. In the last analysis the public had the negative power to veto issues, influence Parliament and in extremity make life intolerable for ministers; it did not have, nor at bottom did it seek, the power to make governments. 'Once in Forty Years', a government journalist commented cynically, 'the *English* Nation is for a *Frolick of Rebellion*'.[56] If nothing else, the excise crisis testifies to the capacity of English society at this time to rise and rebuke its rulers.

[55] *The Rise and Fall of the Late Projected Excise, Impartially Consider'd*, pp. 58–9.
[56] *Hyp-Doctor*, 1 May 1733.

Footnotes 6 to 12 (see pp. 153–4 above).

6 *The figures for Norfolk are as follows:*

Parishes with	Tory Bacon	Tory Wodehouse	Whig Coke	Whig Morden
0–10 voters	1,434	1,389	1,241	1,279
11–25 voters	752	737	680	691
26–50 voters	268	266	199	203
over 50 voters	515	510	745	755
Total incl. out-vote	3,224	3,153	3,081	3,147

7 *The figures for Essex are as follows:*

Parishes with	Whig Castlemaine	Tory Abdy	Tory Bramston
0–10 voters	538	1,033	899
11–25 voters	455	875	800
26–50 voters	221	302	273
over 50 voters	689	728	658
Total incl. out-vote	2,146	3,378	3,056

8 *The figures for Sussex are as follows:*

Parishes with	Govt. Pelham	Govt. Butler	Opp. Bishopp	Opp. Fuller
0–10 voters	412	371	377	309
10–25 voters	620	540	492	493
26–50 voters	541	514	435	397
over 50 voters	698	628	400	382
Total incl. out-vote	2,271	2,053	1,704	1,581

9 *The figures for the Kent towns are as follows:*

Town	Govt. Middlesex	Govt. Oxenden	Opp. Vane	Opp. Dering
Canterbury	143	144	126	137
Chatham	109	106	22	23
Deal	73	81	19	22
Deptford	120	113	26	33
Dover	101	100	54	56
Faversham	45	45	36	36
Folkstone	131	133	52	54
Greenwich	61	56	32	35
Maidstone	73	79	101	102
Rochester	62	61	37	40
Sandwich	65	81	58	59
Sevenoaks	104	81	19	23
Tonbridge	46	33	73	73
Tenterden	59	59	20	21
Westerham	17	15	42	43
Total town vote	1,209	1,187	717	757
Total overall vote for county	3,569	3,450	4,252	4,441

10 *The figures for Derbyshire are as follows:*

	Whig Cavendish	Tory Curzon	Tory Harpur
Esquires	38	53	49
Gentlemen	24	35	31
Clergy	40	51	47

11 *The figures for Essex are as follows:*

	Whig Castlemaine	Tory Abdy	Tory Bramston
Esquires	53	128	115
Gentlemen	5	33	32
Clergy	51	140	126

12 *The figures as as follows:*

Norfolk

	Whig Coke	Whig Morden	Tory Bacon	Tory Wodehouse
Esquires	86	86	83	81
Gentlemen	14	15	60	60
Clergy	164	169	132	131

Sussex

	Govt. Pelham	Govt. Butler	Opp. Bishopp	Opp. Fuller
Esquires	75	65	50	48
Gentlemen	48	42	43	45
Clergy	93	84	51	45

In the above 'Esquires' include Baronets and Knights.

APPENDIX A

(See page 47)

INSTRUCTIONS AGAINST THE EXCISE SCHEME

Bath	Great Bedwyn	St. Albans
Beaumaris	Hindon	Shaftesbury
Bedford	Hull	Shrewsbury
Bideford	Lancaster	Somerset
Boston	Leicester	Southampton
Brackley	Liverpool	Southwark
Bristol	London	Stamford
Canterbury	Newbury	Stratford
Carlisle	Newcastle	Taunton
Chester	Northampton	Towcester
Cockermouth	Norwich	Wareham
Colchester	Nottingham	Warwick
Coventry	Orford	Westminster
Daventry	Peterborough	Whitehaven
Denbigh	Reading	Wigan
Denbighshire	Ripon	Woodstock
Exeter	Rochester	Worcester
Gloucester	Rye	York

APPENDIX B

(*See page 66*)

DIVISION LISTS ON THE EXCISE

The *History of Parliament: House of Commons, 1715–1754*, i. 129, gives the main lists for the division of 14 March 1733. However, the following is an extended and corrected version of the fuller account in M. Ransome, 'Division-Lists of the House of Commons, 1715–1760', *Bull. Hist. Inst. Research*, xix (1942–3), 4–5.

(a) *A List of those who voted For and Against Bringing in the Excise Bill* (n.d.), purporting to give 266 for the excise and 205 against, including Tellers, but in fact giving 262 for and 207 against. This list was reprinted with *An Exact List of all those who voted for and against the late Convention in the House of Commons* (London, 1739), but so altered as to produce actual figures of 266 for and 205 against. Similar, though not identical, versions are to be found in *Political State of Great Britain*, xlvi. 411–26, *Historical Register*, xvii. 298–312, J. Torbuck, *A Collection of the Parliamentary Debates in England from the year MDCLXVIII To the present Time*, xi. 53–70, *Gentleman's Magazine*, iii. 575–80, and later in the standard collections by Chandler and Cobbett.

(b) A list in *The Most Important Transactions of the Sixth Session of the First Parliament of His Majesty king George II, anno Domini 1733*, which claims to give 267 for and 206 against including Tellers, but actually gives 266 for and 204 against.

(c) A list in the *London Magazine*, 1733, pp. 277–81, with corrections (p. 358) and the additions of M.P.s who later voted against the excise (p. 340). The same list was printed with the ballad, *Britannia Excisa, Britain Excis'd* (London, 1733) and *Fog's Weekly Journal*, 7 and 14 July 1733.

A similar list, of those voting against only, appeared in the *Suffolk Mercury*, 16 July 1733.

The discrepancies between these various lists are so numerous that there can be no certainty as to the voting. However, the listing in group (a) appears to be the most reliable, so far as it is possible to judge from comparison with other sources and its general acceptability to the editors of the monthlies. There is one further list of voting on the excise to be found among the papers of Viscount Perceval, at Add. MS. 47000, ff.

67-8. Though it is set out in a somewhat confusing manner, it appears to be essentially a list of the division on 16 March, amended to show voting on 14 March. In the former guise it probably represents Perceval's own observations; in the latter it is more likely to be the result of comparison with the published lists, since it corresponds very closely to those in group (a) above. In any event its main value is as the only extant record of voting on 16 March, though it is open to a variety of objections. At some points it is self-contradictory, allocating the same voter to both sides. At others it stretches credulity, for example citing as supporters of the excise, rabid Tories, who on all the other available evidence, were its unwavering opponents. On the other hand it frequently corresponds with the complementary information about the excise divisions, and must be regarded as generally dependable.

There are no lists for the remaining relevant divisions, which is particularly regrettable in the case of the crucial voting on 10 April. However the lists described above also give the names of M.P.s who voted against the government in later divisions after supporting it in March and if this evidence is collated with the ministry's 'list of absent members' for 10 April (see Appendix C), it is possible to form a clear impression even of the voting on that date.

APPENDIX C
(*See page 80*)

COURT ABSTENTIONS IN THE DIVISION OF 10 APRIL 1733

The following is a transcription of a list endorsed 'List of Absent Members' in the Cholmondeley (Houghton) MSS. Though it is not dated it can be related to the division of 10 April 1733, when the government had very good reason to note the names of those who abstained. Since this identification has not been made previously, and since much of the relevant argument in the text depends on it, the detailed grounds are given below. In the following list the transcription is supplied on the left, the full name and constituency on the right.

Mr Pottenger	Richard Potenger, Reading
Mr Chamberlayne	George Chamberlayne, Buckingham
Mr Hamilton	John Hamilton, Wendover
Sr R. S. Cotton	Sir Robert Salusbury Cotton, Cheshire
Mr Harris	John Harris, Helston
Mr Hughes	Edward Hughes, Saltash
Sr J. Trelawney	Sir John Trelawny, East Looe
Ld Fitzwilliam	Richard Fitzwilliam, Viscount Fitzwilliam, Fowey
Mr Herbert	Thomas Herbert, Newport
Mr Copleston	Thomas Copleston, Callington
Mr Lawson	Gilfred Lawson, Cumberland
Sr C. Wills	Sir Charles Wills, Totnes
Mr Pitt	Thomas Pitt, Okehampton
Sr F. Drake	Sir Francis Henry Drake, Tavistock
Mr Tuckfield	Roger Tuckfield, Ashburton
Mr Treby	George Treby, Dartmouth
Mr Henley	Anthony Henley, Southampton
Sr J. Thornhill	Sir James Thornhill, Weymouth and Melcombe Regis
Mr Doddington Junr	George Bubb Dodington, Bridgwater
Mr T. Tower	Thomas Tower, Wareham
Mr Bond	John Bond, Corfe Castle
Mr Trenchard	George Trenchard, Poole
Mr Hedworth	John Hedworth, County Durham
Mr Thompson of Y.	Edward Thompson, York
Brigadier Tyrrel	James Tyrrell, Boroughbridge
Sr Wm Lowther	Sir William Lowther, Pontefract
Sr P. Parker	Sir Philip Parker, Harwich

APPENDIX C

Col Berkeley	Henry Berkeley, Gloucestershire
Sr R. Meredith	Sir Roger Meredith, Kent
Sr H. Houghton	Sir Henry Hoghton, Preston
Sr T. Lowther	Sir Thomas Lowther, Lancaster
Sr R. Bradshaigh	Sir Roger Bradshaigh, Wigan
Mr Hanbury	John Hanbury, Monmouthshire
Mr Harbord	Harbord Harbord, Norfolk
Mr Britiffe	Robert Britiffe, Norwich
Sr Wm Middleton	Sir William Middleton, Northumberland
Sr Wm Milner	Sir William Milner, York
Mr Bennett	Thomas Bennett, Nottinghamshire
Mr R. Herbert	Richard Herbert, Ludlow
Mr Bridges	George Brydges, Winchester
Norton Powlett Senr	Norton Powlett Senior, Petersfield
and Junr	Norton Powlett Junior, Winchester
Mr Burrard	Paul Burrard, Yarmouth, I.o.W.
Mr Fortescue	William Fortescue, Newport, I.o.W.
Mr Wm Powlett	William Powlett, Lymington
Mr Ja. Lumley	James Lumley, Chichester
Sr R. Mill	Sir Richard Mill, Midhurst
Mr Pelham	Thomas Pelham, Lewes?
Ld Shannon	Richard Boyle, Viscount Shannon, East Grinstead
Sr A. Oughton	Sir Adolphus Oughton, Coventry
Mr Neale	John Neale, Coventry
Mr Wilson	Daniel Wilson, Westmorland
Mr Offley	Crewe Offley, Bewdley
Mr Haskins Styles	Benjamin Haskins Stiles, Devizes
Capt Eyles	Francis Eyles, Devizes
Mr Holland	Roger Holland, Chippenham
Sr R. Austen	Sir Robert Austen, New Romney
Capt. Baker	Hercules Baker, Hythe
Col. Morgan	Maurice Morgan, Yarmouth, I.o.W.
Ld Lisburne	John Vaughan, Viscount Lisburne
Mr Rich Loyd	Richard Lloyd, Cardigan Boroughs
Mr Bevan	Arthur Bevan, Carmarthen
Mr Corbet	William Corbet, Montgomery Boroughs
Mr Dunbar	Patrick Dunbar, Caithness
C. Areskin	Charles Areskine, Dumfriesshire
Ar. Douglas	Archibald Douglas, Dumfries Burghs
Wm Douglas	William Douglas, Roxburghshire
Sr J. Anstruther	Sir John Anstruther, Fifeshire
Mr Scot	Robert Scott, Forfarshire
Drummond	John Drummond, Perth Burghs?

APPENDIX C

Not all these identifications are straightforward. The most useful clue in assigning identities is the fact that the list was made out alphabetically by constituencies, with boroughs listed under the county in which they were situated. Thus the list begins with Berkshire, proceeds through the English counties and ends with Welsh and Scottish constituencies. Though some of the names are out of sequence, this probably means that in the first instance the list was compiled by utilizing the names on a printed schedule of M.P.s. Such schedules were readily obtainable and usually adopted the order explained above. On this basis it is possible to be reasonably certain that the 'Mr. Pitt' referred to is Thomas Pitt, M.P. for Okehampton in Devon, rather than John Pitt, M.P. for Camelford in Cornwall—the Cornish M.P.s are clearly demarcated from Devonians in the list. By similar reasoning 'Mr. Fortescue' must be William Fortescue, M.P. for Newport, I.o.W., rather than Theophilus Fortescue, M.P. for Barnstaple—the county of 'Southampton' being much further down the list than Devon. There are, however, more difficult cases. 'Mr Doddington Junr.' is probably George Bubb Dodington, M.P. for Bridgwater, though the latter, being in Somerset, should have appeared lower down the list. The alternative would be his cousin George Dodington, who was older, but whose constituency of Weymouth and Melcombe Regis in Dorset would be better suited to the place on the list. The solution presumably lies in the mental processes of whoever was responsible for noting the names. The sight of the name Dodington could well have triggered off an entry of a second Dodington in the wrong place on the list, especially in view of the fact that a qualifying 'Junior' was added to the name to make identification clearer. 'Mr. Scott' is also obscure. It is here applied to Robert Scott, M.P. for Forfarshire, rather than James Scott, M.P. for Kincardineshire, on the grounds that the latter would probably have been given his military rank on the list (like others in the armed forces) if he had been meant. The remaining doubtful cases are insoluble. There are two 'Mr. Drummonds', both named John and respectively M.P.s for Perthshire and Perth Burghs. The latter is tentatively suggested here only because he was much better known to government and generally much more active in Parliament than his namesake, who had been absent in earlier divisions and may well not have attended the Commons at all in 1733. Finally there is absolutely no means of knowing which of the Pelhams is indicated by 'Mr. Pelham'. Charles Pelham, M.P. for Beverley, was a Tory and clearly excluded; Henry Pelham, M.P. for Sussex, was, as a very close associate of Walpole's, certainly not absent on 10 April. James Pelham, as M.P. for Newark, should have appeared at another point in the list. However, any of the three remaining candidates, all named Thomas, two of them M.P.s for Lewes and the third for Hastings, might be indicated.

The list was not dated by its author; however, at some recent stage the dates '1730–4' have been suggested in a pencilled endorsement. In fact it is possible to narrow this down a great deal. At the very earliest it could not have been made out before 30 May 1732, since it includes Thomas Bennett who was only returned for Nottinghamshire on that date. Equally it must date from before 24 April 1733 since Maurice Morgan, who appears on the list and was well known to the court, died on that date. In practice this restricts the compilation of the list to the session of 1733, if only because the previous session of 1732 ended on 1 June, the day after Bennett's return. Moreover, if it is accepted that the Mr. Scott named was, as suggested above, Robert Scott, M.P. for Forfarshire, the earliest possible date would have to be made 1 March 1733, since he was not returned until that date. In any event at this point dating ceases to be a matter of certainty and becomes one of probability.

Various arguments indicate 10 April as the likely date. If there was any point in the session of 1733 when the government would be anxious to identify absentees, it was on the division relating to the City's petition against the excise, partly because the court spared no effort to get all its friends to vote, partly because the earlier printed division lists for the division of 14 March made the noting of absentees a much simpler exercise than the recording of voters. Particularly important is the fact that all those listed as being absent were M.P.s who might be expected to support the excise in some circumstances. Not one was a Tory, unless it be Gilfrid Lawson of Cumberland, though he had been long separated from the Tory party of the 1720s and 1730s. A few were friends of opposition, but only such as Walpole, with his rather antiquated views on the nature of party loyalties, might well expect to give support to a Whig ministry in a crisis, for example John Hanbury, M.P. for Monmouthshire. The clinching evidence, however, lies in a comparison of this list of absentees with the division lists of 14 March. In all the absentees amount to precisely seventy. Of these, forty-three had voted for the excise on 14 March, eleven had voted against and seventeen had been absent. On that day government had secured 265 votes as against 214 on 10 April; in short, it suffered a loss of fifty-one supporters between the two dates. Of these a certain number, seven or eight, actually changed sides, voting against the ministry on 10 April. The number of M.P.s who had voted for the excise on 14 March and merely absented themselves on the division of 10 April was therefore forty-three or forty-four. Even permitting a small margin of error to account for uncertainty as to the exact number of those who completely changed sides, and to allow for the inevitable inaccuracies both in the printed and manuscript lists, this figure is very strikingly close to the number arrived at from the manuscript list of absentees. It can scarcely be coincidence that the printed list for 14 March and this manuscript list tally to yield precisely the results which a comparison between 14 March and 10 April would predict. No other division in the session of 1733 can produce anything like such close agreement.

There is, however, one objection to the dating of the list to 10 April. Sir William Lowther appears as one of the absentees on this list, though according to Hervey (*Hervey Memoirs*, p. 162) he was one of those who defected outright on 10 April. There are several plausible explanations of this apparent contradiction. In the first place it is not quite clear from Hervey's wording that by 'defection' he meant actually voting on the opposition side. It is possible that the term comprehended abstention, or that the original informant had implied abstention and that he was subsequently misunderstood. The context in which Hervey reveals the information—idle chatter at court while George II was using the opportunity of the various defections to make some characteristically biting remarks—does not inspire very great confidence in its reliability. It is also possible, indeed likely, that Hervey or George II or their informant simply made a mistake. Hervey confessed in his memoirs to having forgotten the names of all those who defected, and it is possible that his memory was faulty in other respects. Moreover, it is of the utmost significance that not one of the many printed division lists, which gave voting on 14 March and added a list of those who changed their vote subsequently during the excise crisis, concurs with Hervey in attributing a change of mind to Lowther. All the other defections actually named by Hervey (see pages 80–81 above) are confirmed by these lists, but Lowther is the odd man out. The probability is therefore that Lowther in fact abstained on 10 April. This would certainly tie in with his conduct in the Commons on 11 April, when he supported Walpole's face-saving operation to postpone rather than reject the excise scheme (R. Sedgwick, ed., *History of Parliament: House of Commons, 1715–1754*, ii. 228). However, even if this was not the case and Hervey was right, it is not impossible that the manuscript list of absentees itself was mistaken. All in all, the Lowther anomaly is certainly not sufficient to counterbalance the arguments given above for dating the 'list of absent members' to 10 April.

Index

Abingdon, 155
Anne, Queen of England, 17, 99; reign of, 10, 12, 39, 107, 152
Argyll, John Campbell, 2nd Duke of, 150
Arnall, William, political journalist, 1
Atterbury, Francis, Bishop of Rochester, 11
Ayrshire, 140

Bacon, Sir Edmund, M.P. for Norfolk, 41, 126, 153
Bacon, Waller, M.P. for Norwich, 134
Barber, James, Lord Mayor of London, 55 and n., 92, 129
Barnard, Sir John, M.P. for London, 62, 63, 129
Barrymore, James Barry, 4th Earl of, M.P. for Wigan, 137
Bath, 52
Bathurst family, 136
Bathurst, Allen Bathurst, 1st Baron, 125
Bathurst, Hon. Benjamin, M.P. for Gloucestershire, 121, 125
Beaumaris, 159
Beaumont, Sir George, M.P. for Leicester, 75
Bedfordshire, 110
Belfield, John, M.P. for Exeter, 66
Berkeley, Hon. Henry, M.P. for Gloucestershire, 125
Berkeley, James Berkeley, 3rd Earl of, 93, 115, 158
Berkshire, 129, 155
Bertie, Hon. James, M.P. for Middlesex, 115
Birch, John, M.P. for Wembley, 20
Bird, John, M.P. for Coventry, 127–8, 143
Birmingham, 57
Bishopp, Sir Cecil, M.P. for Penryn, 115
Bold, Peter, M.P. for Wigan, 50
Bolingbroke, Henry St. John, 1st Viscount, 12, 14, 94, 106
Bolton, Charles Powlett, 3rd Duke of, 70, 83, 100, 125, 141
Bond, Denis, M.P. for Poole, 20
Bosworth, John, City politician, 130

Bradshaigh, Sir Roger, M.P. for Wigan, 53, 67, 137
Branthwayt, Miles, candidate for Norwich, 134
Brazil, 59
Brereton, Thomas, M.P. for Liverpool, 21
Bridgnorth, 122
Bristol, John Hervey, 1st Earl of, 11, 13
Bristol, opposition to excise scheme at, 56, 77, 93, 152, 160; 1734 election at, 113, 114, 127, 146; dissenters at, 117
Bromley, Henry, M.P. for Cambridgeshire, 112–13
Bromley, William, M.P. for Warwick, 67
Bruce, Charles Bruce, 1st Baron, 116, 146
Bunbury, Sir Charles, M.P. for Chester, 69
Burke, Edmund, 120
Bute, John Stuart, 3rd Earl of, 2
Butler, James, M.P. for Sussex, 112, 153

Cambridgeshire, 112
Camelford, 129
Candle tax, 33
Canterbury, 127, 145, 155
Carlisle, 52 and n., 67
Caroline, Queen Consort, importance to Walpole, 7–9; role in excise crisis, 83–5, 97, 98, 100, 128; burnt in effigy, 91; and 1734 election, 101, 132
Carter, President of Virginia Council, 28
Carteret, John, 2nd Baron, 33, 116, 132
Castlemaine, John Tylney, Viscount, candidate for Essex, 124, 153
Cato's Letters, 14
Cavendish family, 135, 136
Cavendish, Lord Charles, M.P. for Westminster, 80–1, 89–90, 135 and n.
Cavendish, Lord James, M.P. for Derby, 90–1
Champion, George, Alderman of London, 58
Channel Islands, 27
Chapman, William, City politician, 58
Charitable Corporation, 20, 90–1
Chatham, 53

Cheshire, 112, 118, 120, 121, 125–6
Chester, Thomas, M.P. for Gloucestershire, 121, 125
Chester, 69, 117, 122–3
Chesterfield, Philip Dormer Stanhope, 4th Earl of, 6, 70, 83, 84, 96, 97, 140, 166
Chichester, Bishop of, 112
Child, Sir Francis, M.P. for Middlesex, 115, 129
Chippenham, 130
Cholmondeley, Charles, M.P. for Cheshire, 125
Cholmondeley, George, 3rd Earl of, 126
Cider excise, 2
Cirencester, 121, 127
Civil list, 39
Clarendon, Edward Hyde, 1st Earl of, 17, 167
Clarges, Sir Thomas, 50
Clarke, George, M.P. for Oxford University, 18
Clarke, Sir Thomas, M.P. for Hertford, 81
Clinton, Hugh Fortescue, 14th Baron, 84, 96, 97
Cobham, Richard Temple, 1st Viscount, 100
Coke, Robert, candidate for Norfolk, 42, 126, 153
Colchester, 67
Conduitt, John, M.P. for Whitchurch, Southampton, 145
Cornbury, Henry Hyde, Viscount, M.P. for Oxford University, 11
Corn-Cutter's Journal, 22, 128
Cornwall, 82, 117, 129, 140–1, 150
Cotton, Sir Robert Salusbury, M.P. for Cheshire, 125–6
Courtenay, Sir William, M.P. for Devon, 51
Coventry, William Coventry, 5th Earl of, 69
Coventry, opposition to excise scheme at, 52, 59, 67, 71, 81, 87; instructions of for repeal of Septennial Act, 103; 1734 election at, 119, 127–8, 143–4
Cowper, Mary, Countess, 8
Coxe, William, 79
Craftsman, 13, 16, 19, 22, 23, 28–9, 50, 96; and excise scheme, 35n., 44, 45, 46, 48, 49, 53, 54, 61; and 1734 elections, 106, 109, 120, 124, 131, 141, 158, 159, 164–5

Crewe, John, M.P. for Cheshire, 125
Crossgrove, Henry, journalist, 111
Cumberland, 114
Curzon, Nathaniel, M.P. for Derbyshire, 153

D'Aeth, Sir William, candidate for Kent, 69
Daily Courant, 22, 49, 54, 59, 88, 106, 158
Daily Journal, 22
Dalrymple, Sir James, M.P. for Haddington Burghs, 70, 141
Dalrymple, John, M.P. for Wigtown Burghs, 70, 141
Dalrymple, Hon. William, M.P. for Wigtownshire, 70, 141
Danby, Thomas Osborne, 1st Earl of, 167
Danvers, Joseph, M.P. for Bramber, Totnes, 79
Daventry, 50, 52
Dean, Forest of, 155
Delafaye, Charles, Under-secretary, 40, 49, 64, 66, 69, 75, 89, 96, 160, 162
Denbigh and Denbighshire, 52
Derbyshire, 111, 112, 135, 153, 170
Dering, Sir Edward, M.P. for Kent, 69, 115, 124
Derwentwater Trust, 20
Devizes, 130
Devon, 51, 117, 129
Devonshire, William Cavendish, 3rd Duke of, 89
Dissenters, religious, 36, 37, 45, 61, 116–17, 118
Dodington, George Bubb, M.P. for Bridgwater, 6, 82, 103, 140, 142, 146
Dorset, Lionel Cranfield, 1st Duke of, 84, 115, 124, 127, 142
Dorset, 129
Drewe, Francis, M.P. for Exeter, 66
Dunkirk, 9, 25
Dutton, Sir John, M.P. for Gloucestershire, 125

East India Company, 60
Erskine, Thomas, M.P. for Stirling Burghs, 140
Essex, 40, 118, 124, 153, 155 and n., 156 and n., 165, 169, 170
Exeter, 66
Eyles, Francis, M.P. for Devizes, 71
Eyles, Sir John, M.P. for London, 20, 70–1, 130

INDEX

Eyles, Sir Joseph, M.P. for Southwark, 71, 130

Finch family, 12
Flanders, 27
Flint, 122
Flying Post, 164
Fog's Weekly Journal, 23, 106, 107, 109
Fortescue, William, M.P. for Newport I.o.W., 82
Fox, Henry, later 1st Baron Holland, 6, 93
Fox, Stephen, M.P. for Shaftesbury, 145
Fox-North Coalition, 97, 105
Foxites, 163
France, 10, 12, 18, 54, 161
Free Briton, 22, 108, 115, 131
French ambassador, 70, 83
Fuller, John, candidate for Sussex, 115

Gage, Thomas, 1st Viscount, M.P. for Tewkesbury, 119
Garland, Lewes dissenter, 113-14
Gatton, 52n
General Elections, 166, 168
 of 1710, 118
 of 1715, 150
 of 1722, 118, 150
 of 1727, 9, 24, 149, 150
 of 1734, 24, 35-7, 40, 42, chaps. viii, ix, x, *passim*
 of 1741, 1747, 1754, 1761, 150n
 of 1784, 105
George I, King of England, 7, 12, 15, 22; reign of, 4, 5, 150
George II, King of England, accession of, 15-16; and Walpole, 7-9, 33; reign of, 4, 22, 26, 40, 150, 163; and excise crisis, 80, 83-4, 96, 97, 98, 101, 128, 134; court of, 11
George III, King of England, 16, 97, 98, 104, 105; reign of, 152, 163
Gloucester, 56, 57, 121, 136, 137
Gloucester Journal, 56, 106
Gloucestershire, 110, 115, 117, 118, 121, 125
Gooch, Lt. Governor of Virginia, 30-1, 36
Gordon Riots, 148
Grange, James Erskine, Lord, 163
Great Yarmouth, 41, 120, 121
Gregory, George, M.P. for Boroughbridge, 113
Grocers, 58, 88, 101, 102
Grosvenor family, 123

Haddington, Thomas Hamilton, 6th Earl of Haddington, 11
Hague, The, 75
Hales, Sir Thomas, M.P. for Canterbury, 127, 145
Halkett, Peter, M.P. for Stirling Burghs, 140
Hampshire, 41, 110, 116, 124, 144
Harbord, Harbord, M.P. for Norfolk, 42
Hardwicke, Philip Yorke, 2nd Earl of, 3, 6, 10, 144, 147
Harley, Robert, 1st Earl of Oxford, 166
Harpur, Sir Henry, candidate for Derbyshire, 153
Harwich, 52 and n., 67, 71, 142
Haylsham (Sussex), 160
Hearne, Thomas of Oxford, 6
Hedon, 52n.
Hedworth, John, M.P. for County Durham, 71, 75
Hellingly (Sussex), 160
Henley, Anthony, M.P. for Southampton, 68, 75, 145
Hereford, 127
Herefordshire, 121, 129
Hertfordshire, 118
Hervey, John, Lord, observations etc., in Memoirs, 8, 9, 13, 17, 21, 35, 36, 43, 64, 75, 78, 83, 84, 85, 93, 95, 98, 99, 144, 145, 147
Hinton, John Poulett, Lord, 129
Historical Register, 1
Hobart, John, 1st Baron, 121
Holland, 161, 162
Honiton, 51
Houghton, 8
Howard, Hon. Charles, M.P. for Carlisle, 65, 67, 71, 77
Hull, 2
Huntingdon, 55
Hyp-Doctor, 113

Isfield (Sussex), 112, 160
Isham, Sir Justinian, M.P. for Northamptonshire, 52
Islay, Archibald Campbell, 1st Earl of, 109, 140

Jacobitism, menace of, 10-11, 17, 24, 114, 142; and excise crisis, 54-5, 61, 94-5; individual Jacobites, 62, 75; mentioned, 14-15, 108, 117, 165
James I, King of England, 167

INDEX

James III, the Old Pretender, 11, 54, 55
Jekyll, Sir Joseph, M.P. for Reigate, 72, 75
Jenison, Ralph, M.P. for Northumberland, 135, 136
Jew bill, 1, 47, 68, 104, 151, 166
Junto, 12
Justices of the Peace, 154-5 and n., 166

Kemys, Sir Charles, M.P. for Glamorgan, 75
Kemys, Edward, M.P. for Monmouth, 75
Kent, by-election of 1733 in, 69, 72; election of 1734 in, 110, 111, 112, 115, 118, 120, 124, 153, 170; mentioned, 24, 27, 165
Keyt, Sir William, M.P. for Warwick, 67
King, Dr. William, 3, 6
King's Lynn, 41, 52, 111 and n.
Knighton, 122

Lancashire, 24, 129, 137
Lancaster, 117, 128
Land tax, 23, 33, 34, 35, 39, 40, 73, 157, 158-9
Lane, Sir Richard, M.P. for Worcester, 68, 127, 136
Lawton, John, M.P. for Newcastle-under-Lyme, 122
Leeds, 57
Leicester, 57, 60, 75
Leicestershire, 110, 125
Levinz, William, junior, M.P. for Nottinghamshire, 15
Lewes, 113-14, 145
Licensing act, 21
Lichfield, Bishop of, 85-6
Lincoln, Henry Clinton, 9th Earl of, 112
Lisle, Edward, M.P. for Marlborough, Hampshire, 116
Liverpool, 77, 93, 123, 152
Locke, John, 47, 159
Lockwood, Richard, M.P. for Worcester, 127
London, discontent in, 24-5; campaign against excise scheme in, 46, 49, 55, 58, 61, 65, 77, 78, 81, 87, 88, 152; riots in, 91-3; trade, 59; 1734 elections at, 129-30, 136; effects of excise crisis on, 148; mentioned, 28, 30, 41, 50, 56, 71, 111, 115, 117, 124, 155, 165
London Evening Post, 45, 50, 65, 69, 133n., 140, 141

London Journal, 14-15, 22, 23, 48, 53, 131, 132
London Magazine, 27
Lowther, Sir William, M.P. for Pontefract, 71, 80-1
Lumley, Hon. James, M.P. for Chichester, 82
Lyme Regis, 127
Lymington, 141
Lyttelton, Sir Thomas, M.P. for Worcestershire, Camelford, 69, 129, 136

Maidstone, 153
Malcom, Sarah, actress, 91
Malmesbury, 109
Manchester, 57
Manley, Richard, candidate for Chester, 69
Marchmont, Alexander Hume-Campbell, 2nd Earl of, 100, 103
Marlborough, Sarah Churchill, Duchess of, 17, 53, 132-3
Marlborough, 146
Maryland, 28-9
Massachusetts Bay, 2
Meadowcourt, Richard, of Oxford, 95
Meredith, Sir Roger, M.P. for Kent, 69, 72
Merrill, John, M.P. for St. Albans, 54
Methuen, Sir Paul, M.P. for Brackley, 159
Middlesex, Charles Sackville, Earl of, as candidate for Kent, 115, 124
Middlesex, 115, 118, 128, 129
Middleton, Sir William, M.P. for Northumberland, 71, 135, 136
Milner, Sir William, M.P. for York, 71
Minorca, 47, 151, 166
Monmouth, 117
Montrose, James Graham, 1st Duke of, 100
Morden, William, as candidate for Norfolk, 42n., 126, 153

Neale, John, M.P. for Coventry, 59, 67, 127-8, 136, 143-4
Newbury, 56, 57
Newcastle, Thomas Pelham Holles, 1st Duke of, 109, 111, 132, 133-4, 135, 145, 153, 154
Newcastle-under-Lyme, 122
Newcastle-upon-Tyne, 55-6, 57, 113, 117, 128

INDEX

New Shoreham, 144
Norfolk, Walpole family and, 41–2; 1734 election in, 110, 114, 118, 120, 126, 146, 153, 154, 157, 158, 169, 171
North, Frederick, Lord, 17, 93
Northampton Mercury, 46, 48
Northamptonshire, 52, 112, 117, 129, 157
Northumberland, 114, 135
Norwich, 15, 25, 41–2, 134
Norwich Gazette, 111
Norwich Mercury, 108, 111, 143
Nottingham, 87, 113, 114, 136–7

Occasional conformity bill, 116
Old Sarum, 52n
Onslow, Arthur, Speaker of Commons, 72, 95
Ormonde, James Butler, 2nd Duke of, 17
Oughton, Sir Adolphus, M.P. for Coventry, 59, 71, 75, 81, 128
Oxenden, Sir George, M.P. for Sandwich and candidate for Kent, 115, 124
Oxford, 15, 95
Oxfordshire, 129

Paris, 40
Parker, Sir Philip, M.P. for Harwich, 71, 95
Parliament; House of Commons proceedings: on salt duty, 1732, 33, 38; on excise scheme, March 1733, 36, 48, 49, 62–3, 66, 67, 69, 75–6, 107; on excise scheme, April 1733, 77–80, chaps. vi, vii, *passim*; in 1734 session, 54, 101–4; in 1735 session, 130, 132, 133, 144–7
House of Lords, 85, 99–100; effects of excise crisis in Parliament, 148–50; Parliamentary reform, 163–8
Pelhams, 97, 98, 148, 160
Pelham, Henry, M.P. for Sussex, 17, 62, 64, 90, 99, 100, 104, 112, 134, 148, 153
Pelham, Thomas, of Lewes, M.P. for Lewes, 113, 145
Pelham, Thomas, of Stanmer, M.P. for Lewes, 113, 145
Pelham, Thomas, M.P. for Hastings, 96
Penryn, 109
Perceval, John, 1st Viscount Perceval, later Earl of Egmont, see 19n., observations in Diary, 19, 21, 34, 63, 66, 72, 79, 82, 83, 85, 86, 92, 103, 133, 146, 148; and excise scheme, 67, 68–9, 71–2; and 1734 election at Harwich, 142; as pamphleteer, 107; division list drawn up by, 173–4
Perry, Micajah, M.P. for London, 24, 28, 61, 66, 129
Piers, William, M.P. for Wells, 145–6
Pitt, William the Elder, 2, 5, 7, 79–80, 148, 166
Pitt, William the Younger, 2, 17, 105
Pitt-Devonshire Ministry, 151
Pleydell, Edmund Morton, M.P. for Dorset, 75
Plumb, Professor J. H., 5
Plumptre, John, M.P. for Bishop's Castle, Nottingham, 113, 137
Portugal, 59, 61
Post Office, 22, 49, 50
Powlett, Lord Harry, M.P. for Hampshire, 125
Powlett, Lord Nassau, M.P. for Lymington, 70, 141
Powlett, William, M.P. for Lymington, 141
Prendergast, Sir Thomas, M.P. for Chichester, 80–1
Prince of Wales, Frederick, 82, 140, 149, 150
Pulteney, William, M.P. for Hedon, Middlesex, 10, 13, 40, 63, 74, 103, 115, 117, 129, 145, 159, 163

Qualifications bill, 101, 103

Radnor, 122
Ralph, James, writer, 1
Ramsden, John, M.P. for Appleby, 72
Randolph, Sir John, of Virginia, 28–9, 45
Rhode Island, 63, 78
Richmond, Charles Lennox, 2nd Duke of, 144
Riot act, 122
Ripon, 56
Robinson, Thomas, M.P. for Thirsk, 75
Robinson, Sir Thomas, M.P. for Morpeth, 79
Rochester, 53, 54, 112
Rockingham, Charles Watson-Wentworth, 2nd Marquess of, 97
Rockinghams, 163
Rome, 55
Rutland, 125
Rye, 50, 112

INDEX

Sacheverell, Henry, political preacher, 17, 25, 26, 46, 99, 120, 152, 155, 163
St. Albans, 53-4
Salisbury, Bishop of, 36
Salt duty, 33-40, *passim*, 44, 161
Sandwich, Elizabeth, Countess of, 55
Sandys, Samuel, M.P. for Worcester, 6, 127
Saunderson, Sir Thomas, M.P. for Lincolnshire, 61
Savile, Sir George, M.P. for Yorkshire, 15
Scarborough, Richard Lumley, 2nd Earl of, 84, 128
Schism bill, 116, 117
Scotland, 109, 124, 140, 150, 165
Scrope, John, M.P. for Bristol, Lyme Regis, 36, 113, 118, 127, 146
Selwyn, Charles, M.P. for Gloucester, 137
Selwyn, John, City politician, 130
Septennial act, 101, 102, 103
Seven Years War, 163
Shaftesbury, 145
Shepheard, Samuel, M.P. for Cambridgeshire, 112
Shippen, William, M.P. for Newton, 62
Shrewsbury, 117
Shropshire, 110, 112, 122-3
Sinking fund, 33n., 34
Smith, Adam, 2, 3, 161
Somerset, 52, 57, 129
South Sea Company, 11, 20, 71
Southampton, 57, 68, 145
Southwark, 130
Spain, relations with, 68, 101, 151, 166
Speke, George, M.P. for Taunton, Wells, 145-6
Staffordshire, 129
Stair, John Dalrymple, 2nd Earl of, 70, 83, 84, 85, 100, 116, 141
Stamp tax, 22
Stanhope, Hon. Charles, M.P. for Derby, 70
Stanhope, James, minister of George I, 7, 12, 167
Stanhope, Hon. John M.P. for Nottingham, 70
Stanhope, Hon. Sir William, M.P. for Buckinghamshire, 70
Stapylton, Sir Miles, M.P. for Yorkshire, 115, 116, 125
Stephens, John, candidate for Gloucestershire, 125
Stirling, 140, 145

Stout, William, diarist, 24, 160
Stuart, Sir Simeon, candidate for Hampshire, 116, 125
Stukeley, William, antiquarian, 19
Suffolk Mercury, 106
Sugar bill, 63, 78
Sunderland, Charles Spencer, 3rd Earl of, 7, 12, 167
Surrey, 112
Sussex, 23, 165; 1734 election in, 110, 111-12, 115, 117, 118, 120, 133-4, 153, 154, 160, 161, 169, 171
Sutton, Sir Robert, M.P. for Nottinghamshire, 20
Sweden, 11

Temple, Sir William, writer, 159
Test and Corporation acts, 36, 45, 46, 117
Tewkesbury, 119
Thornhill, Sir James, M.P. for Weymouth and Melcombe Regis, 82
Tonbridge, 153
Tory party in early eighteenth century, 10, 12-15, 75; Tories in London, 24, and Norwich, 41; individual Tories, 18, 25, 42 and n., 52, 66, 67, 73, 75, 99; Walpole's Tory policies, 32-3, 72-3; Tory party in 1733 crisis, 81, 94, 95; Tories and country coalition, 105, 106-8, 114-17; Tories in 1734 elections, 121, 122-3, 124-5, 126-8, 129, 135-7, 142-3, 145, 150, 153-6
Towcester, 52
Townshend, Charles Townshend, 2nd Viscount, minister of George I and George II, 9, 10, 33
Treby, George, M.P. for Dartmouth, 82
Triennial act, 167
Tufnell, Samuel, M.P. for Colchester, 67
Turin, 40
Turner, Cholmley, M.P. for Yorkshire, 115
Turnpikes, 121
Tyrconnel, John Brownlow, 1st Viscount, M.P. for Grantham, 61, 81

Vane, William Vane, 1st Viscount, M.P. for Kent, 115, 124
Virginia, 28-31, 36, 45, 61, 64

Waldegrave, James Waldegrave, 1st Earl, 40
Wales, 114, 121, 122, 124, 165

INDEX

Wallingford, 155
Walpole, Edward, M.P. for Lostwithiel, Great Yarmouth, 41
Walpole, Horatio, M.P. for Great Yarmouth, Norwich, 'Horace the elder', 8, 30, 31, 41, 42, 44, 68, 86, 132, 134, 162
Walpole, Sir Robert, prime minister, political personality, ascendancy, and weaknesses, chap. ii, *passim*; and excise scheme, 3, chap. iii, *passim*, 44–5, 72, 74; in Parliament, 48, 49, 62, 66, 71, 76, 101, 102; at Court, 70–1, 83–5; and abandonment of excise scheme, 78–83; and House of Lords, 85–6; political recovery after abandonment of excise scheme, chap. vii, *passim*; and 1734 elections in Norfolk and Norwich, 114, 120, 126–7, 134, 154; position in Parliament after excise crisis, 130–50, *passim*, 151, 156 162, 163; also mentioned, 1, 2, 47, 50, 51, 52, 55, 58, 59, 60, 61, 67, 68, 70, 104, 105, 106, 108, 113, 116, 125, 128, 129, 159, 161, 166, 167, 168
Walpole, Robert, Walpole, 1st Baron, 46
War of Jenkins' Ear, 148, 149
War of Polish Succession, 33, 54
War of Spanish Succession, 22
Ward, Sir Edward, candidate for Norwich, 134
Warren, Borlase, M.P. for Nottingham, 137
Warwick, 67, 103, 145
Warwickshire, 57, 129
Weekly Register, 91
Wellingborough, 157
Wendover, 146
Westerham, 153
Westminster, 65, 80, 124, 159
Westmorland, 114
Whig party, under Walpole, 10–15, *passim*, 94, 149; Whigs in London, 25, 70, 148 and Norfolk, 41 and n., 42 and n.; individual Whigs, 61, 72, 95, 154; Whig opposition, 54, 75, 141, 142, 143; Whigs and country coalition, 105, 106–8, 113–116; Whigs in 1734 elections, 101, 103, 121, 124–32, *passim*, 134–6, 146, 153, 154–7
Whitfield, Lewes merchant, 113
Wigan, 50, 52, 53, 67, 137
Wilkesites, 1, 47, 151
Willes, John, M.P. for West Looe, 127
William III, King of England, 12, 14, 16, 17
Williams Wynn, Watkin, M.P. for Denbighshire, 52, 105, 122–3, 137
Willimot, Robert, City politician and M.P. for London, 58
Wills, Sir Charles, M.P. for Totnes, 82
Wilmington, Spencer Compton, 1st Earl of, 7, 8, 9, 84
Wiltshire, 129, 130
Winn, Sir Rowland, candidate for Yorkshire, 115
Wodehouse, William, M.P. for Norfolk, 126–7, 153
Worcester, 68, 119, 127
Worcestershire, 69, 121, 129
Wortley Montagu, Edward, M.P. for Huntingdon, Peterborough, as candidate for Yorkshire, 115
Wyndham, Sir William, M.P. for Somerset, 48, 52, 57, 73, 161

Yarmouth, Amalie-Sophie, Countess of, 98
Yonge, Sir William, M.P. for Honiton, 51, 103
York, 52, 71
York Building Company, 20, 90
Yorke, John, M.P. for Richmond, 72, 81
Yorke, Philip, later 1st Earl of Hardwicke, M.P. for Seaford, 74
Yorkshire, 112, 115, 118, 120, 125, 146

Lightning Source UK Ltd.
Milton Keynes UK
UKHW041424051118
331810UK00001B/5/P